P9-BVG-210

Profit by Investing in Real Estate Tax Liens

Earn Safe, Secured, and Fixed Returns Every Time

Larry B. Loftis, Esq.

Dearborn™
Trade Publishing
A **Kaplan Professional** Company

This publication is designed to provide accurate and authoritative information in regard to the subject matter covered. It is sold with the understanding that the publisher is not engaged in rendering legal, accounting, or other professional service. If legal advice or other expert assistance is required, the services of a competent professional person should be sought.

Vice President and Publisher: Cynthia A. Zigmund
Acquisitions Editor: Mary B. Good
Senior Managing Editor: Jack Kiburz
Interior Design: Lucy Jenkins
Cover Design: DePinto Studios
Typesetting: Elizabeth Pitts

© 2005 by Larry B. Loftis, Esq.

Published by Dearborn Trade Publishing
A Kaplan Professional Company

All rights reserved. The text of this publication, or any part thereof, may not be reproduced in any manner whatsoever without written permission from the publisher.

Printed in the United States of America

05 06 07 10 9 8 7 6 5 4 3

Library of Congress Cataloging-in-Publication Data

Loftis, Larry B.
   Profit by investing in real estate tax liens : earn safe, secured, and fixed returns every time / Larry B. Loftis.
      p.   cm.
   Includes index.
   ISBN 0-7931-9517-9 (7.25 × 9 pbk.)
   1. Real estate investment—United States—States. 2. Tax liens—United States—States. 3. Foreclosure—United States—States. 4. Real property—Purchasing—United States—States.   I. Title.
   HD255.L64   2004
   332.63′24—dc22

                                                            2004018054

Dearborn Trade books are available at special quantity discounts to use for sales promotions, employee premiums, or educational purposes. Please call our Special Sales Department to order or for more information at 800-621-9621, ext. 4444, e-mail trade@dearborn.com, or write to Dearborn Trade Publishing, 30 South Wacker Drive, Suite 2500, Chicago, IL 60606-7481.

DEDICATION

This book is dedicated to Gemma Dela Rosa, without whose help, support, and encouragement over the last four years this book would never have been written.

Contents

PART THREE
LIST OF STATES

Acknowledgments

My greatest debt of gratitude for this book becoming a reality is to Gemma Dela Rosa, who has worked with me over the last four years. While her official title has been everything from Vice President to National Director, she is best described as my "right hand." She has been with me at the vast majority of tax sales where I've bid or invested, has spoken with county officials in almost all 50 states, and has invested in numerous states herself. She is a tax lien expert in her own right. In short, this book would not exist without her and my thanks to her will never be adequate.

I would like to thank my editor, Mary B. Good, for believing in the project and being the nicest person to work with in the publishing industry. Mary is gracious to a fault and makes a long, arduous task a pleasant and enjoyable process.

I also would like to thank those people who have worked with me, researched for me, or studied under me, including Kerry A. Lucas, Patricia Vallejo, George Smith, Travis Smith, Don Williams, and Harumi Takahama.

Finally, I'd like to thank several county treasurers and tax collectors for their generous help—Kathy Stinn (the nicest county official one could find anywhere), Larry Framke, Bob Knowler, and Earl K. Wood (the dean of all tax collectors and a gentleman of the highest order).

Part One

INVESTING IN TAX LIENS

IF THIS IS SO GOOD, WHY HAVEN'T I HEARD ABOUT IT?

If you picked up this book, you likely already have heard about investing in tax lien certificates. If you are like most people, however, you know little about it. For years, stories have circulated in real estate seminar circles about the fabulous benefits of this type of investment. Unfortunately, the speakers touting the benefits often know little about it and exaggerate the benefits in order to sell a product or service. More often than not, these speakers either have never bought liens at all, or have purchased just a handful of small liens in one state. Sometimes, the misinformation comes from a real estate author who writes a very short section on tax liens to illustrate another way to make money in real estate. In almost every case, these authors have never personally purchased a lien.

I was listening to a seminar not long ago when I overheard a young man at the back tables discussing tax liens with another person. He made several erroneous comments, until finally I could not take it any longer and had to jump in. According to him, you could invest in a lien in Texas and get a guaranteed 25 percent interest rate. In that one sentence, he had made three errors.

First, Texas is a deed state, not a lien state. As such, an investor is buying a deed, not a lien. Second, rates are never "guaranteed." Rates are fixed by statute, but an investor only gets that rate if the owner redeems (i.e., pays off the taxes and penalties). Third, Texas involves a penalty, not an interest rate. With a penalty, one pays the same amount, regardless of when the redemption occurs.

This young man was very confident and matter-of-fact about his knowledge and wanted to impart his expertise to those around him. I knew what had happened. Somewhere, this young man had heard a seminar speaker exaggerate claims about this investment. More than likely, the seminar speaker may himself have just heard this information from another. Like other rumors (what us lawyers call "hearsay"), these stories tend to get bigger as they pass from one person to the next. So I said to him, "Really, have you ever been to a tax sale in Texas?" Knowing the answer, I wanted to see just how far he would go. He stumbled for words for a moment or so and finally admitted that he'd never even been to a Texas sale. "Let me see if I can help you," I said. After spending a few minutes correcting all of his comments about Texas, he finally said to me, "We need to go to lunch."

On several occasions, I've heard seminar speakers state emphatically that a Florida lien pays a guaranteed 18 percent. I will get into specifics of lien investing later in this book, but suffice it to say that the rate is never guaranteed and is seldom 18 percent (Florida is a "bid down" state and bidding starts at 18 percent). Many years ago, it was not uncommon for a Florida investor to get plenty of small liens at 17 to 18 percent (I had plenty in 1999 and 2000). By 2001, people were exiting the stock market and institutional investors were rushing into tax liens and bidding down to 5 to 7 percent. I managed to get a few liens at 18 percent (see Figures 1.1 and 1.2). However, diligent Florida investors now are happy to get 12 to 16 percent.

To be sure, the benefits of tax lien investing are phenomenal, especially when compared to other traditional investments like

FIGURE 1.1 *Orange County Certificate of Sale Billing*

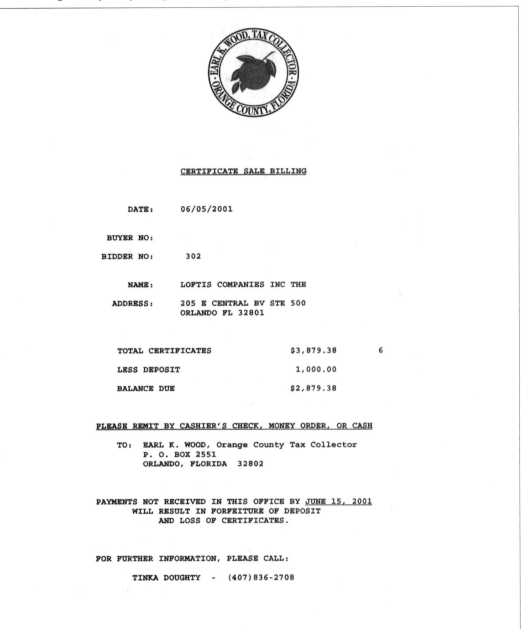

CERTIFICATE SALE BILLING

DATE: 06/05/2001

BUYER NO:

BIDDER NO: 302

NAME: LOFTIS COMPANIES INC THE

ADDRESS: 205 E CENTRAL BV STE 500
             ORLANDO FL 32801

TOTAL CERTIFICATES $3,879.38   6

LESS DEPOSIT   1,000.00

BALANCE DUE $2,879.38

PLEASE REMIT BY CASHIER'S CHECK, MONEY ORDER, OR CASH

TO: EARL K. WOOD, Orange County Tax Collector
      P. O. BOX 2551
      ORLANDO, FLORIDA 32802

PAYMENTS NOT RECEIVED IN THIS OFFICE BY JUNE 15, 2001
      WILL RESULT IN FORFEITURE OF DEPOSIT
           AND LOSS OF CERTIFICATES.

FOR FURTHER INFORMATION, PLEASE CALL:

TINKA DOUGHTY - (407)836-2708

EARL K. WOOD, TAX COLLECTOR
The Sun Trust Center Tower • 200 South Orange Avenue • Reply To: Post Office Box 2551 • Orlando, Florida 32802-2551
(407) 836-2705 • http://www.tax.co.orange.fl.us

FIGURE 1.1 *Orange County Certificate of Sale Billing (Continued)*

```
BYRLST                          EARL K. WOOD
                          ORANGE COUNTY TAX COLLECTOR
                            CERTIFICATE SALE SUMMARY
                    TAX YEAR 2000    SALE DATE  5/25/2001        PAGE     1

BUYER:  302  LOFTIS COMPANIES INC THE


ITEM NO    CERT NO        PARCEL NUMBER          PERCENT         AMOUNT
----------------------------------------------------------------------
   2413   2001-001748    15-21-28-0000-00056      18.00          177.81

   2623   2001-001923    16-21-28-0000-00148      18.00          114.98

   5359   2001-004069    11-23-28-0319-02140      13.00          354.65

   8780   2001-006690    25-22-29-6677-16060      18.00        1,685.03

  13779   2001-010580    07-22-30-5905-00402      18.00          842.94

  16653   2001-012710    17-22-31-2339-11110      18.00          703.97



         SUB TOTAL CERTIFICATES:        $3,879.38              6
```

the stock market. Consider the chart in Figure 1.3 comparing a tax lien certificate to a stock market investment.

Let's look further at these benefits and others.

Rate of return. Even in the days of bull stock markets, most investors were very pleased to receive safe returns of 10 to 15 percent. Over the past few years, however, stock investors have been happy to just retain their principal. Tax lien investors can perform better. In many jurisdictions, the tax lien investor can get returns of 10 to 25 percent, or more. While it is possible to get lower returns because of an investor's desire to buy more liens (spending millions of dollars), savvy investors also can get higher yields by investing in "penalty" jurisdictions (see Chapter 3). I have found that it is fairly easy to get 10 to 16 percent returns in most lien jurisdictions.

FIGURE 1.2 *Orange County Certificate of Sale Billing*

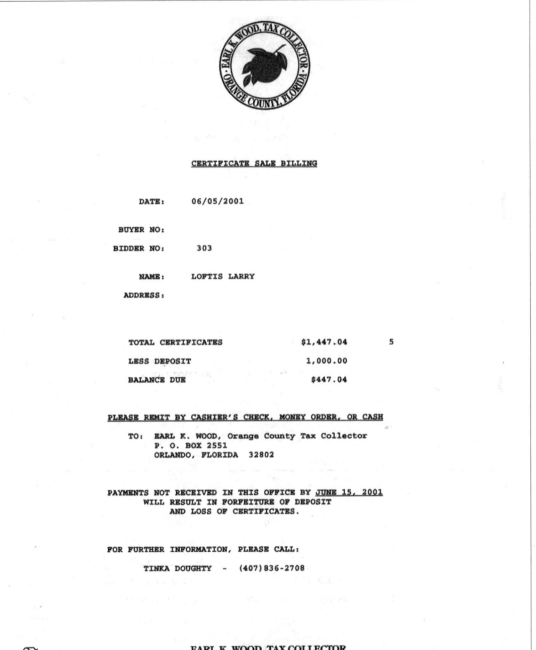

CERTIFICATE SALE BILLING

DATE: 06/05/2001

BUYER NO:

BIDDER NO: 303

NAME: LOFTIS LARRY

ADDRESS:

TOTAL CERTIFICATES $1,447.04   5

LESS DEPOSIT   1,000.00

BALANCE DUE $447.04

PLEASE REMIT BY CASHIER'S CHECK, MONEY ORDER, OR CASH

TO: EARL K. WOOD, Orange County Tax Collector
      P. O. BOX 2551
      ORLANDO, FLORIDA 32802

PAYMENTS NOT RECEIVED IN THIS OFFICE BY JUNE 15, 2001
       WILL RESULT IN FORFEITURE OF DEPOSIT
            AND LOSS OF CERTIFICATES.

FOR FURTHER INFORMATION, PLEASE CALL:

   TINKA DOUGHTY - (407)836-2708

EARL K. WOOD, TAX COLLECTOR
The Sun Trust Center Tower • 200 South Orange Avenue • Reply To: Post Office Box 2551 • Orlando, Florida 32802-2551
(407) 836-2705 • http://www.tax.co.orange.fl.us

FIGURE I.2 *Orange County Certificate of Sale Billing (Continued)*

```
BYRLST                          EARL K. WOOD
                           ORANGE COUNTY TAX COLLECTOR
                             CERTIFICATE SALE SUMMARY
                        TAX YEAR 2000    SALE DATE  5/25/2001         PAGE      1

BUYER:  303  LOFTIS LARRY


  ITEM NO     CERT NO       PARCEL NUMBER          PERCENT            AMOUNT
  -----------------------------------------------------------------------------
     2275   2001-001647   11-21-28-7906-01120       18.00            844.41

     2497   2001-001817   15-21-28-1190-00030       18.00            110.90

     2821   2001-002073   22-21-28-0000-00172       18.00            119.72

     2973   2001-002174   25-21-28-9252-06040       18.00            189.46

     4068   2001-003114   13-22-28-0000-00019       18.00            182.55



        SUB TOTAL CERTIFICATES:          $1,447.04              5
```

Control. Unlike with almost every other high-yielding investment, investors in tax liens have virtually total control in most areas. For example, investors can choose the type of jurisdiction in which they would like to purchase a lien, the size of the lien they would like to purchase, the type of property they would like as collateral, and the interest rate they would like to receive. What these investors cannot control is the time within which the property tax is paid (although it cannot be longer than the statutory redemption period).

Security (collateral). Not only are investors' investments secured by real estate, they also have a *first position* lien. That is, the lien comes before a mortgage or trust deed (i.e., the bank) and any other liens on the property, other than something like a county's "weed lien" (where the property was abandoned and the county had to mow it for sanitary purposes).

Let me now ask you a question or two about banks. First, why do you think banks often escrow property taxes on a new mort-

FIGURE 1.3 *Comparison of Tax Liens and the Stock Market*

Criteria	Tax Liens	Stock Market
Rate of Return	10% – 25% or more (in the better states)	11% average
Control	Total	None
Security (Collateral)	Yes	No
Time Required	Light to Moderate	Light to Moderate
Liquidity	Low	High
Volatility	None	High
Commissions	None	Yes (and/or trade fees)

gage? Answer: Because banks know that the property tax lien comes before their mortgage. If the taxes were not paid, the bank would have to pay the taxes to protect its position, or else be wiped out by a tax lien foreclosure. Second, why do you think banks themselves invest in tax liens? Answer: Because banks intimately know the safety of the investment—tax liens have a higher priority or safety than even their mortgages!

Time required. How long does it take to invest in this type of investment? I listed the time involved as light to moderate. Yes, an investor must spend some time learning how to do this, how his or her county sale works, and must either go to the sale or send a representative (some counties are now allowing an investor to buy online). Yes, this takes time. A stock market investor also spends some time choosing a broker, selecting stocks or mutual funds, making trades, watching the market trends, and so on. My guess is the time is about the same.

Liquidity. Like a certificate of deposit, tax lien certificates are illiquid. Investors cannot expect to receive their principal and interest until the full redemption period has expired. This time is normally one to two years. However, if an investor buys 20 liens in a state that has a two-year redemption period, my experience has been that 10 will pay off over the course of the first year, and the remaining 10 will pay off over the course of the second year. Of those paying off in the first year, probably three or four will redeem a month after the sale (a particularly nice thing in a penalty state).

Volatility. For many people, the tax lien's stability is the most attractive element. Unlike a stock, the tax lien certificate does not fluctuate in value. If you buy a $2,000 lien at 15 percent, that's it; the interest rate is fixed, much like a certificate of deposit. In penalty jurisdictions, you actually have an upside because the "interest" is actually a penalty, which means that your yield will increase if the owner pays off the lien faster.

Commissions. Unlike the stock market, tax lien investing does not involve brokers; thus, no commissions are incurred.

Administration. Many people are comforted by the fact that this type of investment is administered by the government. As such, the investor need not worry about fraud, insider trading, Ponzi schemes, or such other negatives to other investment vehicles. Having said that, I will tell you that many county tax collectors are ruthless in selling liens on worthless properties. I'll help you steer clear of those potential risks in Chapter 7.

Enforcement. As a lawyer, I was most pleased to learn that this type of investment is obviously legal, because it is set forth in the laws of every state. Second, if an owner does not pay the property taxes, the remedies also are set forth in state law. Third, the statutory remedies almost never require any kind of formal legal action, but usually just involve legal notices and county-assisted procedures.

With excellent rates of return, strong collateral as security, no volatility, and these other benefits, tax liens compare very favorably against the stock market and other traditional investments.

With these obvious benefits, how is it that most people know very little about investing in tax lien certificates?

First, this type of investment does not involve brokers. As such, you will not find advertisements in *Fortune, Forbes, Money,* or other financial magazines touting the nice returns or other benefits of tax lien investing. If the big Wall Street firms do not get a broker's fee to sell you this investment, why would they get involved? Having said that, some institutional investors actively invest in these certificates. For example, First Union Bank (now Wachovia) has invested in tax liens for years. So has Bank Atlantic. I've heard that Merrill Lynch has jumped on board as well. But these institutional buyers are buying on behalf of their private banking clients (i.e., wealthy investors).

Second, the element of competition works to keep this investment a secret. All tax lien sales are conducted with some sort of auction bidding process, so that the fewer investors at the event, the better returns or more liens one can buy. As such, every new person who arrives at the lien sale is a potential competitor. Since most sales involve literally thousands of liens costing millions of dollars, the "little" investor is no threat to anyone. However, adding one more institutional investor could affect everyone's success, since that one investor may have over a million dollars to invest that day. Consequently, most tax lien investors do not spread the word on this type of investment.

Third, the government is administering the auction and the process. In most cases, the county municipality is in charge, while in a few jurisdictions the city is authorized to sell liens. Do you think the government goes out of its way to advertise this auction? Has the government ever been very good at marketing? Come to think of it, I have never seen a government advertisement to promote its tax sale. Of course, the county will "notice" the sale (typically several times) in the local newspaper, buried in the back section of the paper. Most people don't even receive a local newspaper at home, and those that do simply assume this section of the paper involves legal notices like foreclosures and other such notices required by statute.

Finally, many people who might know just a bit about tax lien sales shy away from them for lack of knowledge. Some assume that they need a real estate background to buy these liens. Others assume that they might need legal expertise, just as foreclosure investing requires some knowledge of relevant laws. Still others shy away because they assume the investment is too risky. A book agent once told me that this type of investment contains two words that people inherently fear: *tax* and *lien.*Finally, most investors know that some time is involved in understanding the process and going to the actual sale, and they would rather just call their broker to order a stock trade.

For all of these reasons, tax lien investing has remained "under the radar" for the vast majority of investors. Over the past five years, however, more investors have been willing to learn more about this unique investment. In large part, this interest is due to the disastrous bear market of 2000–2003. Most stock market investors have been battered and bloodied over the past few years, and many have been scrambling to find alternative investments.

WHAT IS A TAX LIEN?

Every state and county in the United States levies property taxes on real property. Property taxes are also levied in Canada. With the exception of Indian reservations, every property has taxes due on it each year—vacant lots, residential homes, apartments, commercial properties, shopping centers, and skyscrapers. While you may complain about such taxes on your own property, these taxes allow counties to provide necessary services to the local community, services like police protection, fire departments, libraries, schools, and local roads. In short, your community and mine could not operate and function normally without property taxes.

Each year, the local taxing jurisdiction (usually the county) will assess taxes due on each property and send the owner of that property a bill for the taxes due from the prior year. If the owner does not pay his bill by a certain date, the county (or city in some cases) will levy a lien against that property for the amount of the tax bill. In addition, the county will charge interest and costs to the owner (otherwise, no one would pay their taxes on time!). The county, of course, will send several notices to the owner stating that the taxes are due, and that a late payment will incur additional charges.

Can you see the problem for the county? If many people pay their property taxes late, how does the county make its payroll and provide the necessary services like police and fire protection? Here's how—the county will lien the property and then sell the lien to an investor at a tax lien sale. The investor will have a first position lien (or, in some cases, be second only to a prior *property tax lien*), and that lien will accrue interest and/or penalty from the date of the investor's purchase. When the property owner finally pays his property tax bill, he simply pays the county the delinquent taxes, plus the interest and/or penalty, and the county immediately cuts a check to the investor for his initial principal (the tax bill) plus the interest rate or penalty return. In short, everyone wins. The property owner gets additional time to pay his or her tax bill, the county gets the money it needs now to run the local government, and the investor gets a very nice, safe, secured return. Figure 1.4 illustrates the cycle involved. Figure 1.5 shows the actual tax lien I bought in Iowa on the house in Figure 1.4.

At this point, you're probably wondering how long the property owner has to pay the delinquent taxes and penalty. The time period for this payment is called a "redemption period" and varies by state. While the range varies from six months to four years, most states give the owner one to two years to redeem. This means that the owner could wait until just before expiration of the redemption period and then come in to the county to pay his tax bill and penalty. As such, there is good news and bad news for the investor.

The good news is that the investor does not need to do anything for a year or two (until the owner pays or the redemption

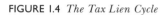
FIGURE 1.4 *The Tax Lien Cycle*

GOVERNMENT

24%

OWNER   **FMV = 80K**

INVESTOR

PROPERTY TAX = $918

FIGURE 1.5 *Iowa Tax Lien Purchase*

```
              CERTIFICATE OF PURCHASE AT TAX SALE NUMBER 01-1772
                 TREASURER'S OFFICE, SHELBY COUNTY, STATE OF IOWA

     I, KATHY STINN              , TREASURER, DO HEREBY CERTIFY THAT ON THE 18 DAY
     OF JUNE,        2001, AT THE REGULAR       TAX SALE PUBLICLY HELD ON THAT DATE,
     THE FOLLOWING PROPERTY SITUATED IN SHELBY COUNTY WAS SOLD TO:
     LARRY LOFTIS;205 E CENTRAL BLVD;SUITE 500;ORLANDO;FL;32801

     FOR THE AMOUNT OF TAXES, INTEREST AND COSTS DUE AND REMAINING UNPAID.

     DIST SH-CP                   TAXED TO: NEUMAN, DAVID B
     ASSHC   PARCEL 832916000003  & GAIL A, SURV

     LEGAL DESCRIPTION:     33-78-40          PT NW SW

     YEAR TYPE  RECEIPT    AMOUNT    INTEREST       COSTS       TOTAL
     1999 RE   90998.0     838.00     76.00          4.00        918.00
                                     SUBTOTAL                    918.00
                                     CERTIFICATE FEE              10.00
                                     GRAND TOTAL                 928.00

     **************************************************************************
     THIS BID WAS FOR A 100% INTEREST IN THE PROPERTY.
     **************************************************************************

     WITNESS MY HAND:
     DATE JUNE 18, 2001              Kathy Stinn
                                  TREASURER OF SHELBY COUNTY,

     **************************************************************************
     ASSIGNMENT:  FOR THE PAYMENT OF $_____, AS PER AGREEMENT, I HEREBY
     ASSIGN ALL RIGHTS, TITLE, AND INTEREST IN THIS CERTIFICATE TO:
     _____  SS _____

     DATE   _____
     01-1772                      ASSIGNOR
```

period expires) and all the while his or her investment is accruing interest at a very nice fixed rate. For most lien jurisdictions, the statutory rates allow for interest ranging from ¼ percent to 18 percent. A few states allow for rates offering much better yields. More on that later.

The bad news is that his investment is illiquid for a period of time matching the redemption period. For example, the redemption period in Florida is two years. While the owner could pay off that lien in one month, the investor might have to wait up to two years until he or she gets paid. Most lien investors actually like having their investment accruing at a good rate for as long as possible. For example, if you bought a lien at 15 percent, you would like for it to stay outstanding for as long as possible.

At this point you probably are thinking, *What if the owner does not pay off his or her tax bill by the end of the redemption period?* Just like any other secured investment, the lien holder will move to foreclose on the lien. Recall that the lien holder is in first position, even ahead of a bank's mortgage on the property. In some cases, the lien holder will force a public sale of the property and get paid the principal plus penalty and costs. In other cases, the owner will get the property, free and clear of all other liens. This subject matter will be discussed thoroughly in Chapter 6.

You also may be wondering if this occurs in all states. The answer is "yes" and "no." Yes, all states have some process for enforcing payment of property taxes. About one half of the states are tax "lien" states, while the other half are considered tax "deed" states. Thus far, the process I've described is the tax lien process. In a deed state, the county is not selling a lien on the property for failure to pay property taxes; rather, the county is actually auctioning the property itself to pay the taxes. Part Two of this book will analyze the process of tax deed sales.

All states will fall into one of three categories:

1. Lien states
2. Deed states
3. "Hybrid" states

A "hybrid" state is technically a deed state. However, it operates like and has much in common with a lien state. In other words, it has aspects of both systems. Let's review the aspects of each.

Lien state:
- The investor has only a *lien* on the property and does not have any other rights in, or title to, the property.
- The investor receives a statutory interest rate until the property tax is received.
- The property owner has a statutory redemption period within which he or she must pay the tax bill.

Deed state:

- The investor actually acquires title to the property.
- No interest rate or redemption period is involved since the investor received the property itself.

Hybrid state:

- The investor actually acquires title to the property, subject, however, to the prior owner's right to redeem and get the property back.
- Should the prior owner redeem (i.e., pay the tax bill plus interest, penalties, and costs), the investor will receive an interest rate or penalty payment on his or her investment.
- The prior owner has a specified redemption period (six months to three years) to redeem the property and re-acquire title.

Figure 1.6 will classify each state into one of these three categories.

LARRY'S REMINDERS

- Tax rates are fixed, but not guaranteed.
- Property tax liens are *first* position liens, even ahead of a bank's mortgage.
- The redemption period is the time during which a property owner must pay off his or her property tax lien. This period ranges from six months to four years.
- A tax lien is only a lien against a property, while a tax deed (acquired through a deed sale) conveys title to the property.
- About one-half of the states are lien states and half are deed states. A few deed states are hybrids, because they operate like lien states.

FIGURE 1.6 *State-by-State Listing of Lien, Deed, and Hybrid States*

Lien	Deed	Hybrid
Alabama	Alaska	Connecticut
Arizona	Arkansas	Delaware
Colorado	California	Georgia
District of Columbia	Idaho	Hawaii
Florida	Kansas	Louisiana
Illinois	Maine	Massachusetts
Indiana	Michigan	Pennsylvania[1]
Iowa	Minnesota	Rhode Island
Kentucky	Nevada	Tennessee
Maryland	New Hampshire	Texas
Mississippi	New Mexico	
Missouri	New York[2]	
Montana	North Carolina	
Nebraska	Ohio[3]	
New Jersey	Oregon	
North Dakota	Pennsylvania[1]	
Ohio[3]	Utah	
Oklahoma	Virginia	
South Carolina	Washington	
South Dakota	Wisconsin	
Vermont		
West Virginia		
Wyoming		

[1]Pennsylvania counties may operate under the hybrid system where the property is improved and has been legally occupied 90 days prior to the sale.
[2]New York City also is allowed to conduct tax lien sales.
[3]Ohio is historically a deed state; however, counties with populations over 200,000 also are allowed to conduct lien sales.

2

THESE LIENS MUST BE ONLY ON CRACK HOUSES, RIGHT?

One of the funniest things I hear when I discuss tax liens with others is the misconception that these liens are only on very bad properties, "crack" houses, for instance. The thinking goes like this: If the owner cannot pay the tax bill on a property, usually only 1 to 2 percent of the property's value, then the owner must be in real trouble and it must be a lousy property. Nothing could be further from the truth. Granted, out of several thousand liens outstanding, certainly some will include vacant lots and small houses in bad areas. Before continuing, let's just analyze that. So what if the collateral is a small lot (as long as it has some value) or small house in a bad area? Taxes still represent 1 to 2 percent of the value of the property. Isn't the risk the same as if it were a very large house, since the 1 to 2 percent tax bill will still apply?

But let's put this all in perspective. Tax liens occur on all types of properties—big houses, small houses, million-dollar homes, condominiums, apartments, shopping centers, commercial buildings, even skyscrapers. I have seen liens on Walt Disney World, McDonalds, Atlantic Gulf Oil, BellSouth Mobility, Amoco, and dozens of other prestigious corporations. See Figure 2.1. I heard that some years ago the Sears Tower in Chicago had a tax lien on it. In my hometown, Orlando, one of the city's landmark properties, Church Street Station, had a tax lien on it. Actually, the property is a complex of buildings, and so there were several liens on the entire complex. See Figure 2.2. At the 2004 sale I bought liens on four properties in this complex. In the late 1970s, this entertainment complex was the number two attraction in Florida, behind Walt Disney World. I've also seen tax liens on virtually every major bank, including Chase Manhattan Bank, LaSalle National Bank, Wells Fargo, Bank of New York, Citibank, Bank One, Sun-Trust, Bank of America, AmSouth, and First Union (I bought liens on Chase and LaSalle). See Figure 2.3. And let's not forget the government itself. I have seen liens on cities (like the city of Hollywood, Florida), the U.S. Post Office, and even the United States of America! See Figure 2.4 for these examples.

A few years back, I bought a lien on a commercial property (see Figure 2.5) that was originally a medical office building. When I went to take a photo of the building, I noticed about 16 sheriff's cars in the parking lot. I also noticed several reserved parking spaces marked "Patrol Lieutenant" and "Patrol Commander." Guess who now was the major tenant of the building? The local Sheriff's Department! Can you connect the dots? If the property taxes were not paid, who would be enforcing my lien? The Sheriff's Department . . . on their own building! In case you are wondering, yes, the lien paid off in due time.

And don't think the wealthy are exempt from this process. I have purchased liens on million-dollar homes and million-dollar commercial properties. I have purchased liens on an NBA Hall of Fame player (Julius "Dr. J" Erving) and a world champion boxer (Hector "Macho" Camacho). See Figure 2.6. I have seen liens on household names such as Wimbledon champion, Steffi Graf, tennis player/model Anna Kornikova, three-time Master's champion, Nick Faldo, NFL football stars Thurman Thomas, Darryl Talley, and Jeff Blake, NBA stars like Dominique Wilkins,

FIGURE 2.1 *Corporate Tax Lien Examples*

	Vizcaya Townhomes		
5891	34 23 28 8883 00030 (U)	Applied Building Devl Of Orl B H Inc	269.28
5892	34 23 28 8883 00040 (U)	Applied Building Devl Of Orl B H Inc	269.28
5893	35 23 28 0000 00060 (U)	Mcdonalds Corp One Mcdonalds Plaza	11,059.82
	Hollywood Plaza		
5894	36 23 28 3787 00050 (U)	Sita Resorts Inc	129,553.04
	Plaza Intl Ut 11		
5895	36 23 28 7165 00018 (U)	Orlando Convention Partners L P	231,835.62
	Plaza Intl Ut 3		
5896	01 24 28 7154 01060 (U)	Ansari Tahir & Ansari Jasmine	19,598.92
	Plaza Intl Ut 5		
5897	01 24 28 7158 01000 (U)	Plaza International Restaurant Inc	76,939.26
5898	02 24 28 0000 00003 (U)	Central Florida Investments Inc	18.51
5899	02 24 28 0000 00009 (U)	Maali Enterprises Inc C/O Park Inc	20,784.06
6926	26 24 28 0000 00036 (U)	Shabel Arleen J & Shabel Jack &	421.49
	Mckoy Land Co Sub		
6927	26 24 28 5357 00491 (U)	Friedman Sam L & Friedman Rita J	217.25
	Lake Bryan Ests		
6928	27 24 28 4336 00110 (U)	Ansari Tahir & Ansari Jasmine	31,712.25
	Lake Bryan Shores		
6929	27 24 28 4340 00010 (U)	Water Sports Management Inc	8,976.37
6930	28 24 28 0000 00030 (U)	Walt Disney World Hospitality & Recreation Corp	88,156.47
6931	34 24 28 0000 00010 (U)	So Yee Kwong & Cheng Janey Chu Fang	5,160.05
6932	34 24 28 0000 00026 (U)	Gonzales Andres	8,226.26
	Munger Willis R Land Co		
6933	34 24 28 5844 00660 (U)	Buena Vista Hospitality Development Partners Lc	25.55
10860	02 23 29 6808 04010 (A)	Carolstan Properties Ltd Lllp	1,583.98
10861	02 23 29 6808 04011 (A)	Carolstan Properties Ltd Lllp	3,974.65
	Poinsettia Park		
10862	02 23 29 7192 0421 (A)	Atlantic Gulf Oil Co	6,615.87
	Westwood Gardens Sub		
10863	02 23 29 9232 00020 (A)	Major Willie Mae	HX 403.34
10864	02 23 29 9232 00050 (A)	Infinity Group International Inc	1,231.84
10865	02 23 29 9232 00130 (A)	Dewitt Clairnel N	HX 193.56
10866	02 23 29 9232 00300 (A)	Inlet Properties Inc	1,141.35
	Westwood Gardens 1st Add		
10867	02 23 29 9234 02140 (A)	Horton Chris & Horton Joanne	926.12
10868	02 23 29 9234 02150 (A)	Hill Jimmie Royal Jr	HX 224.42
	Work Release Ctr Rep		

FIGURE 2.1 *Corporate Tax Lien Examples (Continued)*

14856	25 22 30 8937 00040	(U) Rodriguez David & Alicea Ileana	HX 1,214.87
14857	25 22 30 8937 00210	(U) Llera Dora Alamo	HX 1,365.95
14858	26 22 30 0000 00008	(U) Rotenberger David M Jr &	
		Rotenberger Barbora	13,471.86
14859	26 22 30 0000 00018	(U) Valencia College Shopping Center Ltd	17,626.46
14860	26 22 30 0000 00026	(U) Tischler George W &	
		Tischler Leslie A	2,055.68
14861	26 22 30 0000 00031	(U) Grimsby Orchards Properties Inc	4,686.51
14862	26 22 30 0000 00054	(U) Judd Mary G 1/14 Int &	396.89
14863	26 22 30 0000 00060	(U) Amoco Oil Co	3,360.37
14864	26 22 30 0000 00066	(U) Dade Savings & Loan Association	938.31
14865	26 22 30 0000 00073	(U) Metro Paving & Development Inc	1,359.19
14866	26 22 30 0000 00074	(U) Wiggins Theodore B &	

11373	35 22 29 3772 02030	(A) Miller Theresa	1,482.52
11374	35 22 29 3772 02060	(A) Paul Rinette C/O Arlene Paul	711.48
11375	35 22 29 3772 02080	(A) Laurent Ivertina & Emile Kelly	1,263.51
11376	35 22 29 3772 02150	(A) Hill Robert J Jr & Hill Gladys	HX 565.91
11377	35 22 29 3772 03020	(A) Bell Robert A & Bell Mary S	1,054.13
11378	35 22 29 3772 03051	(A) Anderson Howard	173.49
11379	35 22 29 3772 03060	(A) Hunt Suzie	1,451.29
11380	35 22 29 3772 03070	(A) Hunt Suzie	1,348.85
11381	35 22 29 3772 03140	(A) Brown Michael	2,697.71
11382	35 22 29 3772 03160	(A) Brown Michael	2,486.86

Lamb T A Sub

11383	35 22 29 4956 00010	(A) Bellsouth Mobility Inc	13,763.63

Long L B 1st Add

11384	35 22 29 5200 00100	(A) Trabulsy Solomon & Trabulsy Sy E	3,002.99

Lucerne Oaks Condo

11385	35 22 29 5273 02190	(A) Foster Patrick	761.83

Lucerne Park

11386	35 22 29 5276 03200	(A) Citiwide Distributions Inc	378.63
11387	35 22 29 5276 04230	(A) Mending Hearts Charities Inc	80.36
11388	35 22 29 5276 09080	(A) Lester Daisy Mae Life Estate	

FIGURE 2.2 *Church Street Station, Orlando, Florida*

FIGURE 2.3 *Bank Lien Examples*

19852	22 22 32 0712 16710	(U)	Monroy Herbert	352.51
19853	22 22 32 0712 17006	(U)	Francisco Douglas C	352.51
19854	22 22 32 0712 17011	(U)	Morton Thomas S	427.63
19855	22 22 32 0712 17035	(U)	Perez Evangelina	255.05
19856	22 22 32 0712 17090	(U)	Jablonsky Tracy L	134.02
19857	22 22 32 0712 17290	(U)	Senay Marie A	197.07
19858	22 22 32 0712 17550	(U)	Duke Eula & Oser Barbara J	528.04
19859	22 22 32 0712 17590	(U)	Morton Thomas S	544.29
19860	22 22 32 0712 17680	(U)	Lasalle National Bank Tr C/O Superior Bank	1,196.55
19861	22 22 32 0712 17730	(U)	Carrogan Properties Inc	73.51
19862	22 22 32 0712 18100	(U)	Bailes Leman & Bailes Nancy	255.05
19863	22 22 32 0712 18260	(U)	Clark Debra	224.81

18554	16 22 31 8972 00010	(U)	Garrett Wendy E	677.20
18555	17 22 31 0000 00012	(U)	Farias Jaime & Farias Myrna G	2,153.12
18556	17 22 31 0000 00032	(U)	Suntrust Bank Tr C/O Jones	10,269.67
18557	17 22 31 0000 00055	(U)	White Michael A & White Charlotte Ann	1,268.58
18558	17 22 31 0000 00059	(U)	Pidikiti Nanni	5,102.84
18559	17 22 31 0000 00063	(U)	Masswig Gerhard & Masswig Jean A	HX 247.64
18560	17 22 31 0000 00072	(U)	Sanchez Jose G & Rivera Aurea E	HX 671.14
18561	17 22 31 0000 00075	(U)	Rossman Nancy A C/O Prn Investments	5,350.07
18562	17 22 31 0000 00076	(U)	Pidikiti Nanni	171.82
18563	17 22 31 0000 00093	(U)	Sanchez Jose G & Rivera Aurea E	139.84
Arbor Woods Ut 3				
18564	17 22 31 0230 00711	(U)	Pacholski Joseph	1,241.59

			Mitchell Ronald J	HX 723.06	4
Breezewood Ut 3					
4041	12 22 28 0888 01630	(U)	First Professional Investment Group Inc	HX 968.19	4 / 4
4042	12 22 28 0888 01730	(U)	Solomon Ronnie & Theogene Renee	HX 1,246.06	
4043	12 22 28 0888 01960	(U)	Citibank N A Tr C/O Option One Mortgage Corp	1,667.60	R / 4
Breezewood Ut 4					4
4044	12 22 28 0890 02480	(U)	Davy Leonie	1,622.39	R
4045	12 22 28 0890 02490	(U)	Spencer Jack H & Spencer Kathy A	HX 972.86	4
Bretwood					4
4046	12 22 28 0900 00050	(U)	Gillette Eric	2,115.66	R
4047	12 22 28 0900 00130	(U)	Monnestime Gabriel & Monnestime Jeannine L	HX 1,665.92	4

FIGURE 2.3 *Bank Lien Examples (Continued)*

Angebilt Add

10871	03 23 29 0180 02010	(A)	Gaddy Danny C	1,337.54
10872	03 23 29 0180 02150	(A)	Henry Michael B	1,008.03
10873	03 23 29 0180 03030	(U)	Statewide Capital Inc	801.75
10874	03 23 29 0180 03050	(U)	Federal Home Loan Mortgage Corp	1,526.87
10875	03 23 29 0180 03060	(U)	First Union National Bank Of De	
			C/O Homeq Fidelity	779.29
10876	03 23 29 0180 03101	(U)	Church Orlando Congregational	
			Jehovah Witness Inc	33.77
10877	03 23 29 0180 03150	(U)	Infinity Group International L	

2574	27 23 29 8086 06260	(U)	Jean Ernst E & Jean Mona	HX 1,112.72
2575	27 23 29 8086 06350	(U)	Weeks Thomas B Ii &	
			Whitaker David E	HX 1,086.26

Southland Executive Pk

2576	27 23 29 8194 00001	(U)	Fnb Properties Inc	
			C/O First Union National Bank	23.68
2577	27 23 29 8194 00012	(U)	Amsouth Bank	24,478.02
2578	27 23 29 8194 00020	(U)	Fnb Properties Inc	
			C/O First Union National Bank	45.77
2579	27 23 29 8194 00040	(U)	Fnb Properties Inc	
			C/O First Union National Bank	82.17

Orlando Central Pk No 24

2580	28 23 29 6339 02000	(U)	American Metal Investments Inc	14,583.18

Orlando Central Pk No 34

13131	22 23 29 2792 04010	(U)	Eberle Richard D	HX 1,399.79
13132	22 23 29 2792 05040	(U)	Harvill Joseph R &	
			Harvill Linda J	HX 2,513.07
13133	22 23 29 2792 07010	(U)	Heron Christopher	543.69
13134	22 23 29 2792 07060	(U)	Pedraza Juan R & Pedraza Diane R	HX 995.95
13135	22 23 29 2792 07220	(U)	Wells Fargo Bank Minnesota N A Tr	HX 1,274.43
13136	22 23 29 2792 08010	(U)	Rodriguez Ismael	HX 2,160.90
13137	22 23 29 2792 08050	(U)	Mercado Emilio & Mercado Adelina	HX 652.17
13138	22 23 29 2792 08062	(U)	Ocasio Hugo & Carrasguillo Norma	HX 651.58

Orange Blossom Park

13139	22 23 29 6204 01090	(U)	Colman Frankie S 61 1/2% &	419.86

Orange Blossom Terrace

13140	22 23 29 6208 01120	(U)	Hernandez Milagros	HX 861.23

FIGURE 2.3 *Bank Lien Examples (Continued)*

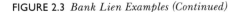

13145	22 23 29 6208 05160	(U)	Williams Rosemary	1,463.88
13146	22 23 29 6208 06130	(U)	Dandrade Kirth &	
			Dandrade Margarita	HX 762.05
13147	22 23 29 6208 08120	(U)	Atlantis Investment Inc	1,082.32
13148	22 23 29 6208 08140	(U)	Diaz Antonio Jr & Diaz Mydia	1,331.66
Prosper Colony Blk 1				
13149	22 23 29 7268 07005	(U)	Yeh Eddie & Yeh Vivien	1,371.48
13150	22 23 29 7268 07014	(U)	Holley William I & Ward W T	38.24
13151	22 23 29 7268 08004	(U)	Chase Manhattan Bank Tr	638.91
13152	22 23 29 7268 21001	(U)	D C Holding Co Inc	748.62
13153	22 23 29 7268 21004	(U)	D C Holding Co Inc	3,640.08
13154	22 23 29 7268 22007	(U)	D C Holding Co Inc	2,155.23
13155	22 23 29 7268 23010	(U)	Zimmer Donald R	HX 870.94
13156	22 23 29 7268 24016	(U)	Kelley Kathy L	HX 595.19
13157	22 23 29 7268 25001	(U)	Wheeler Joseph P Jr Tr	1,508.78

Anfernee "Penny" Hardaway, Dennis Scott, Darrell Armstrong, and Rony Seikaly, and major league baseball stars like Juan Gonzalez and Cy Young and World Series winner Frank Viola. See Figure 2.7. Even celebrities like Wesley Snipes and Carrot Top have had liens on properties. See Figure 2.8. In Figure 2.9, you'll see the Dr. J property on which I bought a lien. Dr. J bought two condos at the top of this nice building and made a penthouse. Since there were originally two properties and two deeds, there were two liens on the property. I bought the first one. Yes, the lien paid off about a month later.

I know what you are asking right now. These people make millions of dollars a year, why aren't they paying their property tax bills? While it is possible that these wealthy individuals did not pay on time because they thought they could invest their money elsewhere and make more than the lien amount in interest, that's unlikely. First, where could they get those kind of returns with relative safety? Second, they are busy people with little time to be snooping around to make a little bit extra return on their money.

FIGURE 2.4 *Government Lien Examples*

4416	18 22 28 0000 00060	(F)	Ramany Robert A	765.77
4417	18 22 28 0000 00062	(U)	King Gladys W & Womack Madeline A &	1,156.52
4418	18 22 28 0000 00079	(F)	Bank Of West Orange Attn: Property Dept	12,254.38
4419	18 22 28 0000 00080	(F)	Environmental Landscape Specialists Inc	2,181.11
4420	18 22 28 0000 00081	(F)	United States Of America C/O Property Manager	1,167.76

Grace Park

4421	18 22 28 3116 01010	(F)	Ocoee Holding Co Inc	1,002.46
4422	18 22 28 3116 01020	(F)	Ocoee Holding Co Inc	2,106.76
4423	18 22 28 3116 02070	(F)	Terry Edward J Tr C/O S A Tarr	4,725.06

11216-PT-01300   12151
ORANGEBROOK VILLAS CO-OP UNIT 13, ABRAHAM,LILLIAN 1/2 INT $609.82

11217-00-00700   12152
17-51-42 SE1/4 LESS SCL RR R/W & LESS PTS SEE TAX ROLL FOR ADDITIONAL LEGA, CITY OF HOLLY-WOOD $146,537.64

11217-01-01100 *   12153
MEEKINS HILLS 32-32 B LOT 22 W1/2,23,24 E1/2 BLK 10, SATCHELL,DEVEN & MARIA $3,278.27

11217-02-08200 *   12154
ORANGEBROOK GOLF ESTATES 99-1 B LOT 7 BLK 9

11219-01-05100
CARVER RANCHES 19-2
MAE &

11219-01-05700 *
CARVER RANCHES 19-2
VIOLA

11219-01-06200 *
CARVER RANCHES 1
BROWN,LOUIS B SR LE

11219-01-06310
CARVER RANCHES 19-2
AIR & NETTIE P

9714	26 22 29 6184 00010	(A)	Lutfi Investment Co Inc	6,651.42
9715	26 22 29 6184 00050	(A)	Burgess Theodore L	660.69

Orange Grove Park

9716	26 22 29 6236 00060	(A)	Deleveaux Wanda D & Deleveaux Vera J	846.12
9717	26 22 29 6236 00590	(A)	Lewis Albert Jr	1,017.18

Not In File

9718	26 22 29 6407 00100	(A)	United States Postal Service	9,916.04

Parramore James B Add To Orl

9719	26 22 29 6716 03011	(A)	Barnes George T Jr C/O Virginia Barnes	168.10
9720	26 22 29 6716 03041	(A)	Peacock J Thomas	4,257.47
9721	26 22 29 6716 07001	(A)	Lutfi Investment Co	422.64

FIGURE 2.5 *Commercial Lien: Medical Office Building*

My guess is that 90 percent of the time these people simply missed the payment deadline. Remember that celebrities and athletes often have little experience in the financial world and often hire someone else to manage their financial affairs. Many of these individuals have a financial company that pays their bills and the financial company may have either missed an invoice or never received it from the athlete/celebrity owner.

In the case of developers or real estate investment companies, many times the developer will hold off on paying the bill until that company finds a buyer for the property (and the tax bill is paid out at closing). Several years ago, the *Orlando Sentinel* ran a story on an upcoming tax sale and interviewed a developer who said he didn't pay his taxes on time because he saw it like a short-term loan, only without bank fees and closing costs.

In 2003, I bought liens on Chase Manhattan Bank and La-Salle National Bank (see Figure 2.3). Why would these national banks own residential properties? This seems easy enough to figure out. Years before, the banks originated or bought a loan on

FIGURE 2.6 *Celebrity Property Liens: Julius Erving and Hector Camacho*

8775	25 22 29 6677 08020	(A)	Halley William J Iii	2,580.69
8776	25 22 29 6677 08060	(A)	Maxwell Bernard & Maxwell Ruth	HX 895.29
8777	25 22 29 6677 13090	(A)	Halley William J Iii &	
			Halley Laura C	HX 1,385.64
8778	25 22 29 6677 15010	(A)	Dong Jeffrey Tr	1,660.88
8779	25 22 29 6677 16040	(A)	Zijl Adolf Everhardus	2,991.35
8780	25 22 29 6677 16060	(A)	Erving Julius W One Magic Pl	1,685.03
8781	25 22 29 6677 16070	(A)	Erving Julius W One Magic Pl	2,991.35

Reeves House

| 8782 | 25 22 29 7340 01040 | (A) | Young Sherwin F | HX 1,865.32 |
| 8783 | 25 22 29 7340 05060 | (A) | 720 Inc | 3,752.54 |

Diamond Cove Ut 2

6016	10 24 28 2035 01230	(U)	Winker Joseph K & Winker Karen L	HX 3,364.95
6017	10 24 28 2035 01710	(U)	Camacho Hector	4,915.39
6018	10 24 28 2035 01820	(U)	Antonov Stoimen & Antonov Anna	3,500.27
6019	10 24 28 2035 01840	(U)	Elorza Lisa Marie	HX 2,066.16
6020	10 24 28 2035 02330	(U)	Pouk Robert	HX 3,808.21

Emerald Forests Ut 1

6021	10 24 28 2491 00050	(U)	Battles Mark D & Battles Tracy L	HX 5,101.78
6022	10 24 28 2491 00120	(U)	Kim Sung Y & Kim Jia S	5,123.18
6023	10 24 28 2491 00450	(U)	Labranche Regina P	5,532.71

Emerald Forests Ut 2

| 6024 | 10 24 28 2495 01740 | (U) | Evans Michael B & Evans Donna E | HX 5,146.11 |
| 6025 | 10 24 28 2495 02410 | (U) | Valderrama Luis A | 4,543.44 |

FIGURE 2.7 *Sports Star Property Liens*

5825	29 23 28 4075 03700	(U)	Daoud Maher & Daoud Tina	3,716.09
5826	29 23 28 4075 03980	(U)	Thomas Thurman L & Thomas Patricia A	35,331.20
5827	29 23 28 4075 04580	(U)	Stamper John G & Stamper Leeanne S	5,408.92
5828	29 23 28 4075 04870	(U)	Baldez Neves Jose Maria & Baldez Sandra Regina Dos Santos	12,802.15
5829	29 23 28 4075 04890	(U)	Christopher Wren Inc	1,388.43
5830	29 23 28 4075 04900	(U)	Christopher Wren Inc	1,388.43
5831	29 23 28 4075 05400	(U)	Riley Maureen S & Welch James Douglas	2,234.85
5832	29 23 28 4075 05430	(U)	Mazza Joseph D &	
5968	03 24 28 7841 00200	(U)	Aurell Stanley O & Aurell Margery J	HX 2,913.28
5969	03 24 28 7841 00330	(U)	Dupuis Gilles P & Dupuis Michele L	3,775.76
5970	03 24 28 7841 00390	(U)	Kim David	HX 5,865.09
5971	03 24 28 7841 00500	(U)	Reyes Jon & Reyes Shirley	HX 5,445.43
5972	03 24 28 7841 00550	(U)	Antonov Stoimen & Antonov Anna	HX 3,303.53
5973	04 24 28 0000 00011	(U)	Viola Frank S Jr & Viola Kathy M	HX 70,961.87
5974	04 24 28 0000 00039	(U)	Mercado Perez Miguel A & Santiago Bonet Damaris G	12,856.67
5975	04 24 28 0000 00050	(U)	Kasu Abdul Ghani & Kasu Sayeeda	HX 9,749.31
5976	04 24 28 0000 00107	(U)	Haddad Jaal & Haddad Mylene	14,501.14

Lake Nona Ph 1 A Parcel 6

17869	07 24 31 4749 00060	(A)	Burton Michael & Burton Lorna	36,260.27
17870	07 24 31 4749 00090	(A)	Smee Roger G	12,066.97
17871	07 24 31 4749 00110	(A)	Oliver Vernon J & Neaves Mary Jane.	14,374.01

Lake Nona Ph 1 A Parcel 7

17872	07 24 31 4750 00150	(A)	Wilkins J Dominique & Wilkins Nicole R	4,167.79
17873	07 24 31 4750 00160	(A)	Wilkins J Dominique & Wilkins Nicole R	4,154.87
17874	07 24 31 4750 00310	(A)	Pierce Russell & Pierce Alison	5,487.10

Live Oak Ests Ph 2

17875	14 24 31 5109 00020	(U)	Gresham Lawrence & Gresham Carolyn &	HX 3,769.51

FIGURE 2.7 *Sports Star Property Liens (Continued)*

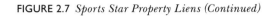

17859	07 24 31 4710 00100	(A)	Isayama Chiyoko	6,813.62

Lake Nona Ph 1 A Parcel 9

17860	07 24 31 4711 00150	(A)	Shaffer Lawrence J & Shaffer Kathleen B	29,213.78
17861	07 24 31 4711 00380	(A)	Faldo Nicholas A C/O Chris Hubman	5,130.20
17862	07 24 31 4711 00390	(A)	Faldo Nicholas A C/O Chris Hubman	5,130.20

Lake Nona Ph 1 A Parcel 4 Rep

17863	07 24 31 4713 00050	(A)	De Voogel Douglas P & De Voogel Lisa Marie	29,969.96
17864	07 24 31 4713 00100	(A)	Fryer John A E & Fryer June	16,203.78

Isleworth

5509	16 23 28 3899 00790	(U)	Bre Capital Group Inc	9,535.20
5510	16 23 28 3899 01030	(U)	Carter Butch	20,537.97
5511	16 23 28 3899 01150	(U)	Gonzalez Juan	HX 22,874.26
5512	16 23 28 3899 01480	(U)	Omicrom Investments Ltd	60,437.55
5513	16 23 28 3899 01500	(U)	Kay Christopher K & Kay Kristine K	HX 18,100.92
5514	16 23 28 3899 01730	(U)	Scott Dennis E	27,620.23
5515	16 23 28 3899 01770	(U)	Harding Victor H & Harding Deborah Lynn	HX 23,825.96
5516	16 23 28 3899 02980	(U)	Tominaga Yasuhiko & Tominaga Yoko	HX 14,172.63
5517	16 23 28 3899 03030	(U)	Lavin Jackie Renault House	15,774.52

5815	29 23 28 4074 01680	(U)	Hanning Franz S & Hanning Kelly M	25,708.19
5816	29 23 28 4074 01690	(U)	Blake Jeffrey C & Blake Lewanna	12,709.24
5817	29 23 28 4074 01800	(U)	Varraux Alan R & Varraux Lorraine P	12,867.22
5818	29 23 28 4074 01890	(U)	Hamilton Thomas E & Hamilton Jackie C	HX 6,881.14
5819	29 23 28 4074 01960	(U)	Griffey George K &	

FIGURE 2.7 *Sports Star Property Liens (Continued)*

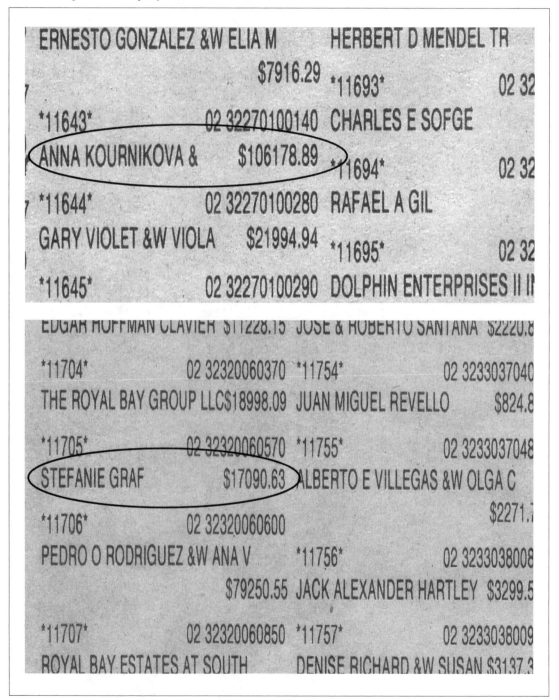

FIGURE 2.8 *Celebrity Property Liens*

5100	34 22 28 0117 00050	(U)	Anderson William L & Anderson Debra L	HX	3,489.
5101	34 22 28 0117 00330	(U)	Buchta Larry J & Buchta Dorothy J	HX	2,559.8
5102	34 22 28 0117 00690	(U)	Peake Donna		3,237.
5103	34 22 28 0117 05000	(U)	Almond Tree Estates Inc C/O Angelia Gordon Property Mngt Inc		139.7
Hamptons					
5104	34 22 28 3313 00280	(U)	Murcia Blanca L	HX	2,903.4
5105	34 22 28 3313 00290	(U)	Snipes Marion J & Snipes Wesley		4,943.0

14016	05 22 30 6654 04407	(B)	W P Park West Llc		754.05
Sylvan Park					
14017	05 22 30 8502 00121	(B)	Carrot Top Inc		4,683.65
Sylvan Park Rep					
14018	05 22 30 8503 00100	(B)	Gray Michael L & Gray Wendy P		4,434.99
Sylvan Hgts					
14019	05 22 30 8504 02072	(B)	Sims Leger Lien Hoa		2,470.51
14020	05 22 30 8504 04031	(B)	Salvation Army		476.93
14021	05 22 30 8504 04040	(B)	Taylor Scott M		2,296.62
14022	05 22 30 8504 04070	(B)	Razzani Russell A	HX	1,721.96

FIGURE 2.9 *Julius Erving's Condos*

a residential property and the loan went into default. What does a bank do when a loan goes into default? Yes, the bank forecloses and gets the property itself, since that was the collateral for the loan. When the bank becomes the new owner of the property, do they also inherit the real estate taxes due? Of course. When the bank takes the property back in a foreclosure, often the bank will not pay the tax bill immediately but will wait until it can resell the property and, like the developers, deduct the property taxes at closing. Don't misunderstand, the bank remains liable for the property taxes, it just delays paying them until it can find a buyer for the property.

At one sale a few years ago, I saw four houses from my own neighborhood listed in the tax lien list. Figure 2.10 will give you some idea of how nice these properties are. I was shocked. This is a small, gated community with only 16 homes. Most of the properties are in the $500,000 to $600,000 range. Twenty-five percent of my neighborhood had tax liens on them! As you can see, I lived in a bad neighborhood!

Can't these people pay their property taxes? I suppose they can. I can only tell you why I think these four properties had delinquent taxes on them. Two houses were in foreclosure (same owner), one involved a divorce, and one had an out-of-the-country owner. There are always a multitude of reasons why property taxes are not timely paid. Figure 2.11 is a million-dollar residence on a beautiful lake in a very exclusive gated community on which I bought a lien in 2003.

In Figure 2.12, you'll see various commercial properties on which I've bought liens.

So let me now ask you, Do you think these liens occur only on "crack" houses?

LARRY'S REMINDERS

- All properties (other than Indian reservations) incur property taxes. These taxes pay for local police and fire service, schools, libraries, roads, and salaries of local officials.
- Tax liens can be found on all kinds of properties—vacant lots, small houses, luxury homes, condos, commercial properties, shopping centers, and industrial properties. At any given sale, you may find liens on well-known companies, athletes, and even other government agencies.
- Lien amounts range from $100 to over $1 million.

FIGURE 2.10 *Four Examples of Residential Tax Lien Properties*

FIGURE 2.10 *Four Examples of Residential Tax Lien Properties (Continued)*

FIGURE 2.11 *A Million-Dollar Residence with Tax Lien*

FIGURE 2.12 *Commercial Properties with Tax Liens*

FIGURE 2.12 *Commercial Properties with Tax Liens (Continued)*

3

10 PERCENT TO 300 PERCENT RETURNS—AND THIS IS SAFE?

"I think stocks will be a great way to make 6 or 7 percent a year for the next 10 or 15 years. But anyone who expects 15 percent a year is living in a dream world."
WARREN BUFFETT

From 1926 to 2000, the stock market averaged 11 percent growth annually (*First Union Perspective,* May 2001). However, as First Union (now Wachovia) points out, the market did not maintain that growth on a steady and consistent basis. Says First Union: "In some years, the market will gain more or less than the average, and in some years it will post losses."

Indeed, years 2000–2002 were horrible years for stock market investors. In fact, according to *USA Today* (March 2-4, 2001), in 2000 the Nasdaq stock index dropped 39.3 percent. If you had invested your money on Nasdaq stocks, on average, you would have *lost* 39 percent of your money! Even the "rock solid" S&P 500 lost 10 percent! As such, an individual investing in the market at the beginning of year 2000 would likely need several years to recoup his or her principal! Perhaps even more startling was the revelation on April 29, 2001, of billionaire Warren Buffett, easily the most-respected name on Wall Street. In front of 17,000 listeners, Buffett stated: "I think stocks will be a great way to make 6 or 7 percent a year for the next 10 or 15 years. But anyone who expects

15 percent a year is living in a dream world" (*Chicago Tribune,* April 30, 2001).

Buffett's prognostication turned out to be optimistic, at least for 2001 and 2002. While 2003 and 2004 showed that the market had turned the corner, the damage to portfolios and retirement accounts from the 2000 to 2002 years was overwhelming. *USA Today* revealed that the S&P 500 lost another 13 percent in 2001 and 23.4 percent in 2002, while the Nasdaq lost another 21.1 percent in 2001 and 31.5 percent in 2002 (January 2, 2003). Rock-solid companies like Coca-Cola and General Electric lost half of their value. Fortunes were lost and were not coming back any time soon. In fact, an article by *BusinessWeek* on March 14, 2003, indicated that many investors in blue chip stocks who came into the market near its peak in 1999 might not recoup their principal for decades. Take a look at these respected companies and how long it may take an investor simply to regain his or her principal, assuming a 7 percent annual growth rate:

	Years to Recover
Microsoft	15
Intel	23
Amazon.com	23
AOL Time Warner	27
Yahoo!	38
Sun Microsystems	45
Lucent Technologies	55

Having been bludgeoned in the stock market, many investors are looking for a safe haven where they can park their money. Unfortunately, the typical choice for most Americans looking for a safe investment is to purchase a certificate of deposit. At the time of this writing, however, CDs are paying a meager 1 to 2 percent, depending on the maturity. Bonds and gold investments have been two other choices for safe-haven investing, but even these investments carry inherent risk. (See "Investors Finding Fewer Safe Havens," *USA Today,* March 5, 2003, and "Bonds: The Risks of Rising Rates," *BusinessWeek,* April 21, 2003.)

Where do investors turn when looking for a decent yield and a fair amount of safety? Is it possible to achieve a safe, steady, and reliable 8 to 15 percent, or even more? Indeed it is! As indicated in Chapter 1, tax lien certificates provide these types of reliable returns with the following safety benefits:

- They are administered by the government.
- They are secured by real estate.
- They are enforced by state law.
- Their rates are fixed.

Consider the chart in Figure 3.1. Notice the possible returns according to state jurisdiction. Keep in mind that these are only the better lien and hybrid states listed. See Part 3 for a complete list of states. In addition, keep in mind that many of the states listed are "bid down the interest" jurisdictions, which means that the bidding starts at a statutory maximum rate but may be bid down to as little as ¼ percent.

Let's start with the downside. In "bid down the interest" states like Florida, Illinois, and the District of Columbia, the statutory rate may be 18 percent, but that is only where the bidding begins. Most liens on good properties will be bid well below that now, since other investments are offering less than 5 percent. At the 2001 sale in Washington, D.C., for example, most liens went for around 9 percent. At recent Florida sales, I've seen rates from ¼ to 17 percent. Since rates on "safe" investments like certificates of deposit are so low, institutional bidders have been bidding most good properties down to ¼ percent. At the 2003 and 2004 sales, for example, institutional bidders competed with each other on most liens over about $1,500. For liens on nice properties, say lien amounts of $2,000 and up, these bidders would bid ¼ percent. For the novice investor this action didn't make any sense. Why would these institutional bidders accept a rate so low? The answer lies in the difference between an interest rate and a yield, or rate of return.

FIGURE 3.1 *Possible Returns on Tax Liens*

State	Statutory Rate	Maximum Return[1]
1. Texas[2]	25%	300%
2. Georgia	20	240
3. Illinois	18	216
4. Delaware[3]	15	180
5. Rhode Island	16	120
6. Indiana[4]	15	120
7. New Jersey[5]	19	90
8. Louisiana	13.7	72
9. Florida[6]	18	60
10. Wyoming	15.75	51
11. Montana	12	34
12. Iowa	24	24
13. Maryland[7]	12–20	20
14. Connecticut	18	18
15. Mississippi	18	18
16. New Hampshire	18	18
17. Ohio	18	18
18. District of Columbia[8]	18	18

[1]The maximum rate of return is determined by a redemption date of one month after the sale, where penalty states are concerned. If redemption occurs faster than one month, those states would show an even higher rate of return.

[2]Texas has a 25 percent penalty and six-month redemption period for nonhomestead, nonagricultural property (shown). For homestead or agricultural properties, the redemption period is two years and the penalty is 25 percent for year one and 50 percent for year two.

[3]Varies by county.

[4]Indiana is a premium bidding state that applies a penalty return. However, on any overbid (i.e., premium over the lien amount), the investor will receive only 10 percent simple interest (with the penalty applied to the lien amount).

[5]New Jersey is a "bid down the interest" state, starting at 18 percent. However, it also adds a penalty based on the size of the lien. Liens under $4,999 have an additional 2 percent penalty, liens from $5,000 to $9,999 have an additional 4 percent penalty, and liens of $10,000 and over have an additional 6 percent penalty. Both figures assume you got the lien under $5,000 and a redemption of two years. The maximum was based on a lien over $10,000 and redemption after one month.

[6]Florida is a "bid down the interest" state, starting at 18 percent. In addition, Florida has a minimum 5 percent penalty (thus, a lien paying off after one month receives a 60 percent rate of return).

[7]Varies by county. Several counties have a rate of 20 percent.

[8]The District of Columbia uses premium bidding (and the investor gets no interest on the premium). At the 2001 sale, the vast majority of liens were bid up (although I did get a couple for the minimum amount and maximum interest rate, although these were on vacant lots). When this occurs, the rate of return is reduced.

Let's say, for example, that I buy a lien in Florida at a rate of ¼ percent. My *yield,* or rate of return, is likely to be around 8 to 10 percent. This is the part that the novice investor misses altogether. Florida has a minimum penalty of 5 percent. As such, even if I bid 1 percent, the minimum penalty to the owner is 5 percent. If the owner pays the lien off one year later, do I get 1 percent or 5 percent? I would receive 5 percent, since that is the minimum.

Can you see that the state inserted this penalty as a safety net for investors? This penalty makes it worthwhile for the investor and also ensures that the county will sell all of its liens. Now let's continue the math. If the investor paid off the lien in one month, what is my rate of return? Since I'll get a 5 percent penalty in one month, that's a 60 percent rate of return ($5 \times 12 = 60$). And if the owner paid off in two months, that's a 30 percent return.

Now let's assume the investor bought 100 liens at a sale. Recall that Florida's redemption period is two years. As such, the investor bidding very low has a risk that some liens will pay off late in the redemption period. For example, if a lien paid off in the 24th month, the minimum 5 percent penalty would only give the investor a return of 2½ percent per year. However, institutional bidders realize that liens will redeem all throughout the redemption period. Some will redeem after 1 month, 2 months, 10 months, 15 months, and so on. Out of 100 liens, you can be assured that liens will redeem every month or so over the two-year period. In addition, many liens on very nice properties tend to redeem faster. As such, the investor will get returns of 60 percent on some liens, 30 percent on some liens, 20 percent on some liens, and, yes, 5 or 2½ percent on other liens.

Here's the second point about those institutional bidders going down to ¼ percent. For those liens that do not redeem, the investor will file for a tax deed (more on that in Chapter 6). In doing so, the investor must buy out the other lien holder (recall a two-year redemption period) at the rate that investor bid and pay the county a processing fee. The county will now take both certificates (his and the other lien holder's) and give the investor a new certificate, at a new interest rate of 18 percent. This aggregate lien will accrue at 18 percent until the tax deed sale, some four to six months away. If you account for some liens paying off quickly and others going to tax deed sale, you will now see why these bidders go down to ¼ percent at the sale. On average, their yield is in the range of 8 to 10 percent. In today's market, to get that yield safely is very attractive.

The good news, of course, is that in every case the investor is choosing the return that is acceptable. If the bidding goes down below the investor's acceptable rate, he or she simply drops out of the bidding and waits on the next lien. In Chapter 5, I'll discuss the different types of bidding systems and how to always get the best rates.

Now for the better news. First, some lien states have a flat rate. For example, Iowa pays a flat 2 percent per month. On an annualized basis, that's a fixed 24 percent per year! Any complaints? Maryland counties have flat rates that range from 12 to 20 percent. The best states, Texas and Georgia, however, are hybrid states and do not have interest rates but penalties. For example, in Texas the penalty is 25 percent and in Georgia, 20 percent. But that rate is neither an interest rate nor a yield, since the penalty is the same regardless of when it is paid. Suppose, for example, that I promise you a 25 percent per annum interest rate on a loan of $10,000. At the end of 12 months, I would owe you $2,500 interest plus the principal, right? At the end of six months, it would be $1,250. At the end of one month, $208.33.

Now let's switch to a 25 percent *penalty*. At the end of one year I owe you $2,500, just like the interest rate. But at the end of six months I still owe you $2,500. And at the end of one month I still owe you $2,500. What is your rate of return, or *yield,* if I pay you the $2,500 in just six months? Fifty percent. What is your yield if I pay you in just one month? *Three hundred* percent!

Now let's apply what we've learned about yields to Texas. If you invest in a Texas deed (recall that it is a hybrid state), the redemption period is either six months for nonhomestead, nonagricultural properties, or two years for a homestead or agricultural property. If the former, that means you have a 25 percent penalty with a six-month redemption period. If the owner redeems at the end of the six-month period, what is your rate of return? Fifty percent! What if the owner redeems after two months? One hundred fifty percent! One month? Three hundred percent!

Now I know what you are thinking: *Yes, that's great, but I still have to reinvest my money again.* Yes, you have to reinvest, but you have made a phenomenal yield, safely, and you can reinvest that money again in more deeds or in some other investment. If you just put the money under your bed, you'd still have a 25 percent yield for the year. My guess is that you wouldn't put the money under your bed but would reinvest it in another deed, lien, or other investment as soon as you received the cash. The good news for Texas is that deed sales occur monthly.

From the tax lien/deed investor's standpoint, penalties offer substantial benefits. In addition to hybrid states, some lien states also add penalties to their interest rates. For example, New Jersey is a "bid down the interest" state, starting at 18 percent. However, the state also adds a 2 to 4 percent penalty, depending on the size of the lien. In Part 3, I'll break down how each state works so you can see the impact of the interest, penalty, and redemption period rules.

I was speaking at a seminar not long ago and someone asked me afterward, "What is the best rate of return you have received on a lien?" I smiled. They guessed, "One hundred percent?" I smiled again. "Two hundred percent?" "Higher," I said. "Five hundred percent?" I smiled and again said, "Higher." "What," they said, "that's impossible."

While this return and scenario is not too common, it does occur. I'll give you the story and you figure out my rate of return. I buy a number of liens in various Florida counties each year. While Florida offers an interest rate (rather than a penalty), recall the minimum 5 percent return. That is, regardless of the interest rate at which you bought the lien, the state will make sure that the minimum you receive is 5 percent. I gave a brief rationale earlier why the state does this, but let's apply it.

Let's assume you bought a lien at 12 percent interest. Not a bad rate of return. But what if the owner redeems and pays it off after one month. What is the amount of interest you receive? Only 1 percent, right? If you bought a $2,000 lien, that's only $20 and is not really worth your while. So the legislature made it a little more palatable by requiring a minimum 5 percent penalty. On this lien, that is only $100, but it helps.

Now let's apply the Florida rule to the following scenario. At the annual sale in Orange County, Florida, the county requires a $1,000 deposit to bid and invoices the investor for amounts due beyond that after the sale (or sends a refund of the balance due if the investor buys less than $1,000 in liens). At the 2001 sale, the auction was held on May 24-28. Since I bought more than $1,000 in liens, the Tax Collector invoiced me for the balance due about two weeks later. The deadline for payment was June 12, as I recall. When I went in to the Tax Collector's office to pay the invoice, I noticed that I had a check in the packet the office assistant gave to me. Seeing a check, I said, "What's this?" "Oh, one of your liens redeemed," she said. It was a check for one of the liens I had purchased; the owner had redeemed and paid off the lien with the 5 percent penalty.

Let's do the math. If I received the 5 percent penalty one month after buying a lien, what would be my yield? Sixty percent ($5 \times 12 = 60$). Recall, however, that this check came in, with my 5 percent penalty, *before* I had actually paid for the lien! So what is my rate of return? Sixty percent? Higher. One hundred percent? Higher. Five hundred percent? Higher. Since I had not actually purchased the lien before I was paid a return, my rate of return would be *infinite*!

I'm often asked, "What's the best state to invest in?" That's like asking where you can find the best pizza. Ask someone from Chicago and someone from New York, and you'll likely get different answers. Once you've got the right city, then you have to choose the best restaurant. This investment scenario is much the same. What's the best state? That depends on your answers to these questions:

- Do you want to invest in liens or deeds?
- If you want to invest in liens, are you willing to invest in hybrid states?
- Where do you reside?
- Are you willing to travel to another state to invest?
- How much do you have to spend?
- Are you willing to do research?
- If you travel to another state, do you realize that you must deduct your expenses from your yield unless you are going there anyway?

I also usually tell people that they can invest based on one of these five options:

1. Invest in your local jurisdiction because it is close and easy.
2. Invest in the jurisdiction that pays the best rates.
3. Invest in the jurisdiction where your relatives live (i.e., you go there anyway).
4. Invest in the jurisdiction where you like to vacation.
5. Invest in the jurisdiction where you can own the property for the best price (i.e., deed sale).

Now let's look at possible answers to these questions. Suppose you tell me that you just want something simple and the best rate of return. I'll tell you to invest in Iowa, since it pays 2 percent per month. But if you live in Florida or California, there will be a plane fare, hotel, and rental car to deduct from your yield. If you live in California and don't have relatives in Iowa, I'll tell you to go to Phoenix and invest in an Arizona lien (16 percent, but a bid down jurisdiction). If you tell me you just want the best return and are willing to do some research, I'll tell you to go to Texas. If you tell me you want to acquire properties for as little as possible, I'll tell you to invest in Kansas or buy liens on properties whose redemption periods have already expired (more on that in Chapter 10).

Keep in mind also that one county may be substantially better (based on crowds or local rules) than the county next door, even though they are in the same state. You also may want to consider investing in jurisdictions that have online sales. There are so many variables to consider, the right investment jurisdiction will vary for each investor. My suggestion is to answer the questions above and look at the details of each state in Part 3.

LARRY'S REMINDERS

- Tax lien investing offers safe and reliable returns of 8 to 15 percent, and, in some jurisdictions, much more.
- Tax lien investing offers the following safety benefits:
  - They are administered by the government.
  - They are secured by real estate.
  - They are enforced by state law.
  - Their rates are fixed.
- Understand the difference between an interest rate (per annum) and a yield, which is your actual rate of return for any given period.
- Jurisdictions that have penalties will significantly increase your yield.
- There is no "best" state. Each state has pros and cons for investors, and each investor has specific needs, wants, and goals. Review the list of states in Part 3 to determine which is best for you.

4

THE AUCTION
Rules, Dates, and Fees

Most lien states will have an annual auction, while deed and hybrid deed states typically have their sales more often. For example, California has biannual sales. Georgia and Texas, both hybrid states, conduct their sales on a monthly basis. Larger counties in Pennsylvania typically hold their deed sales *weekly*!

Keep in mind that a lien state also may have deed sales. For example, Florida, a lien state, also conducts deed sales, since a lien not redeemed requires the lien holder to have the property sold at a deed sale to pay off the lien. In smaller Florida counties, these deed sales will occur quarterly or bimonthly, while larger counties will have monthly deed sales. Orange County, Florida, typically will have two sales per month but may have as many as four sales in a month! The rules and regulations for these auctions vary by state and also by county. You will need to contact the specific county to review its rules.

The remaining information in this section will largely apply to lien jurisdictions. For more information on deed auctions, see Chapters 8 to 13.

FEES

Few counties charge a fee for the right to bid at their auctions, although some of the larger counties do so. For example, Woodbury County, Iowa (second largest in the state), charged a $75 fee at its 2001 sale, while Polk County (Des Moines), Iowa (largest in the state), charged a $100 fee at its 2001 sale. All of the other Iowa counties that I've been to, however, do not charge a fee. Florida counties do not charge a fee, but many require a $1,000 deposit before bidding. The District of Columbia requires a deposit of 20 percent of what you expect to buy at the auction. Indianapolis, Indiana, charges no fee and requires no deposit. Deed auctions typically do not require fees or deposits, although larger counties may require a minimum deposit. Los Angeles County, California, for example, requires a deposit of $1,000 before you are allowed to bid at the annual auction. If a county requires a deposit and you spend less than that amount, the county will mail you a check for the difference.

I know what a few of you may be thinking at this point: *To have better odds of getting a lot of good liens, can I have more than one bidder card at the auction?* Indeed, you may have more than one card. However, most counties will limit you in several ways. First, you must pay your fee or deposit per bidder card. Second, each bidder card must be represented by a different Social Security number or tax identification number (i.e., a corporate or retirement account purchase). Third, many counties will give you only one bidder card per person in the auction. For example, say you have one bidder card representing you personally (with your Social Security number on the W-9) and another card representing your corporation (with its tax identification number on the W-9). Many counties will let you take only one card in at a time. If you bring a friend to hold one card, that solves the problem. Otherwise, when you have finished buying for one card, you must return that card to the county and then go back into the auction room with the second card. This is really not a problem, and I've done it many times; however, you need to know this rule before you try to walk in with two cards at one time.

AUCTION DATES

A disadvantage of lien states, however, is that the auction only comes once a year. For example, you may decide to invest in Iowa liens because of the outstanding rate of 2 percent per month. However, the auctions are all held in June. So what do you do when some of your liens redeem and you want to keep them earning interest? Ideally, you immediately invest in another lien in another state. Since lien sales are held virtually every month of the year, you can keep reinvesting. The problem, of course, is that you don't want to travel to each jurisdiction every time you want to buy another lien. While some counties are moving to allow online bidding, most counties still require a warm body in the auction room (although this is changing rapidly). More on that later in this chapter.

A second potential disadvantage to lien investing is that some counties may be holding their auctions on exactly the same date, and you cannot be in two places at one time, unless you send a friend or family member to one auction and you attend the other. As such, you may be able to visit only one county auction for that month or year. For example, all of the Iowa counties pay the 2 percent per month, but the lien auctions all start on the same day! For the 2001 auctions in Iowa, I reviewed lien lists and spoke to the County Treasurers in Shelby, Monoma, Harrison, and Woodbury counties. I was able to attend, however, only auctions at Shelby, Woodbury, and Polk counties. In case you are wondering how I managed to get in three counties, here was my schedule:

Monday morning—Attend Shelby County sale (smallest county).

Monday afternoon—Drive to and attend Woodbury County sale.

Tuesday morning—Drive to Des Moines (Polk County).
Tuesday afternoon—Attend Polk County sale.

Since smaller counties like Shelby, Monoma, and Harrison would be finished in two hours or less, I had to choose one to attend first. I knew that Woodbury County was large enough to have its sale continue well into the afternoon, so I attended that sale second. Since the Polk County sale would continue to a second or third day, I attended that sale third. There is somewhat of a strategy here, because smaller counties have fewer bidders but also fewer liens. By my estimates, Shelby County had only 20 bidders but only about 75 liens available; Woodbury had about 100 bidders and about 1,500 liens available; and Des Moines had 300 to 400 bidders with several thousand liens available.

Florida auctions take place in late May and early June. The larger counties will hold an auction for one to three weeks, while the smaller counties will hold the auction in two to four days. Since there are 67 counties in Florida, an investor can literally jump around the state to invest more money. In reality, however, only the institutional bidders that have millions and millions to invest do this. Most individual investors will run out of money to spend at one county. The good news for those who don't like to travel is that most of the large Florida counties have changed their auctions to online only.

ONLINE INVESTING

A word about online investing in tax liens—it's coming. Several states are now experimenting with conducting their sales, or some of their sales, online. From the state's (or county's) point of view, this type of administration is much faster and more economical. From the investor's standpoint, there are pros and cons to having an online sale. The benefit is for people who want to invest in another region of the state or country. Instead of actually going there, now they can buy liens over the Internet during the sale week. Someone with a lot of money can be buying liens in several counties simultaneously. The downside is that small, local buyers will likely have additional competition. Second, since bids are placed ahead of time, you really don't have a chance to watch the "feel" of how the bidding is going. These online auctions are new, and time will tell how they play out.

I bought liens in the 2004 online auction for Orange County, Florida (Orlando). The system Orlando used was the same as in Miami and most other major cities. Here's how it worked.

The county directed you to register for the sale at a specific Web site. You then mailed the county a check for $1,000 per bidder number. All liens were listed on the site with lien amount and parcel identification number (allowing you to cross-reference to the appraiser's office). Once registered, you would type in a bid percentage next to the lien you desired. See Figure 4.1. When the auction started, the computer system would award the lien to the bidder with the lowest percentage (bid down system). If two bidders had the same percentage, the computer would pick at random.

The online system actually had one surprising benefit. Let's say you bid ¼ percent and the next lowest bid was 8.25 percent. Because you would only go to 8 percent at a live auction, the computer system would award you the lien at 8 percent. However, because most liens on good properties in my county are now bid at ¼ percent by the institutional bidders (see Chapter 3 for why), many bidders (e.g., Wachovia, Atlantic Bank) had over a dozen bids at ¼ percent. As such, if you have two bids at ¼ and the next lowest bid is 8 percent, the computer only sees two bidders at ¼ and will give you that item at ¼ rather than 7¾ (it happened to me!).

Time will tell if online auctions are here to stay. In my estimation, the trend will continue and more states will adopt it. For the investor, online auctions have advantages and disadvantages. For county administrators and tax collectors, however, online auctions have virtually no downside. Good or bad, I think they are here to stay.

FIGURE 4.1 *Orange County Online Auction*

| Summary | Search | Reports | Budgets | Bid | Results | Upload/Download | My Ac |

You Are: Larry Loftis   Bidder ID: BUYR-LE (# 305)   Last Update: 5:02:43 p

Refresh

Total Security Deposits	Maximum Allowable Budget	Actual Budget Variance (Over/Under Allowable)
$1,000.00	$10,000.00	$0.00

Make Payment

Total Budget: $10,000.00
Budget Used: $0.00
Budget Remaining: $10,000.00

Save Budgets

Batch #	Adv #'s	Award Time	Total Submitted Bids	Batch Budgets
1	1 - 1000	May 19, 2004 9:00 am EDT	$ —	$
2	1001 - 2000	May 19, 2004 10:00 am EDT	$ —	$
3	2001 - 3000	May 19, 2004 11:00 am EDT	$ —	$
4	3001 - 4000	May 19, 2004 12:00 pm EDT	$ —	$
5	4001 - 5000	May 19, 2004 1:00 pm EDT	$ —	$
6	5001 - 6000	May 19, 2004 2:00 pm EDT	$ —	$
7	6001 - 7000	May 19, 2004 3:00 pm EDT	$ —	$
8	7001 - 8000	May 19, 2004 4:00 pm EDT	$ —	$
9	8001 - 9000	May 20, 2004 9:00 am EDT	$ —	$
10	9001 - 10000	May 20, 2004 10:00 am EDT	$ —	$
11	10001 - 11000	May 20, 2004 11:00 am EDT	$ —	$
12	11001 - 12000	May 20, 2004 12:00 pm EDT	$ —	$
13	12001 - 13000	May 20, 2004 1:00 pm EDT	$ —	$
14	13001 - 14000	May 20, 2004 2:00 pm EDT	$ —	$
15	14001 - 15000	May 20, 2004 3:00 pm EDT	$ —	$
16	15001 - 16000	May 20, 2004 4:00 pm EDT	$ —	$
17	16001 - 17000	May 21, 2004 9:00 am EDT	$ —	$
18	17001 - 18000	May 21, 2004 10:00 am EDT	$ —	$
19	18001 - 19000	May 21, 2004 11:00 am EDT	$ —	$
20	19001 - 20000	May 21, 2004 12:00 pm EDT	$ —	$
21	20001 - 20231	May 21, 2004 1:00 pm EDT	$ —	$
Save Budgets		**Totals:**	$	$ —

A STRATEGY FOR THE BIGGER PLAYERS

Want more liens? Recall that the county is going to give one bidder card per Social Security number or tax identification number. If your county is using a "random selection" or "rotational" bidding process (see Chapter 5), the more cards you have in the auction (or online), the better chances you will have to purchase excellent liens. I typically will use one card for my personal investments and another card for my corporate purchases. With this strategy, I have better odds of getting more liens. Some investors use multiple corporations and/or children's and spouse's Social Security numbers to acquire multiple bidder numbers.

At the Shelby County, Iowa, sale I attended in 2001, for example, there were 22 bidder cards issued. However, one individual had some 8 numbers (held by family members). He had the opportunity to buy over one third of the liens offered! At the Woodbury sale, one individual had 20 numbers (held by individuals who were hired for one day to do so). Once these bidders acquired liens for their "boss" (likely using their own Social Security numbers), they would typically assign them to their boss (most counties charge $2 to $10 to do so).

You may want to consider using two cards, even in "bid down" jurisdictions. Here's why. At live auctions, many counties get behind on their timetable and have to "catch up." The county tax collector or treasurer has rented a commercial facility to conduct the auction for, say, one week. The county official knows that to finish on time he or she must complete one fifth of the liens for sale each day. In many cases, if the county gets behind, the county official conducting the sale will begin to start "picking" numbers quickly (or limit bidding to just a few seconds) in order to move through liens and catch up. When this happens, it means the county has just unofficially moved from a "bid down" system to a "random selection" system! Thus, the more cards you have in the room, the better your chances.

REGISTRATION

All counties require registration prior to your investing at a lien auction. The reason for this is because the county will be reporting the interest you receive to the Internal Revenue Service. Typically, this registration just means filling out a W-9 form for each Social Security or tax identification number and a bidder registration form (see Figure 4.2). Because most auctions commence in the morning, you should register at least one day in advance. Keep in mind that some counties may require you to register well in advance of the auction. At the Los Angeles deed auction, for example, the county required registration a week before the auction. You'll need to speak with the county in advance to review its registration policy. In most lien jurisdictions, the county will allow you to register at the sale itself during any auction day.

PAYMENT

Most large counties require certified funds for buying liens. The problem, of course, is that you don't know how many liens you will actually get, or what will be the total dollar amount of those liens before the auction. In most cases, the county will give you a period of time to get the accurate amount of funds. That time is usually 2 to 24 hours. Here are a few examples:

- **District of Columbia.** The investor must always have at least 10 percent (of what you will buy) on deposit with the tax collector. If your purchasing balance drops the deposit below 10 percent, you will be asked to increase your deposit before continuing to purchase liens. You pay the balance in full at the end of your buying or the end of the sale.
- **Indianapolis, Indiana.** No deposit is required. The investor pays for the lien, in certified funds, as soon as he wins the bid. The county's treasurer sits up front, and the winning bidder makes his or her way there immediately to pay for

FIGURE 4.2 *Taxpayer Identification Form W-9*

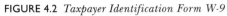

| Form **W-9**
(Rev. January 2003)
Department of the Treasury
Internal Revenue Service | **Request for Taxpayer
Identification Number and Certification** | Give form to the
requester. Do not
send to the IRS. |

Print or type
See Specific Instructions on page 2.

Name

Business name, if different from above

Check appropriate box: ☐ Individual/ Sole proprietor ☐ Corporation ☐ Partnership ☐ Other ▶ .... ☐ Exempt from backup withholding

Address (number, street, and apt. or suite no.)

Requester's name and address (optional)

City, state, and ZIP code

List account number(s) here (optional)

Part I   Taxpayer Identification Number (TIN)

Enter your TIN in the appropriate box. For individuals, this is your social security number (SSN). **However, for a resident alien, sole proprietor, or disregarded entity, see the Part I instructions on page 3.** For other entities, it is your employer identification number (EIN). If you do not have a number, see **How to get a TIN** on page 3.

Note: *If the account is in more than one name, see the chart on page 4 for guidelines on whose number to enter.*

Social security number

or

Employer identification number

Part II   Certification

Under penalties of perjury, I certify that:

1. The number shown on this form is my correct taxpayer identification number (or I am waiting for a number to be issued to me), **and**

2. I am not subject to backup withholding because: **(a)** I am exempt from backup withholding, or **(b)** I have not been notified by the Internal Revenue Service (IRS) that I am subject to backup withholding as a result of a failure to report all interest or dividends, or **(c)** the IRS has notified me that I am no longer subject to backup withholding, **and**

3. I am a U.S. person (including a U.S. resident alien).

Certification instructions. You must cross out item **2** above if you have been notified by the IRS that you are currently subject to backup withholding because you have failed to report all interest and dividends on your tax return. For real estate transactions, item **2** does not apply. For mortgage interest paid, acquisition or abandonment of secured property, cancellation of debt, contributions to an individual retirement arrangement (IRA), and generally, payments other than interest and dividends, you are not required to sign the Certification, but you must provide your correct TIN. (See the instructions on page 4.)

Sign Here   Signature of U.S. person ▶   Date ▶

Purpose of Form

A person who is required to file an information return with the IRS, must obtain your correct taxpayer identification number (TIN) to report, for example, income paid to you, real estate transactions, mortgage interest you paid, acquisition or abandonment of secured property, cancellation of debt, or contributions you made to an IRA.

U.S. person. Use Form W-9 only if you are a U.S. person (including a resident alien), to provide your correct TIN to the person requesting it (the requester) and, when applicable, to:

1. Certify that the TIN you are giving is correct (or you are waiting for a number to be issued),

2. Certify that you are not subject to backup withholding, or

3. Claim exemption from backup withholding if you are a U.S. exempt payee.

Note: *If a requester gives you a form other than Form W-9 to request your TIN, you must use the requester's form if it is substantially similar to this Form W-9.*

Foreign person. If you are a foreign person, use the appropriate Form W-8 (see **Pub. 515,** Withholding of Tax on Nonresident Aliens and Foreign Entities).

Nonresident alien who becomes a resident alien. Generally, only a nonresident alien individual may use the terms of a tax treaty to reduce or eliminate U.S. tax on certain types of income. However, most tax treaties contain a provision known as a "saving clause." Exceptions specified in the saving clause may permit an exemption from tax to continue for certain types of income even after the recipient has otherwise become a U.S. resident alien for tax purposes.

If you are a U.S. resident alien who is relying on an exception contained in the saving clause of a tax treaty to claim an exemption from U.S. tax on certain types of income, you must attach a statement that specifies the following five items:

1. The treaty country. Generally, this must be the same treaty under which you claimed exemption from tax as a nonresident alien.

2. The treaty article addressing the income.

3. The article number (or location) in the tax treaty that contains the saving clause and its exceptions.

4. The type and amount of income that qualifies for the exemption from tax.

5. Sufficient facts to justify the exemption from tax under the terms of the treaty article.

Cat. No. 10231X   Form **W-9** (Rev. 1-2003) the lien. Most investors will give the county a large cashier's check to cover their buying for the entire day.

- **Iowa.** No deposit is required. A few large counties will charge a small fee ($75 for Woodbury, $100 for Polk in 2001) for a bidding card. Payment is made for the purchases at the end of the day in certified funds, although some small counties will allow for personal checks.
- **Florida.** A $1,000 deposit is generally required in the larger counties. Some counties will mail an invoice to the investor about two weeks after the sale (with about two weeks to mail certified funds). Other counties will give the investor one or two days to return with certified funds. See Figure 4.3 for my examples from Orange and Seminole counties in 2003.

As you can see, every county sets its own rules for timely payment. Check with each county before the sale for its rules. Each county will have a "Tax Sale Guidelines" handout setting forth its rules and regulations. See Appendix A.

LARRY'S REMINDERS

- Lien sales typically occur annually, while deed sales may occur biannually, quarterly, monthly, or even weekly.
- Most jurisdictions only have live auctions, but online auctions are becoming more popular with tax collectors.
- Typically, you are allowed only one bidder card per person in the auction room.
- To receive a bidder card, you will need a Social Security number or tax identification number. You can invest personally, or though an entity like a corporation, trust, or retirement account.
- Many counties will require a deposit before allowing you to bid. Review each county's rules prior to attending the auction.

FIGURE 4.3 *Successful Auction Examples*

CERTIFICATE SALE BILLING

DATE: 06/02/2003

BUYER NO:

BIDDER NO: 81

NAME: NATIONAL TAX LIEN INSTITUTE

ADDRESS:

BALANCE DUE $33,237.07   20

LESS DEPOSIT   1,000.00

BALANCE DUE $32,237.07

PLEASE REMIT BY CASHIER'S CHECK, MONEY ORDER, OR CASH

TO: EARL K. WOOD, Orange County Tax Collector
     P. O. BOX 2551
     ORLANDO, FLORIDA 32802

PAYMENTS NOT RECEIVED IN THIS OFFICE BY JUNE 12, 2002
WILL RESULT IN FORFEITURE OF DEPOSIT
AND LOSS OF CERTIFICATES.

FOR FURTHER INFORMATION, PLEASE CALL:

BARBARA HOWE - (407)836-2708

EARL K. WOOD, TAX COLLECTOR
The Sun Trust Center Tower • 200 South Orange Avenue • Reply To: Post Office Box 2551 • Orlando, Florida 32802-2551
(407) 836-2705 • http://www.tax.co.orange.fl.us

FIGURE 4.3 *Successful Auction Examples (Continued)*

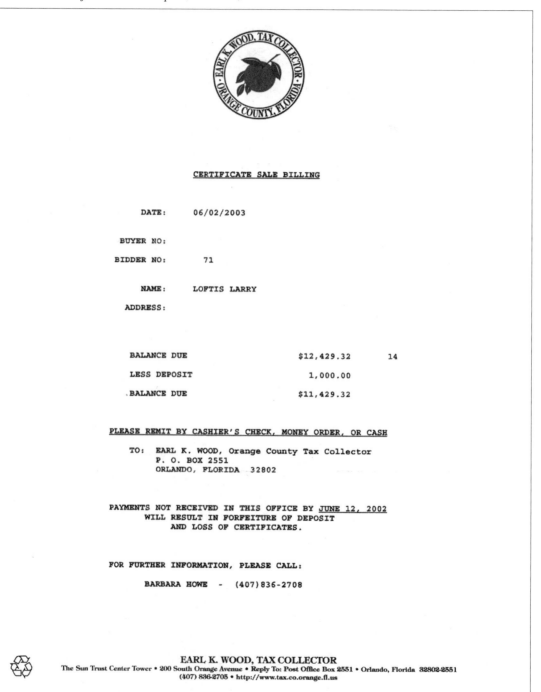

CERTIFICATE SALE BILLING

DATE: 06/02/2003

BUYER NO:

BIDDER NO: 71

NAME: LOFTIS LARRY

ADDRESS:

BALANCE DUE	$12,429.32	14
LESS DEPOSIT	1,000.00	
BALANCE DUE	$11,429.32	

PLEASE REMIT BY CASHIER'S CHECK, MONEY ORDER, OR CASH

TO: EARL K. WOOD, Orange County Tax Collector
P. O. BOX 2551
ORLANDO, FLORIDA 32802

PAYMENTS NOT RECEIVED IN THIS OFFICE BY JUNE 12, 2002
WILL RESULT IN FORFEITURE OF DEPOSIT
AND LOSS OF CERTIFICATES.

FOR FURTHER INFORMATION, PLEASE CALL:

BARBARA HOWE   -   (407)836-2708

EARL K. WOOD, TAX COLLECTOR
The Sun Trust Center Tower • 200 South Orange Avenue • Reply To: Post Office Box 2551 • Orlando, Florida 32802-2551
(407) 836-2705 • http://www.tax.co.orange.fl.us

FIGURE 4.3 *Successful Auction Examples (Continued)*

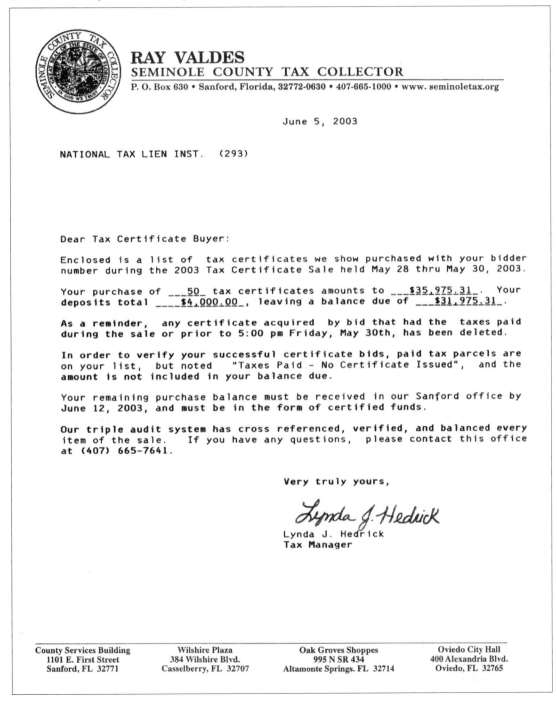

RAY VALDES

SEMINOLE COUNTY TAX COLLECTOR

P. O. Box 630 • Sanford, Florida, 32772-0630 • 407-665-1000 • www. seminoletax.org

June 5, 2003

NATIONAL TAX LIEN INST. (293)

Dear Tax Certificate Buyer:

Enclosed is a list of tax certificates we show purchased with your bidder number during the 2003 Tax Certificate Sale held May 28 thru May 30, 2003.

Your purchase of ___50_ tax certificates amounts to ___$35,975.31_ . Your deposits total ____$4,000.00_ , leaving a balance due of ___$31,975.31_ .

As a reminder, any certificate acquired by bid that had the taxes paid during the sale or prior to 5:00 pm Friday, May 30th, has been deleted.

In order to verify your successful certificate bids, paid tax parcels are on your list, but noted "Taxes Paid – No Certificate Issued", and the amount is not included in your balance due.

Your remaining purchase balance must be received in our Sanford office by June 12, 2003, and must be in the form of certified funds.

Our triple audit system has cross referenced, verified, and balanced every item of the sale. If you have any questions, please contact this office at (407) 665-7641.

Very truly yours,

Lynda J. Hedrick

Lynda J. Hedrick
Tax Manager

County Services Building	Wilshire Plaza	Oak Groves Shoppes	Oviedo City Hall
1101 E. First Street	384 Wilshire Blvd.	995 N SR 434	400 Alexandria Blvd.
Sanford, FL 32771	Casselberry, FL 32707	Altamonte Springs. FL 32714	Oviedo, FL 32765

5

BIDDING

Tricks of the Trade

*"What? You mean that I only get the interest rate on
the lien amount, not on the premium?"*
DISTRICT OF COLUMBIA INVESTOR ON THE *THIRD* AUCTION DAY

In 2001, I attended a tax lien sale in Washington, D.C. I purchased some liens on the first day of the sale and then left to attend another sale the next day. The following day, the third day of the D.C. sale, I returned to D.C. to buy more liens. I arrived during a break, so only a few people were remaining in the room. While looking for a place to sit, I overheard a conversation going on behind me. A lady was discussing the sale rules with another investor. With a look of shock on her face she exclaimed, "What? You mean that I only get the interest rate on the lien amount, not on the premium?" I knew exactly what happened. This lady, who now had been buying liens for three days, just found out that she was not getting any interest on the premiums for her liens.

In D.C. and other jurisdictions, the investor bids a "premium" over the lien amount. The investor receives 18 percent on the lien, but no interest at all on the premium bid. For example, if the lien amount was $1,000 and I bid $2,000, my yield would be 9 percent, since I received 18 percent on the first $1,000 but no interest on the second $1,000. Suffice it to say, this poor lady's overall return was well below what she originally thought. The time for learning the rules for a tax lien sale is *before* the auction, not three days into it!

While bidding procedures are typically dictated by state law, most states give the county official who runs the sale (usually either the county treasurer or tax collector) great leeway in the matter. For example, a state statute might state that the official bidding method is "bid down the ownership," while the county official actually uses a "rotational" system. For that reason, an investor should always review the county's bidding rules and speak with a county official and other seasoned investors before bidding.

BIDDING SYSTEMS

States generally use one of the following five types of bidding systems.

Bid Down the Interest

A "bid down the interest" system means that the state sets a maximum rate, but bidders at the auction may bid a lower amount acceptable to them. For example, Florida is a "bid down the interest" state, starting at the statutory maximum of 18 percent. At Florida live auctions, each bidder will receive a placard with a bidder number on it. When the official announces a particular lien, the investors who want that lien raise their numbers and shout out the interest rates they will accept. The county official typically waits until the bidding stops and awards the lien to the lowest bidder. If no one offers a rate below the statutory rate but several bidders have raised their cards, the county official will sell the lien to one investor at 18 percent by picking the investor at random. See Figure 5.1 for yours truly at work (I'm in the back with card #114)!

FIGURE 5.1 *Yours Truly at Work (I'm bidder #114.)*

I have attended the Orlando tax lien sale every year since 1999 and always seem to pick up interesting stories. In 2003, for example, a lady walked into the sale on the second day of a weeklong auction. I assumed it was her first auction, since she came late in the afternoon of the second day and walked directly to the front of the room to get a seat in the front row. In Orlando (and most cities), institutional investors send representatives at 6 AM (or earlier) to make sure they get seats in the first row, and these seats are always taken shortly after the doors open. Looking around for a while, she finally found a seat in the third row. What happened next will require a little background on the Orlando sale.

Since Florida is a very good lien state, a number of institutional bidders (e.g., Wachovia Bank, Bank Atlantic, and a couple of private funds) will bid at the auctions in the larger cities like Orlando, Miami, Fort Lauderdale, and Tampa. All of the auctions in Florida take place in May and June. Since Orlando is always the first auction in the state, these institutional bidders train their representatives, so that they can invest without supervision in the other cities. I normally see about four or five institutional bidders at this sale. These investors are very aggressive in bidding rates for several reasons:

1. They have millions of dollars to invest.
2. There are many beautiful properties on which to buy liens.
3. Florida has a minimum penalty of 5 percent (which means that even if you bid to 1 percent, if the owner redeems, he or she has to pay a minimum of 5 percent). For example, if I bid 1 percent and the owner redeems one month later, I get 5 percent, or a 60 percent rate of return ($5 \times 12 = 60$).
4. The institutional investors know that most of the nice properties will redeem quickly, triggering the 5 percent minimum.
5. If the owner does not redeem the lien and the investor forecloses on the lien by buying out the other lien (a two-year redemption period means two sales), the county gives the investor a new certificate for 18 percent, which accrues until the actual deed auction to sell the property and pay off the lien holder.
6. Based on numbers 3 to 5 above, these investors know that their total yield will far exceed what their bid amount was at the auction.

Given this information, the institutional bidders in Orlando recently have begun to bid most liens down to ¼ percent, the minimum bid under Florida law. They do this by yelling "Quarter," which means one quarter of 1 percent. My estimate is that their overall yield will be in the range of 8 to 10 percent, if I average out their returns on all liens. Now back to our newcomer at the auction.

After watching the institutional investors bidding "quarter" on many large, expensive properties, this lady began to jump in, also bidding "quarter" very aggressively. It didn't make sense to me, or to the institutional investors sitting in front of me. If she was an institutional bidder, she would have been there on the first day, got a seat in the front row, and had very organized notebooks on the properties coming up (where investor representatives are shown which properties to bid on and to list for their company the percentage at which they bought a lien). After she had bought five or six liens at ¼ percent, the institutional investor in front of me surmised that these would all default, meaning that the investor wouldn't be able to pay for them and they would go back to the county. I agreed. She went on to buy several more liens before the day was over, covering properties valued at over $1 million.

At the beginning of the sale the next day, a county official made an announcement that we all expected. He said, "Folks, remember that you are bidding on the lien *percentage,* not the property itself." Translated: The lady yesterday bidding ¼ percent on all those properties thought she was *acquiring* those properties for one quarter! As absurd as this sounds, it's a true story. She simply did not know the rules or what was going on.

But the story's not over! Later that day when this lady was bidding and buying liens at ¼ percent, she decided to change seats. She wanted to be in the seats where the institutional bidders were sitting. Directly in front of me were three representatives from one institutional bidder company. They were college students on summer break making some extra money working for this company at the auction. One of them, a young man probably 20 years of age, went out of the room for a break. Like most people, he left his bidding placard on his seat so that no one would take his spot while he was away. While he was outside, our aggressive newcomer lady decides she's going to take his seat in the second row. She does and begins bidding and buying again.

After about 30 minutes, she sees a seat open up in the first row so she takes her belongings and moves again.

Shortly thereafter, the college student returns and takes his old seat. Since he's sitting directly in front of me, I see him begin to look around for something—under his seat, next to him, on the floor around him. He has a very worried, if not distraught, look on his face. I realized what had happened. The rookie lady who had taken his seat also had taken his bidding card with her to the new seat in the front row! I tapped the young man on the shoulder and explained that the lady had taken his seat while he was outside and that she might inadvertently have taken his number. I might as well have told him that he had cancer! Since everyone knew this lady was clueless, he knew of the danger of her having his bidding number. So he politely tapped the lady and asked, "Ma'am, you don't have my bidder card, do you?" She fumbled through her belongings and, finding it, said, "Oh, I'm sorry, I sure do; here you go." Horrified, the young student exclaimed, "You didn't buy anything with it, did you?" She didn't *think* so. So the second lesson from this story is to always have your bidding card with you or with a trusted associate!

Premium Bidding

Premium bidding occurs where the county awards the lien to the investor bidding the highest premium above the lien amount. For example, on a $500 lien, the winning bid may be $1,000: the $500 lien plus a $500 premium. What will differ, however, is how the county will treat the interest rate for the winning bid. Counties generally use one of the following five systems:

1. The premium and the lien both receive the same interest rate or penalty.
2. The premium and the lien both receive interest, but at different rates.

3. The lien amount receives interest, while the premium amount does not.
4. The premium amount receives interest, while the lien amount does not.
5. The premium is lost (the investor does not receive his principal back on any premium paid).

The example at the beginning of this chapter shows that the District of Columbia offers no interest on the premium portion (#3). In other areas, like Texas for example, the investor will receive his or her interest rate or penalty on both the lien amount and the premium (#1). This system is the best scenario for the investor, since the investor really does not care what the bidding goes to because he'll get his penalty or interest return on the entire amount.

Indiana uses system #2, paying a different rate for the premium and the lien. Indiana has a penalty return on the lien amount (10 percent or 15 percent, depending on the redemption date). However, any premium amount (which they call an "overbid") receives only 10 percent simple interest. While this tends to reduce your overall rate of return, a small overbid carrying 10 percent interest will not disappoint too many investors. One additional note about the Indiana system: in Indianapolis, the county official uses a PowerPoint system to list liens for sale on the screen (as do many counties). An unusual aspect of their sale, however, is that they list 25 liens at a time on the screen, and any interested bidders simply voice their interest in one of the liens. If others want to bid on the one you just announced, they do so by raising their bidder cards to acknowledge a premium bid. If no one else raises his or her card, you get it at the minimum bid.

In systems #2 through #5, prepared investors simply adjust their bids before bidding so that they get their acceptable rates of return. For example, if your jurisdiction pays no interest on your premium but pays 18 percent on the lien amount, someone who wants at least a 9 percent rate of return cannot bid more than $2,000 for a $1,000 lien. If you can acquire that lien for bidding only $1,500, so much the better, as you'll be getting a return of 12 percent.

Random Selection

In a random selection jurisdiction, the county official will randomly select a bidder number and ask that investor if he or she wants the particular lien up for sale. If that bidder declines, the official will select another bidder and once again ask if the bidder wants the lien. This process continues for several rounds. If none of the bidders selected wants the lien, the county official will typically ask, "Does anyone want this lien?" If anyone wants it, that bidder is awarded the lien.

The method used for random selection will depend on the number of bidders in attendance at the sale and the sophistication of the county administration. Several years ago, I was investing in Shelby, Iowa, a small but very quaint and friendly town. While Iowa is officially a "bid down the ownership" state, most of the counties use the random selection process. The day before the Shelby sale, I spoke with the county treasurer. She confirmed that Shelby was officially under the "bid down the ownership" system, but that I could "ask" for the random selection system publicly before the sale began the next day. I did, and naturally the other investors did not oppose the motion.

Since there were only 22 bidders at the Shelby County sale (actually about 10 if you consider families as one bidder), the county put 22 Ping-Pong balls in a large KFC bucket with a bidder's number on each ball. A county official then simply reached into the bucket, picked a ball, and announced the number of the bidder selected. Since this method is not too scientific, one Ping-Pong ball near the top might get a larger number of liens. As I recall, bidder number 8 was chosen a disproportionate number of times, once in succession!

In a large county like Polk County (Des Moines), Iowa, the county employs a computer to randomly select bidder numbers. Under this method, the county simply displays the number selected on a large screen, together with the lien being sold. Once displayed, the investor simply announces whether he or she desires to purchase the lien. If he or she declines, the computer selects another bidder.

One other aspect of this bidding is worth mentioning. Some counties will switch to this system without notice if they get behind schedule. For example, Florida officially uses the "bid down" method. However, the county tax collector has only a few days to sell thousands of liens. If every lien is slowly bid down, this consumes valuable time. Say we have a lien that comes up and one bidder says 17 percent, the next says 16¾ percent, the next says 16¼ percent, then 16 percent, then 15¾ percent, and so on. If most of the liens are bid this way in the first day or two, the county will likely get behind schedule and not finish on time (often a problem since the auction hall for a large county will be rented). The county official in charge only has one option—to sell a lot of liens very quickly to catch up. How does the official do that? I've seen it many times. The official just takes the first bidder card he or she sees, or the first number that he or she hears. In essence, the official has just switched to a random selection system in order to catch up. I have found this switch to occur late in the day, since that is when the official gets an accounting of where he or she is in the overall sale. My advice to you: Stay until the very end every day!

Rotational Bidding

When I bought liens in Woodbury County, Iowa, I found the rotational system very fair. Under this system, each investor receives the same number of chances to purchase a lien. Here, the county official simply looks at the list of liens, starts at the top, and asks bidder #1 if he or she wants the first lien on the list. If bidder #1 declines, bidder #2 is asked, and so on. Let's suppose that bidder #2 declines but bidder #3 takes the lien. Bidders #2 and #3 don't lose their "turn," however, since they were responding to the lien allocated to bidder #1. So, when the official gets a taker on the first lien, the next lien is offered to bidder #2.

This type of system is probably most fair, since bidders will get an equal number of opportunities to buy liens. But here's the downside—if on your turn you get a $150,000 lien that you cannot afford, too bad; you now have to wait another cycle for your turn again. The same holds true if on your turn you get a $190 lien on a vacant lot. The upside, of course, is that under this system, like the random selection system, everyone gets the same, maximum return. In the case of Iowa, that's a nice 2 percent per month, or 24 percent annual return.

Bid Down the Ownership

This system is the least desirable of all the systems, and both investors and county officials dislike it. Under the "bid down the ownership" system, investors bid down how much of the property the lien will encumber. For example, if there is no bidding, the lien is sold at face value, earns the statutory interest rate, and encumbers 100 percent of the property. However, a bidder may say he or she will buy the lien accepting an encumbrance on only 75 percent of the property, or 50 percent, or 25 percent, or even 1 percent! How crazy is this? How would an investor possibly enforce the lien or foreclose on it? In short, it would require a court order to sell the property and apportion the proceeds according to percent of ownership!

While Nebraska and Iowa both "officially" use this system, most counties try to avoid it. During my visit to Iowa for the 2001 sale, for example, I saw that Shelby, Monoma, Harrison, and Polk counties used the random selection bidding system, while Woodbury used the rotational bidding system.

Over-the-Counter

Over-the-counter is not an official bidding system. This method is used to buy liens after the sale occurs. For example, if the county has liens left over after a sale, an investor can come to the county and purchase any liens in "inventory." Literally, investors can buy liens over-the-counter at the tax official's office. I purchased a lien in Omaha, Nebraska, this way. Keep in mind that if you are buying over-the-counter, no one is bidding against you. As such, you will always get it at the statutory maximum rate (14 percent for my Nebraska lien). If the state you are thinking about has a very high interest rate, it is likely that all of the liens will be purchased at the sale. However, what most people forget is that a certain number of liens purchased at the sale will default. For example, an investor may have bought the lien thinking it was for another property, and the county allowed him or her to void the sale. That lien may not be offered for sale again at the auction. Likewise, an investor may have purchased 20 liens at the auction but failed to come up with the cash at the end of the sale (some counties will bill you). If so, the county will have to take those liens back as well. All of these defaulted liens will be returned to the county's "inventory" and typically can be purchased for the statutory maximum rate, after the sale, over-the-counter.

In Figure 5.2 you will see the Nebraska lien that I purchased over-the-counter. Notice at the top of the lien it states "Private Sale." That just indicates that the sale of this lien occurred privately (to me) and not at a public auction.

TRICKS OF THE TRADE

I'm often asked by new or prospective lien investors, "How can I compete with the institutional investors that are at the tax sales?" The question, of course, makes several assumptions. First, it assumes that institutional investors are at this sale. Typically, in-

FIGURE 5.2 *Nebraska Over-the-Counter Lien Purchase*

PRIVATE SALE   01-05612

COUNTY TREASURER'S CERTIFICATE OF TAX SALE

STATE OF NEBRASKA
COUNTY OF DOUGLAS   *I, JULIE M. HANEY Treasurer of the County of Douglas, in the State of Nebraska, do hereby certify that the following described Real Estate in said County and State, to wit:*

0139-5568-16

LAKE CUNNINGHAM HILLS   LOT   285   BLOCK   0
IRREG

was, on the 21ST DAY OF JUNE, A.D. 2001   duly sold by me in the manner provided by law at Private Sale at my office, for the Delinquent Taxes

          99/00 $270.32 +   40.23 + 5.00 = $315.55
          WEEDS   1 $110.00 +   24.98 = $134.98

amounting to 450.53   *Dollars, including interest and penalty thereon, and the costs allowed by law, to* LARRY B. LOFTIS
for the said sum of 460.53   *Dollars. And I further certify that such Real Estate has been offered at public sale for taxes but not sold for want of bidders, and that unless redemption is made of said Real Estate in the manner provided by law, the said* LARRY B. LOFTIS
heirs or assigns, will be entitled to a deed therefor on and after the 21ST DAY OF JUNE, A.D. 2004
on surrender of this Certificate and Compliance with the provisions of the Revenue Law.
     IN WITNESS WHEREOF, I have hereunto set my hand this 21ST DAY OF JUNE, A.D. 2001

                    COPY   *Julie M. Haney*
     $460.53   100%   *Treasurer of Douglas County, State of Nebraska.*

stitutional investors appear only at sales of large counties (a metropolitan area, say, with a population of over 500,000). Second, it assumes that you are bidding on the same properties as the institutional investors. In many cases, that competition may not occur. Many prospective investors also are intimidated by large crowds and assume they will not be able to get good rates of return. Let's look at some of the tricks of the trade that will assist you in getting the jump on the competition, or competing with institutional investors. These tips apply to the most common bidding system, "bid down the interest," or its variation of "bid up the premium."

Buy at Smaller Counties

Institutional investors typically have several million dollars to spend at a single tax lien sale.It would not make sense for them to attend a sale for a small county that only has, say, $750,000 in liens to sell. For example, at the 2003 sale in Orange County, Florida, several institutional investors purchased over $3 million of liens over the four days of that sale. Keep in mind, of course, that these large counties will have tens of thousands of liens to sell. To avoid competing against these bidders, just go to the counties where they will not be going—small counties. In most states with good rates, you will find two to four very large metropolitan areas where institutional investors likely will attend the sales. In Florida, these investors will invest in the Miami/Ft. Lauderdale area, the Tampa/St. Petersburg area, Orlando, and Jacksonville. But Florida has 67 counties. So, rule number one is to consider going to (or investing online, if available) a sale in a smaller city. I typically go to smaller counties to get higher yields.

In Figure 5.3, I'm training colleagues how to play the bidding game. The first photo is from a deed sale in Los Angeles, while the second photo is from a small county in Florida. You can probably see from the photo that the room is very small, because smaller counties attract fewer bidders. At this sale, there was only one institutional bidder. I ended up getting all that I wanted in

FIGURE 5.3 *Training Others to Play the Bidding Game*

the 12 to 16 percent range. As you'll see below, I got these nice rates also because I was buying smaller liens (i.e., $400 to $1,200).

Buy Smaller Liens

Assume you decide to go to a sale for a large jurisdiction. How do you compete with institutional investors who are buying large numbers of liens at very low rates? Buy smaller liens. Most institutional investors only buy liens above a certain dollar threshold, typically between $1,000 and $1,500. In most cases, you can buy liens of $300 to $1,000 that are usually "below the radar" of these institutional bidders. In essence, you are trading off the quality of the property for a higher interest rate; that is, the house behind a $700 lien will not be nearly as nice as the house on a $2,000 lien. The numbers are relative, of course, since you are still looking at a lien that represents 1 to 2 percent of the fair market value of the property. If you buy a $300 lien, you're probably looking at a vacant lot. Again, it's the same adage, "Greater risk, greater reward." You'll get the best rates on those small liens, because they will be more likely not to redeem since no one lives on a vacant lot. I usually try to stay above about $450. If no institutional bidders are present, I try to stay above about $750.

Buy Liens on Nonhomestead Properties

Here's another tip to avoid competing with institutional bidders. Probably one-half of the institutional bidders (sometimes more) will not buy a lien on residential property that is not a "homestead" property. A homestead designation means that the property is someone's personal residence, and that person filed for the exemption with the county. In my estimation, maybe 25 percent of people who would qualify for a homestead exemption never do, for whatever reason. By filing for the exemption, the county deducts a certain number (in my state, $25,000) off of the county's appraised value of your home, thus lowering your property tax bill. Institutional bidders know that a homestead property has a higher likelihood of redemption because it is a personal residence. In addition, the designation assures the investor that the property is not a vacant lot. Because you can find out if the property is improved with the appraiser's office, I buy many liens that are not homesteads.

Stay during "Off" Times of the Sale

What are "off" times of a sale? An off time is when most of the other bidders are not in the room. When is that? Lunchtime! The majority of counties will bid right through the lunch hour by just alternating county officials conducting the bidding process. Most of those in attendance have been in the sale room since early in the morning and are hungry! As such, they get a bite to eat from noon to 1 PM. What is another off time? After 5 PM! Most people are creatures of habit, and the workplace normally says that the day ends at 5 PM. Remember that institutional bidders do not have vice presidents at the sales. Rather, they hire college students or agents whom they may use every year. Most of these people have been at the sale since 8:30 AM and are ready to leave at 5 PM. Also, parents may leave around 4:30 PM to pick up a child from school or day care. Other investors are just worn out from sitting all day and leave around 5 PM. *Use these off times to your advantage!* Some of the best rates will occur then because there are few people in the room.

My favorite trick of the trade is to stay after the posted closing time of the sale. For example, the county may hand out a flyer that says the auction will run from 8:30 AM until 5:00 or 5:30 PM. When the clock hits the official closing time, however, the county official realizes that he or she is behind schedule to finish the sale in the set number of days. To solve this problem and catch up, the official announces then that the sale will continue until 6 PM or 7 PM. Most investors are long gone by then.

Another off time is the last day of the sale. Oftentimes, the county will only need a few hours in the morning of the last day to finish the sale. Since most bidders have been there for several days and have bought their fair share of liens (or, in the case of individual bidders, have run out of money!), they either do not show up on the last day or leave an hour or so before the end.

I recall being at a sale last year where I missed most of the first day and the mornings of most days. It was now the last day. Most days there were about 25 bidders in the room. This last day there were 15. Four or five institutional bidders were at the sale, and the rates for liens in the $400 to $1,000 range were about 10 to 14 percent. At about 11 AM, an amazing thing happened—all of the institutional bidders and most of the other bidders left. But the sale was not over! I looked around the room, and there were only three of us left! One of the other bidders was an attorney friend who buys liens for his own account and is a seasoned investor. We looked at each other, smiled, and the bidding continued with just the three of us.

Why did everyone leave? At 11 AM, the county had finished its published list of liens. This is the official list that appears in the newspaper. However, the county also had a new, unpublished list that did not make the formal published list. There were maybe 50 liens on this list. The institutional bidders left because they had not been authorized by their employers to buy any of these liens. Since their employers never saw this small list, the agents knew they could not buy them. I do not know why the other bidders left—perhaps they thought the sale was over, were not interested in these new liens, or had run out of money. It did not matter to the three of us left in the room. We all purchased the remaining liens at between 14 and 18 percent.

You may be wondering why the three of us didn't just alternate liens and not bid against each other so we could get 18 percent on each lien. While this "secret" procedure does sometimes occur in some small counties, it is illegal under most state statutes, including Florida where we were bidding. Two of the three of us bidding were attorneys, so we know better than to do this. I also just wanted to have some fun with my friend. We'd been bidding at these sales for years and usually told each other which counties were looking good ratewise. So the prankster in me wanted to play with him a little bit. When he opened the bid at 17 percent, for example, I responded with 16¾ percent, and so on. . . . We had fun seeing who would go the lowest, but kept most of the liens in the 16 to 18 percent range.

Don't Hesitate

Have you heard the adage, "He who hesitates, loses"? This could not be more true than in tax lien investing. Auctions move—very fast! If you are not prepared, you will miss a good property or make a mistake. I have bought liens (and deeds) at great rates because other bidders hesitated. I've also lost good liens because I hesitated!

Let me illustrate a typical auction flow in a "bid down" lien state. The county official announces the lien and dollar amount and waits. Someone will yell out the interest rate at which they will take the lien, followed by others who yell out consecutively smaller numbers. For example, one person yells "16 percent." Then you hear "15¾ . . . 15½ . . . 15¼," and so on. After hundreds or thousands of liens have been sold, the crowd expects a certain tempo for this bidding. Some wait for the institutional bidders to start the bidding. I was at a large sale once where the institutional bidders were bidding down almost all of the excellent properties (say, values of $100,000 or more) to 5 percent or under. The institutional bidders were scooping up so many properties that many of the individual bidders left. A friend of mine who is a seasoned bidder came into the room in the afternoon and sat down next to me. A few minutes after he came in, a lien for over $9,000 was announced. At this particular sale, the institutional bidders were bidding down comparable liens to ¼ percent. My friend yelled out "17 percent." There was a one-second pause before the county official announced his bidder number.

The audience was stunned. All liens over $1,500 had been bid down to 5 percent or below all day long. My friend just hit a home run! The crowd instinctively responded with "Wooooo."

Why did the institutional bidders ignore this big lien? The property was a gas station, and they were not allowed to bid on it. All of the other bidders had been lulled to sleep by the constant barrage of institutional bidders going down to very low rates very quickly. Most bids opened at 5 or 6 percent. Before any of the individual bidders (probably 95 percent of the room) could respond to my friend's bid, it was gone. Everyone just assumed the institutional bidders would bid it down. Believe me, 20 people in that room would have loved to bid on that lien.

Always remember that the county cannot wait for others to jump in. If there is a slight pause in bidding, too bad, it's gone. The county does this for two reasons. First, there are hundreds or thousands or tens of thousands of liens to process, so the pace of the auction must move quickly to finish. Second, it would not be fair if county officials sometimes paused just because they thought a lien should be bid down further. Furthermore, once they have announced a winning bidder, they will not go back. On many occasions I've heard someone say, "What was the bid?" Too bad, too late. I've also heard people offer a lower rate; however, since the county official had already awarded the lien to another person, it was too late. You snooze, you lose! The good news is that, if you are at the auction long enough, this process will also work in your favor. Just be alert and be patient!

Keep in mind that if you are attending your first auction, watch for a while. Learn the tempo. Watch how fast it moves. Not long ago, I was training someone to bid for me at an auction. He watched me for a while and then I told him, "OK, I'm going to circle the one here that I want you to get. Go down to as low as 14 percent." He said, "OK." I watched him as it came up. The county official announced the lien and someone jumped in at 16 percent! Then another at 15½. I nudged him, "Jump in!" He froze. Then another, "15 percent." Gone. Someone got it for 15 percent. So I told him, "Jump into the fray when it gets going." I gave him another lien, and as soon as the bidding began at 16½ percent, he yelled, "14 percent!" Yes, he got it, but he jumped from 16½ to 14. I had to teach him to see where the opening bid comes in and go just below that. He eventually got the hang of it, but it takes a few runs to be comfortable with the timing, tempo, and process of yelling out bids. It's also fun and exhilarating . . . the chase of the hunt!

A Word about Online Investing

As of this writing, a number of counties around the country are experimenting with online sales. One county in California has already had a tax deed sale online. In 2004, Florida counties experimented with online sales. I bought liens in my area online. Buying liens this way was a little strange, but it was also fun. It allowed me to avoid racing to the auction location at 8 AM. It also allows you to invest in counties simultaneously. As I mentioned in Chapter 4, there are pros and cons for investors with online sales. In my opinion, online auctions are coming. Because it is so efficient for the county, and more people now have access to the Internet, I think more states will be using online auctions to conduct at least some of their sales.

Personally, I like the old, traditional method of getting a placard and going to the auction. It's more exciting and fun than watching your computer screen. In addition, many of the "tricks of the trade" are inapplicable in an online auction. I think the small counties (particularly rural) will continue the traditional auction method for the near future.

LARRY'S REMINDERS

- States generally use one of five bidding systems: 1) bid down the interest, 2) premium bidding, 3) random selection, 4) rotational bidding, 5) bid down the ownership.
- To get better rates, buy liens at smaller counties, buy smaller liens, buy liens on nonhomestead properties.
- Many counties are experimenting with online auctions, which may become a trend.
- All auctions move very quickly. The auctioneer or county official must sell an enormous number of liens in a relatively short period of time. *You must pay careful attention at all times or you will end up missing your lien altogether or bidding on the wrong lien!* I certainly have missed my fair share of liens and have bid on, and purchased, the wrong lien on more than one occasion! If this ever happens to you, see the person conducting the sale at the *first* break and let him or her know of your mistake. In my experience, the county official will almost always let you off the hook if you mention it at the first break. If you wait until the end of the day, you'll get off the hook about 50 percent of the time. If you wait until the next day, you'll almost always be stuck with that lien. As such, check every lien that you purchased in *your* records with the county's printout of what you bought *before* you leave for the day.
- Before investing in an auction, review carefully the county's registration and bidding rules. See Appendix A for examples.

6

WHAT IF THEY DON'T PAY? FORECLOSING ON YOUR SECURED INVESTMENT

A property tax lien is one of the most secured investments you'll ever find. In fact, your property tax lien is in first position, even ahead of a bank's mortgage on the property. Typically, liens against a property are set in a priority order, depending on the date the lien was recorded at the courthouse. For example, a house may have a first mortgage held by a bank in the first position, a home equity loan mortgage in second position, a mechanic's lien for repairs in third position, and so on. However, a property tax lien almost always takes priority over all other liens. Why is that? In short, property tax liens pay for virtually all county services—police and fire protection, schools, libraries, local roads, and local official salaries. If counties can't collect property taxes, you would not be able to call 911 for emergency service.

Let's assume a property has a fair market value of $200,000. Let's also assume that the property has a first mortgage with a balance of $120,000, and a second mortgage from a home equity loan with a balance of $15,000. Assume also that the property taxes are $2,500 per year (typically, property taxes are 1 to 2 percent of the fair market value). In the event of a foreclosure by any-one, here's the lien priority, or payout order, once the foreclosure sale occurs:

1. County property taxes: $2,500 (plus interest if paid late)
2. First mortgage (ABC Bank): $120,000
3. Second mortgage (XYZ Bank): $15,000

Let's assume that ABC Bank forecloses on its loan because the loan is in default for nonpayment. Let's further assume that the property taxes are delinquent and that an investor buys that lien at a tax lien sale. At the bank's foreclosure auction, the prop-erty tax lien holder will be paid before the bank, simply because the tax lien has a higher priority.

Now let's change the scenario. Assume that the bank's loan is not in default, but the property taxes are delinquent and that lien is bought by an investor at the tax lien sale. Now let's assume that the redemption period is about to expire and the owner has not redeemed or paid off the tax lien. At this point, the bank will al-most always come in and pay off that tax lien to protect its posi-tion. That is, the bank knows that if the lien holder forecloses on the tax lien, the bank's mortgage will be wiped out. Accordingly, the bank will pay off a $2,500 lien, with interest, to protect its $120,000 mortgage behind that lien. Since banks inherently know the security of property tax liens, some banks, like Wachovia and Bank Atlantic, regularly invest in them.

Here's another twist. What if the state in which you are buy-ing liens has a two- or three-year redemption period? What hap-pens to the other lien holder(s)? Assume you are in a state with a two-year redemption period. Using our earlier example, here's the priority at payout:

1. Tax lien from year one: $2,500 (plus interest)
2. Tax lien from year two: $2,500 (plus interest)
3. First mortgage (ABC Bank): $120,000
4. Second mortgage (XYZ Bank): $15,000

We know that the lien bought in year one will have a redemption period expire one year before the lien bought in year two. Assuming that neither the property owner nor the two banks pay off the property tax liens, what happens? When the redemption period of two years runs out on lien #1, that lien holder can foreclose on his or her lien. While redemption of the lien can and will wipe out the mortgages (except in New Mexico, which is a deed state and would not involve this scenario), a lien holder cannot wipe out another *property* tax lien. So, if lien holder #1 wants to proceed with a tax lien foreclosure, he or she must pay off tax lien holder #2 (with interest). Thus, a tax lien holder is always protected. Lien holder #2 will be paid his or her principal investment, plus the statutory interest or penalty. Lien holder #1 now will either acquire the property free of all liens or have the property sold at a tax deed sale and be paid for his redemption of lien #2, plus his or her original investment and interest, depending on the jurisdiction.

FORECLOSURE TYPES

Generally speaking, states use one of two types of tax lien foreclosures. In the first type, the lien holder will acquire the property free and clear. For the purpose of this analysis, I'll refer to these jurisdictions as "administrative filing" states. In the second type of state, the lien holder will force the sale of the property at a tax deed sale and be paid off (or acquire the property if no one bids past the lien holder's credit for monies owed). I'll refer to these types of jurisdictions as "tax deed sale" states. Let's look at each type in detail.

Administrative Filing States

In an administrative filing jurisdiction, a lien holder desiring to foreclose on his or her lien must do the following:

1. Wait until the redemption period runs.
2. Notify the county of his or her desire to foreclose, which may include the requirement to:
   - pay a small administrative fee to the county;
   - fill out and sign some paperwork with the county;
   - send a notice to the property owner; and/or
   - publish a legal notice in the local newspaper.
3. Pay off any other *property tax liens,* if applicable, and, in some cases, any "weed" lien imposed by the county for mowing the property.

In essence, upon completing the administrative procedures outlined above, the foreclosing lien holder will acquire the property free and clear. This type of procedure is used by most lien states.

Tax Deed States

In another type of foreclosure system, the lien holder only forces a tax deed sale. Florida uses this type of system. Here, the lien holder must follow the steps outlined above, except that the county will handle all notices. The county will then set the property for a tax deed sale. In Florida, this sale will occur about four months or so after filing for the sale with the county.

At any time up until this sale, the property owner may come in to redeem, or pay off, all the liens and costs. If the property owner does not, the sale will occur on the specified date. At the sale, the lien holder will be given a credit for his or her first position lien, plus interest; the second lien (which he or she bought out), plus the interest paid to that person; and the filing fee, plus any other costs the county may have charged. If the bidding does not exceed this credit, that lien holder now owns the property free and clear. If the bidding does exceed his or her credit and the lien holder does not wish to bid, he or she will be paid the credit amount, and the winning bidder will get the property free and clear.

This brings up a second investment option. Some real estate investors do not invest in tax liens but go to tax deed sales to acquire properties. Investors at tax deed sales can generally acquire properties for much lower sales prices than at a mortgage foreclosure. Mortgage foreclosure properties generally sell for 60 to 85 cents on the dollar, while tax deed foreclosure properties generally sell for 10 to 65 cents on the dollar. As you would expect, vacant lots will sell near the lower end of that spectrum while nice properties will sell closer to the higher end of the spectrum.

You would be surprised by what shows up at these sales. Of course, there are many residential lots being auctioned but also a few houses. I was at a sale a few years ago where a large commercial lot, several acres in size, was being sold. The property was on the corner of a busy intersection in one of the fastest-growing areas of town. In short, it was a prime commercial location. The ironic part is that the property was the parking lot for a huge Walgreens store! How did Walgreens let that happen? I don't know, but I can speculate. My guess is that the lot was separately deeded to Walgreens. Perhaps it was a different owner who sold that portion of land to Walgreens. I presume that the financial person who paid the property tax bills for Walgreens was in the corporate headquarters, probably located in a different state. Maybe the bill for this property never made it to that person's desk. I do know that the taxes for the store itself were paid, just not for the parking lot.

The bidding was frenzied. Two parties went back and forth for what seemed like hours (more like ten minutes, really). As I recall, the property sold for over $700,000. Remember, this was a huge commercial lot in a prime area of town. Perhaps the winning bidder wanted to develop part of the lot. In any event, that winning bidder knew that he could hold Walgreens hostage, because that was the only parking available for the store. In all likelihood, the new property owner will offer Walgreens a lease renewal at a very high rent. What choices does Walgreens now have? Walgreens can now either pay the high lease rate or close a store in a prime location, which it had spent hundreds of thousands, if not millions, of dollars to develop. Now if Walgreens decides to close the store and sell the property, who would buy a big retail store that has no parking? Leverage is an amazing tool in negotiation.

LARRY'S REMINDERS

- A property tax lien is a priority lien and takes precedence over other types of liens (except in New Mexico and state liens in Arizona).
- If a state has a redemption period of two or more years (and two or more tax liens will be sold), the buyer of the first lien has priority over the others. To foreclose on the lien, this investor must pay off the other property tax lien holder(s). A property tax lien cannot be extinguished by another lien.
- States generally use one of two systems to process foreclosure of a tax lien:
  1. Administrative filing
  2. Tax deed auction

Structall

Alabama 12%
Arizona 16 90
Minnesota ?! my mail
Montana 10% + 2% penalty
Nebraska 14%
Oklahoma 8% list available
South Carolina 8 n 12 90
South Dakota 12

Texas 25%
West Virginia 12%
   Deputy LandCommission 304-343-4441

W Yoming 15 + 3 penalty

Willow Hill Sunrooms

(813) 780-9826 • Fax (813) 788-4314

Lic. # CBC 058878

FREE ESTIMATE

Date: _____

Homeowner's Name: _____

Address: _____

City: _____ **State:** _____ **ZIP:** _____

Home Phone: _____ **Work Phone:** _____ **E-Mail Address:** _____

Best time to call: ☐ Morning ☐ Afternoon ☐ Evening

Type of house: ☐ One-story ☐ Two-story ☐ Condominium ☐ Townhouse ☐ Mobile Home

My house is: ☐ Block ☐ Wood Frame ☐ Brick

We already have: ☐ Concrete Slab ☐ Roof Size of room you are considering _____

Appointment Time: _____ **Appointment Date:** _____

7

NOTHING IS RISK-FREE, BUT
THIS IS AS CLOSE AS IT GETS

You've probably heard the expression "the greater the risk, the greater the reward." Generally, this is true. In tax liens, however, you can achieve very high rates of return for very little risk. The last chapter illustrated how a property tax lien has priority over all other liens, including even a bank's mortgage. Because of that safety, some banks invest in tax lien certificates. But we all know that everything has some level of risk. Even certificates of deposit, or CDs, carry some risk (since they won't keep up with inflation, I prefer to call them certificates of depreciation). They are insured by the FDIC up to $100,000. But what if the FDIC goes bankrupt? What if there is a run on banks? These are unlikely events, of course, but still possible. Just ask the people who lost millions in the savings and loan crisis a few years back. So what are the potential risks with a tax lien investment?

THE INTERNAL REVENUE SERVICE

People often ask me, "Isn't the IRS ahead of you?" That is, will the IRS have a higher priority than a property tax lien? The answer is "yes" and "no." Under federal law (Section 7425(d), USC Title 26, Internal Revenue Service Code), the IRS has 120 days from the date of a public auction of the property (e.g., deed sale) to "redeem" or "buy out" your position. If the IRS chooses to redeem the property, it must pay:

- The actual amount paid for the property by the purchaser (i.e., the lien amounts), plus interest at 6 percent per annum from the date of the sale.
- The expenses of the sale, including protection and maintenance of the property that exceed any income received from the property.

So, if you purchase a lien on a property that has an IRS lien on it, the IRS lien "rides" with the property during your statutory redemption period. If the owner of the property does not redeem and you foreclose on your lien by forcing a tax sale (where the property transfers to you), the IRS clock starts ticking from the date of the sale. If the IRS does not redeem you, their lien on the property is extinguished.

So is the IRS *ahead* of you in the order of priority? Not really. Your lien cannot be wiped out by an IRS lien; your lien is not really "junior" to the IRS lien. The IRS just has a short window of time within which they can buy out your position. Your only "risk," if you want to call it that, is just getting a lower interest rate.

Here's the reality of the IRS "risk." I have bought hundreds of liens, and I have yet to see an IRS lien attached to one of the properties on which I purchased a lien. While I have seen IRS liens on properties at *deed* sales, I simply choose not to bid on those properties (in most cases, they are flagged as having the IRS lien).

BANKRUPTCY OF THE PROPERTY OWNER

In my estimation, maybe one lien in 200 (or more) will involve a bankruptcy of the property owner. That is, between the time you buy the lien and the time the redemption period expires, the owner files for bankruptcy. What happens to your lien if the owner files for bankruptcy?

Under federal bankruptcy law, once a person files for bankruptcy, the assigned federal judge will "stay" or stop all pending claims against that person and bring all actions into the judge's jurisdiction. This stay order will apply to all liens against that person or that person's assets. As a lien holder on the bankrupt person's property, you will receive a notice from the bankruptcy court to confirm your lien. The judge will separate all creditors into secured and unsecured creditors. Since you have a lien on real property, you are a secured creditor. And since your lien is a first-position lien, you have the highest priority against that property. In most cases, the judge will allow your lien to continue in first position against the property, and you will be paid your principal and the interest due. As such, your legal rights have not been impaired, only delayed. It is possible, however, for the judge to order the sale of the property and pay all secured creditors only a percentage of their claims.

Having said that, you want to avoid this potential risk if at all possible. In one scenario, the judge may only ask you to fill out a form indicating what your lien is and the interest you are owed. However, if the debtor names all creditors in the petition, you will need to file an "answer" with the court setting forth your claim, which will require the services of an attorney. If your lien is very small, it may not be worthwhile to even pursue the claim.

What's the best way to avoid getting a lien on a property that may later be encumbered with a bankruptcy? Buy larger liens. In general, a property tax lien represents 1 to 2 percent of the fair market value of a property. Accordingly, if you buy a $400 lien, the property is worth $20,000 to $40,000. If you buy a $3,000 lien, the property is worth $150,000 to $300,000. Which homeowner do you think is more likely to file for bankruptcy? Your risk of the owner filing for bankruptcy is small; nevertheless, it is possible.

WORTHLESS LOTS THAT WILL NOT REDEEM

Buying liens on worthless lots is the biggest potential risk in tax lien investing. This risk is totally avoidable, however, so pay careful attention to this section. Counties (and cities, too, when they conduct sales) are ruthless in both lien and deed sales. They have one purpose and one purpose only in selling a lien or deed—to collect property taxes due. Ninety percent of tax collectors could care less about what that lien is on. Ten percent really do care and do not want you to buy a lien on a worthless lot. For that reason, many tax collectors will not sell liens under $100. Unfortunately, the 90 percent of ruthless tax collectors will gladly sell you a $500 lien on a worthless lot.

What is worthless property? Imagine a vacant lot that is 10 feet wide by 100 feet long. What can you do with that lot? Because it is so small, you cannot build on it. I have seen many of these types of properties sold at lien and deed sales—lots that are side yards to residential houses; lots that are basically a drainage ditch; lots that have very odd configurations; and lots next to a transformer. Got the point?

If you buy a lien on a property like this, the property owner is not likely to pay off the lien. So what if you foreclose and even get the property; what will you do with it? To whom will you sell the property? I have learned this lesson the hard way!

How do you avoid these liens? First, don't buy small liens. If you have a $200 lien, it is most likely a vacant lot. Sure, you can buy a $2,000 lien on vacant property, but you will be dealing with a large piece of property in all likelihood. Second, the safest bet to avoid buying liens on vacant lots is to physically inspect the property before the sale. However, because you may be buying many liens, may not know the liens on which you will win the bidding, or may not know the area, this option may be impractical.

Third, another safeguard is to buy liens only on properties that are listed as "homestead." This designation means that it is someone's principal residence. This assures you that it is a house and that someone lives there. If so, the chances of the lien being redeemed are extremely high. Some institutional investors will invest only in properties listed as homestead. I don't personally take this route, because I also like liens on houses that are not homestead properties, as well as commercial properties. However, many investors do take this precaution to give them the most security.

A fourth safe way to avoid vacant lots is to buy in an area that you know. For example, in my county and the surrounding counties, I can tell from the listing in the newspaper where the property is and what type of property it is. In my newspaper, for example, the lien listing may show that the property is listed in a very nice subdivision, a good commercial area, or on a desirable street. I can tell from the entry if it is a residential house or commercial building. By the same token, I also know what the bad areas are and what to stay away from. Don't get me wrong—buying a lien on a house is still a safe and good investment, even in bad areas, because the lien still represents only 1 to 2 percent of the fair market value. Nonetheless, if I have a choice, I'll go for liens on nicer properties in nicer areas.

Many times I will buy in areas that I do not know, which means I do not know good areas from bad ones or good streets from bad ones. What do I do in this case? I look for liens over $1,000 in size. I look for properties that are shown as homestead or have an obvious commercial address. For example, a listing may reveal that it is in the First State Commerce Center. The name tells me that it is commercial. I've also seen plenty of liens on properties owned by companies you may have heard of—Walt Disney World, McDonald's, BellSouth Mobility, and virtually every major bank. I've bought liens on properties owned by Chase

Manhattan Bank and LaSalle National Bank. In short, liens on properties owned by major corporations are typically very safe liens.

When in an unfamiliar area, there's one other thing you can do: check out the property with the county appraiser's office. In most instances, this can be done online. Just get the Web site for the appraiser's office and go to the search engine for properties. Normally, you can pull up a property by the owner's name, the street address, the lot and block number, or the parcel identification number. For example, Figure 7.1 shows the appraiser's information on a property on which I bought a lien a few years ago.

Notice that the county's page gives me a photo of the property (somewhat unusual), the square footage, year built, assessed value, and other helpful information. While very few counties will provide a photo of the property, almost all will give you the square feet, year built, and assessed value. Keep in mind that the county's assessed value is normally around 80 to 85 percent of the fair market value.

If you buy using these guidelines, you can easily avoid buying liens on vacant lots. That's the good news. Here's the bad news. Remember the axiom "the greater the risk, the greater the reward"? Which liens do you think will command the highest rates of interest in a bidding jurisdiction? That's right, the smallest liens. But that's OK, because there's something for everyone. The institutional buyers like the big liens on the big properties and may bid them down very low, because the risk is almost zero. Likewise, many small investors prefer to invest in small liens for two reasons:

1. They can buy small liens that are affordable.
2. They can get the best rates of return.

FIGURE 7.1 *Appraiser's Information on Lien Property*

Parcel Appraisal Summary - 832916000003

Page 1 of 1

Parcel Appraisal Summary - Shelby County Assessor

Shelby County, IA

Reference Number: 832916000003
Contract Holder: NEUMAN, DAVID B & GAIL A, SURV
BOX 135, ROUTE 1
SHELBY, IA 51570
Property Address: 700 BORDER ST
Legal Description: 33-78-40 PT NW SW

Class: R - RESIDENTIAL
School District: SHELBY-TENNANT COMM

Residential Dwelling		Sketch (click to enlarge)
Lot Area:	1.89 Acres; 82,161 SF	
Occupancy:	Single-Family / Owner Occupied	
Style:	2 Story Frame	
Year Built:	1920	
Exterior Material:	Aluminum/Vinyl	
Above-Grade Living Area:	1,920 SF	
Attic:	None	
Number Rooms:	12	
Number Bedrooms:	0	
Basement Area Type:	Full	
Basement Finished Area:	0 SF	
Number of Baths:	2 Full Baths	
Central Air:	No	
Number of Fireplaces:	None	
Garage:	220 SF - Det Frame (Built 1920)	
Porches and Decks:	Wood Deck-Med (296 SF); 1 S Fr Opn (88 SF)	
Yard Extras:	SHEDS; CATTLE SHED 13 X 35	

Values	2000 Assessment		Sales Date	$ Amount	Sale Type (NUTC)
			1/17/1996	$0	038
Land:	$21,035				
Buildings:	$0				
Ag Dwelling or M&E:	$41,489				
Total:	$62,524				

Disclaimer: *The information in this web site represents current data from a working file which is updated continuously. Information is believed reliable, but its accuracy cannot be guaranteed.*

EARLY REDEMPTION WITHOUT PENALTY

One downside of tax lien investing is that a lien may redeem very quickly, and the jurisdiction may not have a penalty for early redemption. Here's what I mean. Let's say you buy a lien at 12 percent interest. This means that it is 12 percent *per annum*. That's a nice rate of return, but what if it redeems after just one month? Yes, you will get a 12 percent return, but the dollar amount you receive will only be 1 percent of your principal. Now you will have to find another investment vehicle in which to park your money. Because of that disincentive, many states include a penalty, either on top of a per annum rate or in lieu of an annual rate. Let's consider an example of two states.

Assume you purchased a $1,000 lien in Iowa. This state has a very nice interest rate of 2 percent per month. That's an annual fixed return of 24 percent, right? Now let's assume that you purchased another $1,000 lien in Florida at 6 percent. If both liens redeem after one year, what do you have? In Iowa, you made $240 for a 24 percent return. In Florida, you made only $60, for a 6 percent return. But what if both liens redeemed after only one month? In Iowa, you would have made 2 percent, or only $20. In Florida, however, you would have made $50, or a 60 percent *yield* because Florida has a minimum penalty of 5 percent. This penalty is just a small reward that Florida adds to make it a little more worth your while to invest there.

So, early redemption is not really a "risk" in tax lien investing. Rather, early redemption is just the downside of this type of investing. You still get a nice rate of return; however, you didn't make a lot of money in just one month and now you need to reinvest that money.

LARRY'S REMINDERS

- Property tax liens do not wipe out IRS liens, and vice versa. However, once a tax lien holder forecloses on his or her lien, if the IRS has a lien on the underlying property, the IRS will have 120 days from the date of the foreclosure sale to redeem and pay off the tax lien holder his or her principal, 6 percent interest, and all costs. After 120 days, the IRS lien will be extinguished from the property.
- If a property owner files for bankruptcy while a tax lien is outstanding (i.e., during the redemption period), a bankruptcy judge will stay all actions against the debtor and notify all creditors, including the tax lien holder. Depending on the action taken by the debtor, the lien holder will need to either file an informal form with the bankruptcy judge (supplied by the court), or file a formal answer.
- Avoid buying liens on vacant lots, unless you have seen the property and know that it is buildable or salable.
- To diminish your risk, buy larger liens and liens designated as "homestead."
- For additional information on a property, go to the county appraiser's Web site. You normally can retrieve valuable information on a property by searching by parcel identification number or street address.

INVESTING IN TAX DEEDS

8

ATTENTION ALL
REAL ESTATE SCAVENGERS!

About one-half of the states are tax lien states, and the other half are tax deed states. Recall that I categorize ten states as "hybrid" states (see Chapter 1). These states, like Texas and Georgia, are deed states, but they have many aspects in common with lien states and operate much like a lien state.

We know that a tax lien state is one where a lien is filed on a property by the local jurisdiction for failure to pay the property taxes. The investor who buys that lien does not own the property. Rather, that investor only has a lien on the property. The investor is waiting for the owner to pay the taxes due, with interest or penalty, so that the investor can receive a nice rate of return on the investment.

A tax deed, however, is very different. If you buy a tax deed at a sale, you *own* the property from that day forward. With the exception of Arizona (which does not extinguish a prior state lien) and New Mexico (which does not extinguish any liens), and possible local special assessments, you own the property free and clear of other liens (save a county's mowing or "weed" lien to reimburse the county for mowing it, or in extreme cases, a demolition lien). You can now do what you want with this property—rent it, resell it, or even live in it. In the normal tax deed state—what I will call a "pure" tax deed state—the owner has no chance to redeem. Keep in mind that the tax sale was no surprise to the owner. In most instances, that owner had notices and warnings from the county for years. So if you buy a tax deed, you own the property.

HYBRID DEED STATES

In hybrid states, however, the previous property owner still has a chance to redeem. Notice that I said "previous" owner. You own the property; however, the previous owner has a right to redeem for six months to two years, depending on the state and the type of property involved. For example, in Texas, if the property is nonagricultural and nonhomestead, the prior owner has just six months to redeem. If the property is agricultural or homestead, the prior owner has two years to redeem.

Keep in mind what the prior owner must do to redeem. First, he must come up with all of the back taxes, which he could not pay in the first place. Second, he must pay you off on any premium you may have paid at the sale. Third, he now has to come up with your penalty rate, which covers not only the lien itself, but your "overbid," plus county administrative costs.

In our Texas example, let's say we have a $200,000 piece of property. Let's also assume that the taxes are $3,000 per year. Assume also that the owner is two years behind at the time of the sale, or $6,000 in arrears. In most cases, the bidding starts at the back taxes, or $6,000 (which typically also includes the county's administrative costs in bringing the sale, omitted for this example). Now let's assume that you paid $60,000 for the property at the sale, or $54,000 over the back taxes. If the prior owner is to redeem, he or she must now pay the $6,000 in taxes, plus your

$54,000 overbid, plus county administrative costs, plus a 25 percent penalty on top of everything! What is the likelihood of that? If the property is not agricultural or homestead, he or she would also have to come up with this amount in six months, since that's the redemption period for this type of property!

Yes, if the prior owner finds a lost rich uncle, he or she could possibly redeem. Are you crying about it? With a 25 percent penalty (a 50 percent rate of return at the worst, if it's nonagricultural and nonhomestead property) on your investment, you're not losing any sleep. In fact, you could have rented out the property during the months that you owned it, thus increasing your yield even more. But since the prior owner has this redemption right, however unlikely, you probably wouldn't want to put a new roof on a house. But there's nothing wrong with adding a few coats of paint and renting the place out while the redemption period runs.

STATES WITH BOTH LIEN AND DEED SALES

Florida is a lien state but also has monthly deed sales due to its foreclosure system. Ohio is a deed state but counties with populations over 200,000 are also allowed to have lien sales. New York is a deed state, but New York City is also allowed to have lien sales. Note again the breakdown of categories in Figure 8.1.

Investing in tax deeds, or properties, carries far more risk than investing in a lien on the property. But what generally comes with more risk? More reward! Assuming that you can buy the property at the right price, you can make a phenomenal rate of return on your money. What is the right price? The answer depends on what type of property it is, and what it will cost to put the property in prime resale condition. The answer also depends on how much money you have to invest. You may be able to get a $300,000 property for $50,000, but if you cannot come up with $50,000 for the auction, it doesn't matter what the property is worth. That's the first downside to this type of investing; it gener-

FIGURE 8.1 *State-by-State Categorization*

Lien	Deed	Hybrid
Alabama	Alaska	Connecticut
Arizona	Arkansas	Delaware
Colorado	California	Georgia
District of Columbia	Idaho	Hawaii
Florida	Kansas	Louisiana
Illinois	Maine	Massachusetts
Indiana	Michigan	Pennsylvania[1]
Iowa	Minnesota	Rhode Island
Kentucky	Nevada	Tennessee
Maryland	New Hampshire	Texas
Mississippi	New Mexico	
Missouri	New York[2]	
Montana	North Carolina	
Nebraska	Ohio[3]	
New Jersey	Oregon	
North Dakota	Pennsylvania[1]	
Ohio[3]	Utah	
Oklahoma	Virginia	
South Carolina	Washington	
South Dakota	Wisconsin	
Vermont		
West Virginia		
Wyoming		

[1]Pennsylvania counties may operate under the hybrid system where the property is improved and has been legally occupied 90 days prior to the sale.
[2]New York City also is allowed to conduct tax lien sales.
[3]Ohio is historically a deed state; however, counties with populations over 200,000 also are allowed to conduct lien sales.

ally takes a considerable amount of money to get into the game. In the following chapters, we'll take a look at what kind of properties you can find, and just how much money you'll need to have a decent shot at getting them.

LARRY'S REMINDERS

- While a tax lien is only a lien on property, a tax deed conveys *ownership* of the property.
- A hybrid state is a deed state that operates like a lien state. While ownership of the property is conveyed, the prior

property owner still has a period of time to redeem the property.

- In almost all cases, a property acquired through a tax deed sale will be acquired free and clear of all liens (save a possible "weed" lien or demolition lien).
- See Part Three for a detailed list of states.

9

LOTS, DITCHES, AND A FEW GEMS

Over the years, I've seen a fair amount of hype in seminars and on television about getting nice properties for "pennies on the dollar." When I first got into tax lien investing, I thought this scenario would be quite common. After years of buying liens and deeds around the country, however, I've seen that getting a nice property for pennies on the dollar is quite rare. In most cases, properties sold at tax deed auctions are not "nice" properties. Makes sense, right? Why would someone lose a nice property at a tax deed sale?

At most tax deed sales, you will find many vacant lots, including a number of worthless lots, containing irregular or small parcels. In many cases, the county will readily sell you a drainage ditch. Because of this, it's always imperative for the investor to actually see the property before bidding. You will also see a few houses and even some commercial properties. The houses that I've seen at deed sales are typically vacant, often boarded up, and usually in disrepair. Investors at these sales buy such properties knowing that they will require a fair amount of rehabilitation. I've also bid on a few gems. While in Texas, for example, I bid on

FIGURE 9.1 *Commercial Building on Which I Was Outbid*

a set of seven condominiums. While I did see the outside of the complex, I could not get into the units. As such, I kept my bidding conservative and was outbid by another investor.

In Figure 9.1, you'll see a commercial building in New York that I bid on. Each section of the building was separately deeded. It was in a nice commercial area and across the street from a Mc-Donald's restaurant. I was outbid there as well.

In my estimation, most deed properties sell at auctions for around 50 cents on the dollar. Oftentimes, however, it sells for more or less, depending on the quality of the property and the number of bidders present. In Figure 9.2, you'll see a property that I purchased in Kansas for only $4,100. The purchase price was in the area of about 8 cents on the dollar (given the sales prices in the neighborhood), but the property needed a lot of work. Nevertheless, it was a safe investment. Figure 9.3 shows the Sheriff's Deed awarded.

FIGURE 9.2 *A Safe Investment in Kansas*

At the same sale, I also purchased a couple of vacant lots. These were residential lots in decent areas, but the lots were very small. One lot required a variance from the building code, since it was five feet smaller than the code would allow for building. Since I bought these for only $75 each, these were also very safe investments. See Figures 9.4 and 9.5.

LARRY'S REMINDERS

- Most properties sold at tax deed sales will be vacant lots. Many of these lots will be worthless properties. However, a few nice properties may also be sold at a tax deed sale.
- Keep in mind that tax deed properties are sold for cash, and almost always will require rehabilitation.

FIGURE 9.3 *Example of Sheriff's Deed*

SHERIFF'S DEED

KNOW ALL MEN BY THESE PRESENTS, THAT a certain action to foreclose tax liens on certain real property in the County of Leavenworth, State of Kansas, has heretofore been filed in the District Court of Leavenworth County, Kansas, and is titled: The Board of County Commissioners of Leavenworth County, Kansas v. JL Clark Plumbing & Heating, Inc, et al, Case No. 0107 CV 224; and Judgement was thereafter rendered by said court in the above entitled action on 19 October, 2001.

In compliance with, and pursuant to this Judgment, the Clerk of the District Court of Leavenworth County, Kansas, issued an order to Sheriff Herbert F. Nye, Sheriff of Leavenworth County, Kansas, to advertise and sell tracts of land, lots, or pieces of real estate described below, all according to law.

The Leavenworth County Sheriff gave notice of this sale by advertisement and publication notice of sale in The Tonganoxie Mirror newspaper printed in Leavenworth County, Kansas, and which had been continuously and uninterruptedly published in Leavenworth County, Kansas, not less than fifty (50) weeks for a period of five years prior to the first publication notice, all according to the law. The Leavenworth County Sheriff, Herbert F. Nye, thereafter sold to Larry Boyd Loftis for the highest and best bid obtainable on 11 December, 2001, the following described real property; for the amount shown by each particular tract, lot, or piece of real estate.

DESCRIPTION: The South Half of Lot 26, and all of Lots 27 and 28 in Block numbered 33, Macaulay's First Addition to the City of Leavenworth according to the recorded plat thereof.

Price: $4,100.00

THEREAFTER, on the 17th day of December, 2001, the order of sale and the proceedings of sale were returned to the Leavenworth County District Court and after examination of the proceedings, and finding that the sale was made in all respects in conformity with the law applicable, the District Court of Leavenworth County confirmed the sale, and the proceedings made thereto, on the 18th day of December, 2001.

THEREAFTER, and according to law, the Sheriff of Leavenworth County was ordered to execute this good and sufficient deed to the purchaser(s) Larry Boyd Loftis.

I, Herbert F. Nye, Sheriff of Leavenworth County, Kansas, therefore do hereby give, grant, sell and convey to Larry Boyd Loftis, their heirs and assigns, forever, all the above-described real estate located in Leavenworth County, Kansas, together with all and singular tenements, hereditaments and appurtenances thereto or in any way appertaining, subject to zoning regulations, easements, restrictions, and mineral interests of record.

TO HAVE AND TO HOLD THE SAME UNTO THE SAID Larry Boyd Loftis, their heirs and assigns forever.

IN WITNESS WHEREOF, I, Herbert F. Nye, Sheriff of Leavenworth County, State of Kansas, have hereunto set my hand this 18th day of December, 2001.

Herbert F. Nye
Sheriff of Leavenworth County, Kansas

STATE OF KANSAS)
)   SS:
COUNTY OF LEAVENWORTH)

This instrument was acknowledged before me the 18th day of December, 2001 by Herbert F. Nye as Sheriff of Leavenworth County, Kansas.

K. Janette Nessmith - Eyerly
Notary Public - State of Kansas
My Appt. Expires 01-24-2004

Notary Public

My Appointment Expires:
01-24-2004

FIGURE 9.4 *Vacant Lot Purchased for $75*

FIGURE 9.5 *Example of Sheriff's Deed*

CORRECTED **SHERIFF'S DEED**

KNOW ALL MEN BY THESE PRESENTS, THAT a certain action to foreclose tax liens on certain real property in the County of Leavenworth, State of Kansas, has heretofore been filed in the District Court of Leavenworth County, Kansas, and is titled: The Board of County Commissioners of Leavenworth County, Kansas v. JL Clark Plumbing & Heating, Inc, et al, Case No. 0107 CV 224; and Judgement was thereafter rendered by said court in the above entitled action on 19 October, 2001.

In compliance with, and pursuant to this Judgment, the Clerk of the District Court of Leavenworth County, Kansas, issued an order to Sheriff Herbert F. Nye, Sheriff of Leavenworth County, Kansas, to advertise and sell tracts of land, lots, or pieces of real estate described below, all according to law.

The Leavenworth County Sheriff gave notice of this sale by advertisement and publication notice of sale in The Tonganoxie Mirror newspaper printed in Leavenworth County, Kansas, and which had been continuously and uninterruptedly published in Leavenworth County, Kansas, not less than fifty (50) weeks for a period of five years prior to the first publication notice, all according to the law. The Leavenworth County Sheriff, Herbert F. Nye, thereafter sold to Larry Boyd Loftis for the highest and best bid obtainable on 11 December, 2001, the following described real property; for the amount shown by each particular tract, lot, or piece of real estate.

DESCRIPTION: Lots 14 and 15, Block 101, Day and Macaulay's Subdivision, City of Leavenworth, Leavenworth County, Kansas.

Price: $75.00

THEREAFTER, on the 17thday of December, 2001, the order of sale and the proceedings of sale were returned to the Leavenworth County District Court and after examination of the proceedings, and finding that the sale was made in all respects in conformity with the law applicable, the District Court of Leavenworth County confirmed the sale, and the proceedings made thereto, on the 18th day of December, 2001.

THEREAFTER, and according to law, the Sheriff of Leavenworth County was ordered to execute this good and sufficient deed to the purchaser(s) Larry Boyd Loftis.

I, Herbert F. Nye, Sheriff of Leavenworth County, Kansas, therefore do hereby give, grant, sell and convey to Larry Boyd Loftis, their heirs and assigns, forever, all the above-described real estate located in Leavenworth County, Kansas, together with all and singular tenements, hereditaments and appurtenances thereto or in any way appertaining, subject to zoning regulations, easements, restrictions, and mineral interests of record.

TO HAVE AND TO HOLD THE SAME UNTO THE SAID Larry Boyd Loftis, their heirs and assigns forever.

IN WITNESS WHEREOF, I, Herbert F. Nye, Sheriff of Leavenworth County, State of Kansas, have hereunto set my hand this 3rd day of January, 2002.

Herbert F. Nye
Sheriff of Leavenworth County, Kansas

STATE OF KANSAS   )
)   SS:
COUNTY OF LEAVENWORTH)

This instrument was acknowledged before me the 3rd day of ~~December, 2001~~ January 2002 by Herbert F. Nye as Sheriff of Leavenworth County, Kansas.

K. Janette Nessmith - Eyerly
Notary Public - State of Kansas
My Appt. Expires 01-14-2004

Notary Public

My Appointment Expires:

10

PENNIES ON THE DOLLAR?

Seminar speakers often suggest the possibility of buying a property for pennies on the dollar in tax deed or lien investing, as if anyone could do it at any sale on any type of property. Is it possible? Yes, I've done it. Is it common? No. As I mentioned in Chapter 9, most tax deed sale properties generally sell for around 50 cents on the dollar, in my experience. However, some areas are better than others; some auctions have fewer investors than others; and there are a few things that will increase your odds of getting a property extremely cheaply. Let's look at a few ways to really steal a property.

FORECLOSURE OF A TAX LIEN

The best way to acquire a property for pennies on the dollar is not to buy it at a tax deed sale—but at a tax lien sale. Here's why. At a tax deed sale, you will be competing with other bidders. Many of these bidders may be willing to buy it for 50 cents on the dollar, sometimes even more. If you purchased a lien at a tax lien sale, however, you are really buying for a rate of return. However, if the lien does not redeem, you may get the property for little more than one or two years of back property taxes.

While this situation is very rare, it does happen. In most lien states, the foreclosure process does not involve a public sale of the property but only a statutory requirement to send certified letters to the owner and lien holders—and typically a notice in the legal section of the local newspaper. In most cases, a foreclosing property tax lien holder is only paying off a subsequent property tax lien holder (if applicable), paying the back taxes, and reimbursing the county for its administrative fees for publication. In almost all cases, you should be wiping out any other liens. In short, you will be acquiring the property for pennies on the dollar. The downside, of course, is that you have to wait one, two, or even three years for the redemption period to run and to process the administrative foreclosure process with the county.

Is this scenario likely to happen on a nice property? No. First, what owner would let a property go like that? Second, if there is a mortgagee on the property, such as a bank, that mortgagee would step in and pay off the property tax liens to protect their position. In most cases, the owner will be either out-of-state, an entity such as a corporation or trust, or perhaps an heir who inherited the property but did not want it.

A few years ago I bid on an intercoastal property in Merritt Island, Florida. It was a normal house that needed some rehab, but was on a huge lot right on the intercoastal river. Most of the neighbors had nice sailboats moored at their docks. When I looked in the county's file on this property, I figured out what likely had happened. First, I saw that the owner, who was a woman, was living in the Northeast—Maryland as I recall. When I dug deeper in the file, I found a divorce decree. Apparently, many years before, the husband and wife had purchased this property as a winter home. My guess is that they likely had a nice sailboat or powerboat at their dock. While I didn't read the entire divorce decree (and the distribution of assets would not have been in this file), I assumed that the wife got this winter home as part of the settlement. However, since it was far away and she would be traveling alone, this waterfront property was not nearly as much fun as it used to be. In addition, perhaps the husband received the boat in the asset distribution. In any event, it appeared that the wife just didn't want it any longer and didn't want to continue paying the property taxes. Why not just sell the property? Your guess is as good as mine. Perhaps she was independently wealthy and elderly, or perhaps the house brought back too many bad memories. For whatever reason, the taxes were not paid and the county sold it at a deed auction.

In addition, the property did not have a mortgage. If it did, the mortgagee would have stepped in, paid the taxes, and then foreclosed on the mortgage. So, as a second requirement to stealing a property, you need to buy a lien on a property that is not encumbered by a mortgage or trust deed.

BUYING VACANT LOTS

The best deals at tax deed sales are almost always on vacant lots. It's common sense really. Would you lose a house for back taxes? Would you lose a commercial property? You might lose a lot if you were in some financial trouble and couldn't pay taxes due from two or more years. This asset is certainly less important.

As mentioned previously, many of these lots are of questionable quality or value. To be sure, though, you can buy them for pennies on the dollar—at least to the tax-assessed dollar value. I've bought them for as little as $75. I've also spent as much as $900 for a vacant residential lot. However, that lot was assessed by the county at $16,000 when I bought it, and was assessed at $20,000 the next year.

Does this mean that the property is worth $20,000? Not necessarily. While the tax-assessed value is typically in the range of 85 percent of the true fair market value, vacant lots are much harder to value. In some cases, they are completely worthless. I still have the lot I bought for $900. It's two and a half acres of residential property outside of Los Angeles—*way outside* of Los Angeles! I bought it on speculation that the city would continue to grow, and that developments would reach my lot and greatly increase its value. In the meantime, I've spent $900 and I have a small property tax due each year. Eventually, a developer will come in and purchase large blocks of land for a subdivision, and my lot will be necessary for that development. So I hold and wait.

I live in Orlando, home of the world-famous Walt Disney World. This resort is the number one tourist destination in the world. The Disney property is larger than most counties and occupies thousands of acres. Growing up in Orlando, I know well the history of the development. Walt Disney and his team worked in great secrecy in the late 1960s to purchase hundreds of small acre lots to piece together the thousands of acres necessary for the development of Disney World. At the time, this land was very obscure and close to nothing. Today, the land is priceless. So who knows, maybe Disney will rebuild Disneyland in Los Angeles in the area where I have my little two-and-a-half-acre tract!

HANDYMAN SPECIALS

The third way to get great deals is to look at houses or properties that need much work. As you might expect, if a property is going to be sold at a tax deed sale, it needs a lot of work! Since I'm not particularly handy, I don't really like these properties. Yes, you can hire workers to do what is necessary, but you will reduce your profit and increase your out-of-pocket costs.

In the last chapter, I mentioned the house I bought for $4,100. I debated whether to get it for two reasons: One, it was in Kansas and I live in Florida. If I am an out-of-state owner, can you imagine the trouble I will encounter rehabbing the property? Second, the house needed a lot of work, and I didn't have time to get estimates from a general contractor. The prices in the area were around $50,000 (a very rural area), so I knew it was a safe investment. I was back in Florida the day after I bought it. In fact, I was very busy at the time and didn't have time to fool around with rehabbing or even thinking about it.

After sitting on it for a few months, I decided to put an ad in the paper to flip it for a few thousand more than I had paid, which I did. Had I been local to the property, I would have hired a general contractor and made much more. Nevertheless, it was a nice return on investment and represented only a few hours of work.

COUNTY MINIMUM BIDS

One last note to increase your odds of stealing a property. Most deed jurisdictions will open the bidding at the outstanding back taxes and county administrative costs. A few jurisdictions will have a higher amount. For example, if the property is a homestead residential property, some counties will require that bidding start at 50 percent of the tax-assessed value (maybe 35 to 40 percent of the fair market value). However, other counties allow opening bids *below* the outstanding back taxes. For example, when I was in Kansas, the county where I bought properties allowed for opening bids of only 50 cents!

Keep in mind that other bidders will be there but sometimes bidders run out of money. Sometimes, they are there to buy the property next to their own property and leave once that property is sold. In any event, all things considered, your preference would be to bid where the county has low opening bids.

In the list of states in Part Three, I give a few personal notes related to opening bids in a few states. There you will also find all pertinent information regarding bidding at sales for each state.

LARRY'S REMINDERS

- The best deals on acquiring properties is not on tax deeds, but on tax liens where the redemption period has expired.
- At tax deed sales, the best deals will usually occur on vacant lots, since fewer bidders will be interested in acquiring them.
- Be wary of tax-assessed values on vacant lots, because those figures may not be indicative of the lot's true fair market value.
- If you seek to acquire a property at a tax deed auction, you may want to invest in counties that have low minimum bids.

11

CAVEAT EMPTOR! RISKS AND HOW TO AVOID THEM

In the last chapter, I mentioned that many properties can be bought for very low prices, perhaps for even pennies on the dollar. However, many properties are not worth buying! For example, you might buy a vacant lot that is so small it is unbuildable. Or the lot is configured in such a strange way that it is also unbuildable, except possibly for use as a parking lot. In other cases, the property might be under water or next to or part of a drainage ditch! So, in tax deed investing, rule number one is always to personally view the property. Put your own two feet on the property being sold. Let's examine further this potential risk.

BAD PROPERTIES

When it comes to property taxes, counties have a double standard. On the one hand, the county insists that you pay property taxes each year. Those taxes are based on someone else's appraisal or assessed value (the county assessor). Oftentimes, that tax-assessed value may be way out of line with reality. I've seen drainage ditches assessed at $20,000! And what can you do about it? Nothing. Oh sure, you could challenge a tax assessor's valuation, but that requires some of your time finding out how to challenge it, arguing your case, and so on. On top of that, the assessor may just say that you are wrong and extract a tax from you for whatever he or she thinks is appropriate. In most cases, the assessor has never been to or even seen the property. The assessor is usually only looking at the historic records of what it has been assessed for and just adjusting for inflation.

A few years back, I was at a deed sale in Pennsylvania. I looked at a few properties before the sale. One of the properties listed by the county was a condominium in a very nice complex. Going by my rule to always personally see the property, I drove over to take a look at it. The complex sat on top of a hill with a gorgeous view of the city. The design was modern and of a beautiful traditional architecture. Each building had a nice foyer with a huge brass chandelier. It was nice—very nice. Any condo in this complex would certainly be new, nice, and somewhat expensive.

The unit listed with the tax lien was unit 10, so I went to that building. While I might not be able to go inside the unit, at least it would give me the comfort of knowing that I saw unit "10" on the door. But I had one small problem: all of the buildings were secured (I told you it was nice!). Outside of each building was a keypad listing the last names of the tenants to open the front door. Now I had a dilemma: I couldn't get inside the building. Do I follow my rule of always visually inspecting every property, or do I rely on the quality of the building and complex? A stickler for rules, I decided to insist on seeing the unit. Since I knew I couldn't get in without a code, I waited for someone to exit the building. About ten minutes later, someone came out and I gracefully entered.

The building was not large, so I knew it would just take a minute to find unit 10. I just turned right and walked down the hall. The units were all numbered sequentially. I saw units 1, 2, 3,

4, and 5 and this side ended. Going the other way, I saw that I was headed in the right direction. Unit 6, 7, 8, 9 . . . end of hall. Hmmm, did I go the wrong way? I went back the other way again, and sure enough, that side ended at unit 5. Guess what? There was no unit 10! My guess is that a unit 10 existed in the original architectural plans filed with the county when the complex was built. But it was never built. The county was selling a lien on something that did not even exist! What's worse, the building was secure and most people would not have waited around to get in.

Obviously, a county assessor never visited the property. Nevertheless, it was listed with a value and a tax due just like all the other units. Had I not stuck with my rule of always visually inspecting every property, I would have bought that property and been a very *un*happy camper! Always, always, always visually inspect every property that you intend to buy at a tax deed sale.

ENVIRONMENTAL PROBLEMS

While the vast majority of properties sold at deed sales do not have environmental issues, you will eventually run across a property that does have some issues. In almost all cases, the county will put a special note next to that property indicating that it either has or may have an environmental problem. Figure 11.1 shows such a case from a sale I went to in Los Angeles. If you see something like this, you obviously don't bid on it!

Is it possible to get a property that has an environmental issue but was not flagged by the county? Yes, you could get a property like that if the county did not know of the problem. Here's an easy way to stay clear of these potential problems. One, visually inspect the property. Two, don't buy a gas station property or a property next to a gas station. Three, buy liens only on residential or commercial properties with buildings. Stay away from vacant lands, especially those with industrial zoning.

FIGURE II.I *Property Listing Showing Potential Environmental Problem*

```
                                                      MB   PG   PCL
   ITEM         LEGAL LATEST                        LASTEST  PARCEL
    NO   NSB#   DESC  ASSESSEE    LOCATION   MIN BID.  IMPS EARLIEST PARCEL


   3719    176    E J   BALDWIN'S   FIFTH   $87,553       Y    8741 011 002
          SUBDIVISION OF  A    PORTION   OF                 81/8741 011 002
          RANCHO LA PUENTE LOT   COM   AT  S
          TERMINUS OF A COURSE IN  W  LINE
          OF VALINDA AVE   PER   MB533-48-49
          HAVING A BEARING OF S 0¢39'50"  W
          AND A LENGTH OF 473.38 FT   TH   N
          0¢39'50" E TO A PT N 0¢39'50"   E
          150 FT FROM E PROLONGATION OF   N
          LINE OF MAPLEGROVE ST PER CSB119     THIS PROPERTY MAY BE CONTAMINATED
          TH N 86¢02'49" W   150   FT   TH   S INVESTIGATE BEFORE YOU PURCHASE
          0¢39'50" W TO SD  N  LINE   TH   E
          THEREON TO A PT  S  47¢18'35"   W
          23.44 FT FROM BEG TH N 47¢18'35"
          E TO BEG   PART   OF   LOT   349
          ASSESSED    TO    SEIRAFI,MOHAMED
          LOCATION COUNTY OF LOS ANGELES
```

INTERNAL REVENUE SERVICE LIENS

In Chapter 7, I discussed the situation with IRS liens. In almost all cases, a tax deed property with an IRS lien will be disclosed by the county. Figure 11.2 shows a list of properties with IRS liens on them. This was disclosed by Los Angeles County in the front of its deed sale catalog. My advice is to just skip these properties!

Because most counties will disclose this information, it is easy enough to avoid these properties. If you end up with a property that does have an IRS lien on it, the IRS has 120 days to act on that lien. Since you are not the debtor (owing the IRS money), the IRS will often exclude the property from its list of assets for the debtor if you ask. In some cases, you may want to discuss the matter with your attorney. Just remember that the IRS must redeem the property within the 120-day window (from the date of the sale) or lose its lien against the property. See Chapter 7 to review.

FIGURE 11.2 *List of Properties with IRS Liens*

2001B IRS LIEN

Item #	Parcel #	Item #	Parcel #	Item #	Parcel #
74	2537 012 006	93	2569 010 003	114	2644 026 004
124	2819 019 005	130	2825 014 057	131	2825 018 045
294	3064 016 040	371	3084 014 018	377	3089 005 003
385	3089 028 029	386	3091 004 009	400	3109 002 075
410	3116 011 019	413	3117 005 036	414	3117 005 037
415	3117 005 038	416	3117 005 039	425	3123 013 036
432	3137 005 029	440	3145 031 040	477	3214 031 013
518	3228 026 014	529	3234 012 003	530	3234 012 004
550	3247 027 001	551	3248 021 025	552	3248 021 045
611	3270 006 007	617	3270 014 011	621	3270 017 047
657	3278 007 001	662	3278 015 031	663	3278 015 032
696	3310 006 005	697	3310 006 041	710	3310 023 009
713	3310 023 020	715	3310 023 024	716	3310 023 025
725	3314 007 064	731	3314 008 068	750	3316 002 001
759	3316 012 008	761	3316 012 048	774	3316 014 041
780	3316 018 051	782	3316 020 044	825	3318 014 062
838	3322 009 022	854	3322 016 003	857	3322 021 038
883	3326 002 117	884	3326 002 127	888	3326 004 053
894	3326 005 084	910	3326 011 063	921	3326 015 068
932	3326 024 001	936	3326 026 014	975	3334 011 033
993	3336 005 052	1004	3336 011 019	1008	3338 002 022
1011	3338 006 021	1057	3346 008 065	1073	3346 022 003
1105	3350 019 014	1109	3350 020 072	1142	3362 006 004
1156	3363 004 029	1158	3363 010 018	1184	3366 012 017
1220	3370 001 028	1224	3370 009 022	1233	3372 004 025
1255	3374 020 021	1265	3376 006 012	1266	3376 010 020
1354	4031 027 014	1363	4061 013 007	1386	4337 020 007
1389	4350 003 007	1395	4371 001 002	1396	4371 003 004
1398	4371 020 017	1404	4371 032 011	1405	4371 036 009
1414	4379 013 006	1427	4380 017 019	1498	4440 003 003
1502	4440 017 001	1521	4442 008 011	1530	4442 014 011
1558	4442 030 014	1574	4444 011 013	1603	4451 011 007
1634	4461 017 046	1636	4461 018 023	1639	4461 018 038
1642	4461 023 003	1647	4461 027 017	1677	4465 005 009
1678	4465 005 024	1775	4490 006 019	1778	4493 001 009
1797	5024 013 011	1810	5037 002 005	1819	5049 013 044
1827	5058 023 046	1861	5137 018 011	1863	5142 015 012
1870	5155 012 178	1892	5207 024 014	1900	5208 013 018
1932	5209 014 010	1943	5209 021 021	1956	5213 023 006
1979	5216 013 017	1985	5217 003 008	1989	5217 011 007
1990	5217 011 008	1993	5217 015 016	1994	5217 015 017
1995	5217 015 018	2010	5225 020 012	2035	5228 019 008
2039	5228 023 011	2062	5243 005 009	2063	5243 007 005
2055	5244 025 005	2096	5302 027 001	2102	5304 004 017
2123	5305 026 035	2125	5305 029 006	2152	5355 009 028
2158	5364 018 019	2166	5381 018 019	2182	5405 007 026
2186	5405 004 016	2191	5415 008 018	2192	5415 008 026

In short, the risks associated with deed investing are all avoidable. Just remember to always see the property before bidding. If you have an interest in a vacant lot, visit the county to see if a property is buildable. County rules vary here, so check with the county first. I once found a lot that was 55 feet wide, but the county's minimum for building was 60 feet. The time to ask the county about this is *before* you bid at the auction, not after you own the property!

LARRY'S REMINDERS

- Counties are ruthless in selling worthless properties at tax deed sales. Always, always, *visually* inspect every property that you intend to buy at a tax deed sale.
- In almost all cases, counties will disclose if a property has, or may have, environmental problems or issues. *Do not bid on these properties.*
- Most counties will also disclose if a property is encumbered by an IRS lien. While your property tax lien will not be extinguished by an IRS lien, I would also avoid these properties.

12

THE BIDDING BATTLE—
NOT FOR THE TIMID

Bidding at tax lien and deed auctions is fun, if not exhilarating. Because it is an auction where you bid against others, your competitive juices may start flowing. That can be both good and bad. Active competition tends to focus your attention and heighten your reflexes. However, competition often encourages us to win, which might lead us to bid above our planned figure in the heat of battle. Most of the people at the auction will be seasoned investors. A few will be rookies, and a few more will be at their first sale. Most important, the sale will move very, very fast. If you have seen auctions where professional auctioneers are used, you'll get the point. In fact, some counties employ professional auctioneers to run the sale. So, let's look at a few points for preparing for the auction.

DO YOUR HOMEWORK

In my estimation, 90 percent of mistakes made at deed auctions are due to the bidder's lack of due diligence, or homework.

Some bidders never look at the property. This is the biggest mistake of all, as I discussed previously. Here's my checklist of things to do before the sale.

1. Check the file for the property at the county offices. For a tax deed sale, counties will usually have a big file on each property. This file will normally include information about the taxes due, the owner, and other liens. Sometimes, the file will also have an appraisal from the assessor's office, and sometimes a survey. Normally, the file also will reveal if the property is a vacant lot or an improved lot (i.e., with a building on it). The file may also reveal if the property is a homestead property. If so, there's a great chance that the property tax lien will be paid before the deed sale. In some cases, you also can get detailed information, such as the number of bedrooms and baths, the square feet, year built, and so on. Check to see if the assessor's information is available online as well. I like properties where the monies due (normally the starting point for bidding) are no more than 20 percent of the assessed value. Recall that property taxes are about 1 to 2 percent of the fair market value, and that you will be paying two or more years of back taxes (in most jurisdictions). The county will also add administrative fees and costs.

2. Contact the assessor's office for "comps." Comparables, or sales of comparable properties in the area, will assist you in knowing what you can resell the property for. If the assessor's information is online, the comps can be seen oftentimes there as well.

3. If a vacant lot, locate the physical address. In many instances, a vacant lot will not have a street address. Instead, the county will have a legal address and a parcel identification number. Ask the county official to help you at this point. Normally, you'll go to a plat map to locate the property. You can usually locate the vacant property by the physical street address of the adjacent properties.

4. Now check out the property. Once you have done your homework on the property, you can proceed to view the property. This means you have determined that the property either has a structure on it or is a vacant lot of buildable size. You've looked at the value vis-à-vis the assessed or appraised value. You've made a determination that the property is a good one and that you might be able to get it for a reasonable price. What is reasonable will vary for each person. Those really wanting to "steal" it will look for 10 cents on the dollar. Those who may be in the business of rehabbing and flipping properties may be willing to go up to 50 cents on the dollar or more.

Now a word about when to check out a property. You really should look at all properties a day or two before the sale. Leave a business day before the sale in case you have any questions about the property. Why wait until a few days before the sale? Because at least one half of the properties will redeem just before the sale. If you see six properties you really like, you'll probably only have three to bid on at the sale. So, if you don't want to spend time driving around town looking for the three properties that were not even at the sale, wait until a day or so before the sale.

For example, if the sale is on a Wednesday, go by the county office to look at the files on Monday, and look at the properties Tuesday morning. If the sale is on a Monday, go by the county on Friday and look at the properties late Friday or Saturday. Many counties will show their updated listings on the Internet, so that you can first check there to see if a property has redeemed and been taken off the sale list.

SET YOUR MAXIMUM AHEAD OF TIME

At every deed sale I've been to, there are always some properties that sell for more than they should have. This occurs for two reasons. First, the bidder did not set a maximum price before the sale that he or she would bid. Second, the bidding moves fast and people want to *win!* The bidding is normally competitive and people get excited. You'll be surprised what people will do in the heat of the bidding battle. Here is one more reason why people bid more than they should. Let's say you come to an auction intent on bidding on four properties. One redeems just before the sale, so now you're down to three. The first one comes up and you're outbid. The second one comes up and again you're outbid. As the third and last one comes up, you're likely saying to yourself, "By golly, I'm not going to be outbid on this one! I'm going to go home with something!" Don't do it! There will be other properties and other auctions. Stay the course with your guidelines.

BE ASSERTIVE!

Like lien auctions, deed auctions move fast and only people who are ready with their number and final bid will stay in the game. When it's time for you to jump in, you have to yell your bid as if someone has just stolen your wallet or purse! This goes for lien bidding, too. I've seen too many properties missed because the bidder was too timid in his or her bid. I've trained several people how to do this, and, without exception, the first mistake they all make is to either hesitate with their bid or to say it as if they were talking to the person next to them. Yell it!

WHAT SOME SEASONED INVESTORS DO

Here's the scenario. Say you have a nice property worth $75,000. Suppose the bidding starts at $8,000. You have five bidders actively going at it: "$9,000 . . . $10,000 . . . $10,500 . . . $11,000 . . . $11,500 . . . $12,000. . . ." At this point, we're down to three bidders: "$13,000 . . . $13,400 . . . $13,800. . . ." Now there are only two bidders: "$14,000 . . . $14,300 . . . $14,500 . . . $14,700. . . ." Silence. The auctioneer then says, "$14,700 going once, $14,700 going twice. . . ." Then, from the back of the room: "$20,000." What? Where did that come from? A new bidder! Where's this guy been? He hasn't said a word the whole time and just now comes in, some $5,300 over the last bid! The guy who has been bidding all along and thought he was going to get it at $14,700 just winces. This new guy, this "mole" in the back of the room, just got it at $20,000, while everyone else in the room stares in shock.

What just happened? The late-entry bid is common bidding practice for some seasoned investors who think that with more bidders, the more a frenzy builds and the higher the price will eventually go. So they sit back and let the other investors weed themselves out. At the final moment, when bidding has stopped, they jump in at a huge increase in bid. So they've done two things. First, they didn't add to the bidding frenzy. Second, they gauged their bid to *shock* the last bidder, who was about to win. Before the last bidder can readjust his or her thinking to this new bid of $20,000 and consider whether to stay in the game, the bidding is over. It's a shrewd strategy, and I see it at almost every deed auction I attend. Be aware of this strategy, either to recognize it, or to use it to your advantage!

LARRY'S REMINDERS

- Do your homework before the sale:
  —Check the file for the property at the county offices.
  —Contact the county assessor's office for comps.
  —If a vacant lot, locate the physical address.
  —Personally inspect the property.
- Set your maximum bid ahead of time.
- Be assertive—yell out your bid as if someone has robbed you.
- Be aware of the late bidding "shock" investors and their strategy.

13

FREE AND CLEAR, BUT CAN I SELL IT?

Whenever you acquire a property through either a tax lien or tax deed scenario, you have both good news and bad news. The good news is that you typically own it free and clear. The better news is that you probably bought it for somewhere between pennies on the dollar and 50 cents on the dollar. The bad news is that your title is not the same as when you buy a house through a normal sale with an individual seller. Actually, it's not bad news; it just means you may need to do a little bit of work to "perfect the title."

PERFECTING THE TITLE

When you acquire a property from a taxing entity, you are not getting the same title as you would if you just bought a property from an individual seller. In the individual-to-individual scenario, the buyer will demand a certain type of deed, namely a "warranty" deed. What that means is that the seller is giving you a warranty (or guarantee, if you will) that the title is good, marketable, and insurable. Essentially, this means that the title is "clean," or free from any encumbrances (or the title company may "except" an encumbrance from coverage in its title insurance policy).

In a property acquired from the county, however, you will not receive a warranty deed. The county is not giving you *any* warranties. That's not its job. The county tax collector or treasurer is not a title insurance company. The county official's job is to collect the taxes due on that property. Period. You typically will get a *sheriff's deed, tax deed, constable's deed,* or similar deed of conveyance. Figure 13.1 shows a copy of the sheriff's deed I received on the house I bought at the Kansas deed sale.

If you plan to resell the property for full fair market value (called a "retail" sale in real estate lingo), however, most title companies will not accept this type of deed. You likely will need to have an attorney file what is called a "quiet title action." This is a fairly simple "pleading" that the attorney will file with the local court. If anyone claims to have rights in the property, he or she will have to respond to this pleading or forever lose any potential rights. Absent a scenario where you acquired a deed before a redemption period had run, it is highly unlikely anyone will claim rights at this point. Depending on your area of the country, you may pay an attorney $1,000 to $3,000 to do this. Once this is completed, you will be able to sell the property with a warranty deed and can ask for full fair market value. Since you acquired the property far below fair market value, spending another thousand dollars or so to perfect the title should not bother you. You simply need to factor in this amount as a cost of doing business, the same way you would consider brokers' commissions.

However, if you buy a property for 10 to 50 cents on the dollar, you may want to consider selling the property "wholesale" to a "retail" seller. A retail seller is someone who wants to rehab the property and sell it for fair market value. These retail sellers generally buy properties for 50 to 75 cents on the dollar from wholesalers.

FIGURE 13.1 *Example of Sheriff's Deed*

SHERIFF'S DEED

FILED FOR RECORD
2001 DEC 19 P 12: 36

KNOW ALL MEN BY THESE PRESENTS, THAT a certain action to foreclose tax liens on certain real property in the County of Leavenworth, State of Kansas, has heretofore been filed in the District Court of Leavenworth County, Kansas, and is titled: The Board of County Commissioners of Leavenworth County, Kansas v. JL Clark Plumbing & Heating, Inc, et al, Case No. 0107 CV 224; and Judgement was thereafter rendered by said court in the above entitled action on 19 October, 2001.

In compliance with, and pursuant to this Judgment, the Clerk of the District Court of Leavenworth County, Kansas, issued an order to Sheriff Herbert F. Nye, Sheriff of Leavenworth County, Kansas, to advertise and sell tracts of land, lots, or pieces of real estate described below, all according to law.

The Leavenworth County Sheriff gave notice of this sale by advertisement and publication notice of sale in The Tonganoxie Mirror newspaper printed in Leavenworth County, Kansas, and which had been continuously and uninterruptedly published in Leavenworth County, Kansas, not less than fifty (50) weeks for a period of five years prior to the first publication notice, all according to the law. The Leavenworth County Sheriff, Herbert F. Nye, thereafter sold to Larry Boyd Loftis for the highest and best bid obtainable on 11 December, 2001, the following described real property; for the amount shown by each particular tract, lot, or piece of real estate.

DESCRIPTION: The South Half of Lot 26, and all of Lots 27 and 28 in Block numbered 33, Macaulay's First Addition to the City of Leavenworth according to the recorded plat thereof.

Entered in the transfer record in my office this 19 day of Dec, 20 01
County Clerk

Price: $4,100.00

THEREAFTER, on the 17th day of December, 2001, the order of sale and the proceedings of sale were returned to the Leavenworth County District Court and after examination of the proceedings, and finding that the sale was made in all respects in conformity with the law applicable, the District Court of Leavenworth County confirmed the sale, and the proceedings made thereto, on the 18th day of December, 2001.

THEREAFTER, and according to law, the Sheriff of Leavenworth County was ordered to execute this good and sufficient deed to the purchaser(s) Larry Boyd Loftis.

I, Herbert F. Nye, Sheriff of Leavenworth County, Kansas, therefore do hereby give, grant, sell and convey to Larry Boyd Loftis, their heirs and assigns, forever, all the above-described real estate located in Leavenworth County, Kansas, together with all and singular tenements, hereditaments and appurtenances thereto or in any way appertaining, subject to zoning regulations, easements, restrictions, and mineral interests of record.

TO HAVE AND TO HOLD THE SAME UNTO THE SAID Larry Boyd Loftis, their heirs and assigns forever.

IN WITNESS WHEREOF, I, Herbert F. Nye, Sheriff of Leavenworth County, State of Kansas, have hereunto set my hand this 18th day of December, 2001.

Herbert F. Nye
Sheriff of Leavenworth County, Kansas

STATE OF KANSAS)
) SS:
COUNTY OF LEAVENWORTH)

This instrument was acknowledged before me the 18th day of December, 2001 by Herbert F. Nye as Sheriff of Leavenworth County, Kansas.

K. Janette Nessmith - Eyerly
Notary Public - State of Kansas
My Appt. Expires 01-24-2004

Notary Public

My Appointment Expires:
01-24-2004

Have you ever seen the signs that say, "We Buy Ugly Houses"? These are wholesalers. They will advertise to find people in a real jam who need to sell a house quickly. They'll buy these ugly (because they need work) houses quickly with cash. Then they'll put an ad in the paper that says something like "Handyman Special." This ad will draw out the retailers who want to buy it for 75 to 80 cents on the dollar, fix it up, and resell it for full fair market value.

If you choose this wholesale method, you can sell the property by way of a *quit claim deed,* which gives no warranties. Since you are selling it at a significant discount, buyers know they have plenty of profit margin to work with. Your buyer can later perfect the title if he or she so chooses. In most cases, they'll just invest the $1,000 to $3,000 to file the quiet title action and get a clean deed. You can find rehabbers (or retailers) by advertising a handyman special in the paper, or by attending your local real estate investors' club.

YOU HAVE THE PROPERTY, NOW WHAT?

Once you acquire a property, here are your options: (1) rent the property; (2) sell the property with a broker; (3) sell the property "for sale by owner"; or (4) simply hold it for investment purposes. If you decide to use a broker to resell the property and do not know of anyone in the area, you can probably get a referral from your local title company. Another way is to just use one of the national brokerage firms like Watson, Century 21, or RE/MAX. I have sold a couple of properties using RE/MAX. I like RE/MAX, because it is national but each office is independently owned. The RE/MAX brokers I have used to sell properties have been outstanding.

If you decide to sell the property "by owner," you will eliminate any broker commissions. This may be less practical where the property is not vacant land, however. For example, if you live out-of-state, how will you show the property? If the property is local or is vacant land, the sale by owner also has an additional benefit. Since you own the property outright, you can sell it with owner financing. For example, you could get, say, 10 percent down (or the amount you paid for the property), and finance the balance at, say, 8 percent for 5, 10, or even 30 years. If you don't want to wait this long, you also can put in a balloon where the balance will be due in three, four, or five years. One thing is certain: If you finance the property, you will sell it faster and can ask a higher price. I used this approach to sell a large home in Orlando. I sold it quickly and got my exact asking price. I've also used a lease option to entice renters/owners (basically renting with an option to buy at some point in the future).

SELLING YOUR REAL ESTATE NOTE

If you choose the seller financing option and take back a mortgage and promissory note from the buyer, you now have another option. You can sell that note for cash. In some cases, you can even do a "simultaneous close," where the sale of the property and the sale of the note occur at the same time. In actuality, the note is sold a few minutes after the property, but the seller leaves with a check in hand for the note.

WHAT NOT TO DO

Let me add one last bit of advice. If you do get a property, whatever you do, don't sit on it. That is, do not just let it sit there without taking some action, whether selling it, rehabbing it, or renting it. If you do sit on a property, three things will happen (I learned this the hard way). First, any improved property that sits without occupants (and air-conditioning) will deteriorate. Rodents may find their way in. If you're in the South, roaches certainly will. Second, weeds will grow. In addition to making the house look unsightly, it will become a health hazard and the county will mow it for you and charge an outlandish fee—like $200 each time. Third, property taxes (and insurance, if you have it) will accrue each month, just adding up month after month. If you let a property sit for months, you'll quickly be eating into your original profit margin. In short, decide what you want to do with the property and get on it!

LARRY'S REMINDERS

- If you acquire a property at a tax deed sale, you will not acquire it with warranties.
- If you want to resell the property for full fair market value, you will need to "perfect" the title.
- Perfecting the title will require hiring an attorney to "quiet the title."
- If you want to sell the property quickly, consider selling it wholesale to a "retailer" through a quit claim deed.
- Never sit on a property after acquiring it. Your property will deteriorate and each day will mean costs in insurance and mowing.

Part Three

LIST OF STATES

ALABAMA

Sale Type:	Lien
Interest Rate:	12% per annum
Bid Method:	Premium bid (premium also receives 12%)
Redemption Period:	3 years
Sale Date(s):	May
Statute Section(s):	Code of Alabama Sections 40-10-15, 20, 120, 121, 187
Over-the-Counter?	Yes (See "Comments")

Comments:

Over-the-counter sales in Alabama are handled on the state level. Tax certificates not purchased at the county level are delivered to the Alabama Commissioner of Revenue. You may contact the state commissioner at:

Alabama Department of Revenue
Property Tax Division
P.O. Box 327210
Montgomery, AL 36132-7210

ALASKA

Sale Type:	Deed
Interest Rate:	N/A
Bid Method:	Set by municipality
Redemption Period:	1 year minimum (set by municipality)
Sale Date(s):	Varies by municipality
Statute Section(s):	Alaska Statutes, Chapter 48
Over-the-Counter?	No

Comments:

Alaska is a bit different than most deed states in two respects. First, the only "bidders" at a tax sale are the municipalities. Properties are generally transferred to the municipalities for the lien amount. Thereafter, a minimum redemption period of one year must transpire. Properties then may be sold by the municipalities under procedures set by local ordinance. Second, the sale by the municipality likely will set the sale price at the fair market value.

Thus, Alaska is *not* one of the better deed states.

ARIZONA

Sale Type:	Lien
Interest Rate:	16% per annum
Bid Method:	Bid down the interest
Redemption Period:	3 years (if judicial foreclosure)
	5 years (if nonjudicial foreclosure)
Sale Date(s):	February
	Coconino (Flagstaff)—3rd Thursday
Statute Section(s):	Arizona Revised Statutes Sections 42-312, 390, 393, 410, 451, 462
Over-the-Counter?	Yes

Comments:

In Arizona, *the tax lien does NOT take priority over a* state *lien.* As such, you could foreclose on your tax lien and get the property, only to find out that there was a large lien held by the State of Arizona, which would run with the land. Check with the county involved to be sure there is no state lien (or a very small one) on your property before purchasing the lien.

ARKANSAS

Sale Type:	Deed
Interest Rate:	N/A
Bid Method:	Premium bid
Redemption Period:	30 days (from auction date)
Sale Date(s):	May 1 (Little Rock)
Statute Section(s):	Arkansas Code, Chapter 38
Over-the-Counter?	No

Comments:

In Arkansas, the minimum bid for a tax deed property is not only the lien amount (i.e., delinquent property taxes, penalties, interest, and costs), but also the county assessor's assessed value. Under Arkansas law, the assessed value of a property is 20% of the assessor's "true market value." Since property taxes typically run 1% to 2% of the property's value, the minimum that you could purchase a property for would likely be 25%. Check also to see the number of years of delinquent property taxes.

CALIFORNIA

Sale Type:	Deed
Interest Rate:	N/A
Bid Method:	Premium bid
Redemption Period:	N/A
Sale Date(s):	Varies by county
	Fresno—1st Monday in March
	Kern (Bakersfield)—March/July/November
	Los Angeles—February/August
	San Diego—February
	San Francisco—April
Statute Section(s):	California Revenue and Taxation Code
	Chapter 7, Sections 3691, 3698, 3712
Over-the-Counter?	No

Comments:

1. A property acquired at a tax deed sale in California would be acquired *free of all liens and encumbrances,* except for any special assessments, easements (which always run with any property upon conveyance), and possibly an IRS lien. In the vast majority of cases, none of these items is present, so the property may be acquired for as little as pennies on the dollar (bidding permit).

2. I purchased one property at the August 2001 sale in Los Angeles and bid on several others. There was an enormous amount of properties sold (over 3,900 properties in the sale book, although probably half of those redeemed and half of those remaining were bad properties). My guess is that about 1,000 good properties were sold. There appeared to be 300 to 400 bidders at the sale. For improved properties (i.e., those with a house or other building on them), the bidding was fairly active. The property I purchased (my assistant purchased one also) was a vacant lot and was bought at the opening bid. As it turned out, the assessor's appraised value was far above what my California

broker says it can be sold for (but far in excess of what I paid, $900). Beware of erroneous assessor values!

3. *Carefully inspect your properties beforehand!* I also tried to look at several lots that were impossible to find because of their remote mountain location, or were probably unsuitable for building due to mountain conditions. The county is irresponsible for selling these, but they do anyway. *Always, always, check out the property closely before you bid on it.*

COLORADO

Sale Type:	Lien
Interest Rate:	9 points above the federal discount rate set in September, rounded to the nearest full percent. See "Comments" on the effect of premium bidding.
Bid Method:	Premium bid (See "Comments")
Redemption Period:	3 years
Sale Date(s):	1st Thursday in November
Statute Section(s):	Colorado Revised Statutes, Sections 39-12-103, 39-11-120, 122
Over-the-Counter?	Allowed (but not mandatory) by statute; check with each particular county. Denver is "no."

Comments:

NOTE: Under Colorado's premium bidding system, *the investor does NOT receive back any premium bid over the lien amount or any interest thereon.* For example, suppose the lien amount was $1,000. If an investor bid $1,500 for that lien, he would receive his interest rate only on the $1,000. He would *LOSE* the $500 premium and receive no interest on that amount. Since this system certainly reduces the attractiveness to investors, some counties utilize the *rotational* bidding system.

CONNECTICUT

Sale Type:	Deed (a hybrid state; see "Comments")
Interest Rate:	18% per annum
Bid Method:	Premium bid (premium also receives 18%)
Redemption Period:	1 year
Sale Date(s):	June
Statute Section(s):	General Statutes of Connecticut Section 12-157
Over-the-Counter?	No

Comments:

Technically, Connecticut is a deed state with a one year right of redemption. However, it operates much more like a lien state. Within two weeks after the tax sale, the county collector will execute a deed to the purchaser or municipality; however, this deed will not be recorded for one year (the redemption period). If the owner redeems, he or she pays the total amount paid by the purchaser, plus 18% per annum. If the owner does not redeem, the deed is recorded and the purchaser gets the property.

In some areas (e.g., New Haven), the city collects the taxes and sells the liens. However, New Haven only sells them to qualified buyers in very large bulk sales.

DELAWARE

Sale Type:	Deed (a hybrid state; see "Comments")
Interest Rate:	15% penalty (See "Comments")
Bid Method:	Premium bid
Redemption Period:	60 days
Sale Date(s):	Varies by county (only 3) Kent County—Jan., Apr., July, Oct. Sussex County—varies (3 or 4 per year) New Castle—varies
Statute Section(s):	9 Del. Code Sections 8721, 8728, 8749, 8750, 8758
Over-the-Counter?	No

Comments:

1. Delaware is a deed state but operates like a lien state (thus, it's a hybrid state).

2. Delaware is a very interesting state. I spoke with the county attorney who has handled the sale for Sussex County for several years. The state's statutes give the counties more than one way to execute their tax sales. For example, Section 8776 of Title 9 (9 Del. C. § 8776) provides one way to execute their sale–20% interest with a one-year redemption. However, Sections 8728 and 8758 allow for another system–the one actually used by the counties. Under this system, the owner has only *60 days* to redeem, it is a *15% penalty,* and it is a priority lien (i.e., ahead of all other liens and extinguishes them). Once the sale is completed, the county attorney will petition the Superior Court for an order approving the sales. This will be a routine matter unless a mistake or some extraordinary event occurred. Once the sale is approved by the court, the 60-day period begins.

3. Recall how the penalty system works. The owner must pay that penalty, regardless of when the lien is redeemed. Accordingly, the faster the owner pays, the greater your rate of return. Now let's examine the rate of return under the system used in Delaware–15% penalty and 60-day redemption period. Let's assume that it took the county attorney a month to get the court approval. What's your rate of return?

Month	Activity	Return if Redemption after end of month
1	Court approval	180%
2	1st 30 days	90%
3	2nd 30 days	60%

You determine your rate of return by multiplying the percentage received each month by the number of months per year (12). Thus, in month one, you received 15% times 12 = 180. If redemption occurred after two months, you still get the same amount (i.e., 15%), but it now took two months to receive. Thus, you received 7.5% each month times 12 = 90.

DISTRICT OF COLUMBIA

Sale Type:	Lien
Interest Rate:	18% per annum
Bid Method:	Premium bid (premium does *not* receive interest)

Redemption Period:	6 months (See "Comments")
Sale Date(s):	July
Statute Section(s):	D.C. Code Section 47-1304
Over-the-Counter?	No

Comments:

1. <u>Redemption:</u> The six-month redemption period is not self-executing. After waiting four months, the investor may order a title search on the property from a qualified title company. After six months, and upon completion of the title search, the investor may file an action with the District of Columbia Superior Court to foreclose the owner's right of redemption.

2. <u>Sale observations:</u> I attended and bought liens at the 2001 sale. I made two observations from the sale. First, most of the properties were bid at premiums, thus reducing the investor's yield below 18%. In D.C., the premium does not receive the 18% interest. For example, an investor buying a $1,000 lien for $2,000 would only receive a 9% rate of return, since the $1,000 premium received no interest at all. On average, most investors were willing to accept a 9% to 10% return. I wanted the 18% returns, so I purchased liens on vacant lots (less interest from bidders). One lot was actually owned by a local college.

The second observation I made was how *unfriendly and unprofessional* the city employees were. While there were probably four to six city employees standing (or sitting) around at all times, none of them could assist with any questions. All of the government workers said questions would have to be answered by the tax sale manager, Connie Hogue. However, Ms. Hogue stayed out of sight for most of the sale and refused to meet with or answer questions from investors. I never even saw her. Given the city's objective to sell liens, I found this very unusual. I have attended lien and deed sales all over the country. Most city and county officials are courteous and helpful. A few are not. The D.C. employees are the worst of those in the latter category.

FLORIDA

Sale Type:	Lien
Interest Rate:	18% per annum, but 5% minimum (See "Comments")
Bid Method:	Bid down the interest

Redemption Period:	2 years
Sale Date(s):	May–June
Statute Section(s):	Florida Statutes Annotated Section 197
Over-the-Counter?	Liens—no; deeds—yes

Comments:

1. Florida Statute Section 197.472(2) provides in pertinent part:

> When a tax certificate is redeemed and the interest amount earned on the certificate is less than 5 percent of the face amount of the certificate, a mandatory charge [i.e., penalty] of 5 percent shall be levied upon the tax certificate. The person redeeming the tax certificate shall pay the interest rate due on the certificate or the 5 percent mandatory charge, whichever is greater.

What this means is that, regardless of the interest rate bid, the investor will get a minimum of a 5% penalty rather than the annualized interest rate. For example, if I purchased the lien at 18%, that is 1.5% per month on an annualized basis. So what if the owner redeems after only one month? I still get an 18% interest rate, but that is not much in actual dollar amount since it is only 1.5%. The Florida legislators realized the disadvantage to investors, so they made sure the investor would get a minimum of 5% return in actual dollars. Thus, if an owner redeems after only one month, the investor realizes a 60% return (5% × 12 months = 60%). I have received not only a 60% return on some of my Florida liens, I also have received an infinite return since one paid off (with a 5% penalty) before I actually went down to the county to pay the invoice for the lien!

If you attend a sale (now online) at a large county like Orange County (Orlando), you'll notice that many of the corporate investors will bid the lien down to ¼%. The reason is because they know that a number of these liens, particularly the larger ones, will pay off in the first or second month. Thus, their overall return is much higher and will balance out those liens that run the full redemption period.

While the Florida counties have an annual lien sale, they also have deed sales. This is because the foreclosure of the tax lien is not "self-executing" (as in Texas, Connecticut, and other states). The lien holder must file for a "tax deed" with the county. The county will then place that property for sale at a tax deed auction, where the actual property will be sold to pay off the lien (with interest, of course). Smaller counties will have deed sales every two months or so, while larger counties will have sales monthly. Orange County typically has two to four deed sales each month. One disadvantage—if the property is a homestead property, the bidding must start at *one-half* of the county's assessed value!

2. Florida's redemption period is two years. However, if your lien does not redeem, *you must file for a tax deed within seven years* (from the date of purchase) or lose your lien (i.e., you've made a nice donation to the county!).

GEORGIA

Sale Type:	Deed (a hybrid state)
Interest Rate:	20% penalty
Bid Method:	Premium bid
Redemption Period:	1 year (not self-executing)
Sale Date(s):	1st Tuesday of each month (large counties)
	Appling (Baxley)—1st Tuesday in October
	Decatur (Bainbridge)—3 or 4 sales per year
	Dougherty (Albany)—1st Tuesday in August
	Glynn (Brunswick)—1st Tuesday in July
	Ware (Waycross)—1st Tuesday in August
Statute Section(s):	Official Code of Georgia Annotated Sections 48-2-40; 48-3-19, 20; 48-4-42, 45
Over-the-Counter?	No

Comments:

1. Technically, Georgia is a deed state, but it operates much like a lien state. At the tax sale, the property is sold, subject to a one-year right of redemption. Furthermore, foreclosure on the right of redemption is not "self-executing." Rather, after the one-year period expires, the investor must terminate the redemption right by

   • sending by certified or registered mail a notice to the owner of the property, any occupant of the property, and any other lien holder (or one having any right or interest in the property); and

   • publishing in the local newspaper (where the county sheriff advertises) once a week for four consecutive weeks immediately prior to the week of redemption deadline identified in the notice.

2. Since Georgia's 20% rate is a penalty rather than a per annum interest rate, the faster the redemption, the better the rate of return. Here's what your rate of return would look like based on a redemption between months 1 to 12 (rounded to the nearest whole number):

Redemption After Month:	Effective Rate of Return
1	240%
2	120%
3	80%
4	60%
5	48%
6	40%
7	34%
8	30%
9	27%
10	24%
11	22%
12	20%

Recall that the redemption right is not automatically terminated. What happens if the owner does not redeem after one year? If the owner doesn't pay the first year, he or she incurs an additional penalty of 20% for the second year (even though it may be only one day after the one-year period elapses). O.C.G.A. Section 48-4-42 provides in pertinent part:

The amount required to be paid for redemption of property from any sale for taxes . . . shall be the amount paid for the property at the tax sale . . . plus a premium of 20 percent of the amount *for each year or fraction of a year* which has elapsed between the date of sale and the date on which the redemption payment is made. [emphasis added]

Accordingly, if the redemption occurred after 13 months, your rate of return would be 36.9%! However, it gets better than that. Section 48-4-42 goes on to provide:

If redemption is not made until after the required notice has been given, there shall be added to the redemption price the sheriff's cost in connection with serving the notice, the cost of publication of the notice, if any, and the *further sum of 20 percent* of the amount paid for the property. . . . [emphasis added]

As such, a redemption after the first year and after the notice was given would be required to pay

- the amount paid for the property at the sale (i.e., your principal investment),
- 20% penalty for year one,
- 20% penalty for year two,
- *20% penalty after notice is given,* or
- 60% in addition to your principal!

Let's assume you have an owner who has not redeemed after the first year and you send out your statutory notices. Assume that the owner redeems after the second month of the second year. Here's what your return would look like:

60% ÷ 14 months = 4.2857%/month
Annualized: 4.2857 × 12 months = 51.43% return!

Overall, then, Georgia is an excellent state. It has the extra work of the statutory notice to terminate the right of redemption but has a sale *monthly* and provides an investor 20% to 120% return!

GUAM (Territory of)

Sale Type:	Deed (a hybrid state)
Interest Rate:	12% per annum
Bid Method:	Premium bid
Redemption Period:	1 year
Statute Section(s):	11 Guam Law Section 24812
Over-the-Counter?	No

HAWAII

Sale Type:	Deed (a hybrid state)
Interest Rate:	12% per annum
Bid Method:	Premium bid
Redemption Period:	1 year
Sale Date(s):	Two sales a year, typically June and November or December
Statute Section(s):	Hawaii Revised Statutes Section 246-60
Over-the-Counter?	No

Comments:

1. Not a bad place to mix a little pleasure with business!
2. For Hawaii County, there are two offices (East and West). We contacted the East county office and found out that the West area is the place to get the better properties. According to the county official, if you buy in the East area, "you'll need a jeep to find it!"

IDAHO

Sale Type:	Deed
Interest Rate:	N/A
Bid Method:	Premium bid
Redemption Period:	N/A
Sale Date(s):	May
Statute Section(s):	Idaho Statute Sections 31-808; 63-1003 through 63-1011
Over-the-Counter?	No

Comments:

1. Idaho is a "pure" deed state, since you get the actual property after the sale. Since the delinquent taxes are a priority lien, any other liens will be extinguished by a tax deed sale (the exception, as in most other states, would be for lien holders who were not given notice of the sale—a rare occurrence).
2. The *minimum bid* is determined by the county commissioners. The county treasurer will submit a minimum bid recommendation to the commissioners; this minimum bid will include the delinquent taxes (with penalty and interest), pending issue fees, certifications and special assessments, costs of publication of the notice of the sale, and recording fees. In Ada County (Boise), the bid recommendation will also include a current market value for the property as determined by the Ada County assessor.

ILLINOIS

Sale Type:	Lien
Interest Rate:	18% penalty (See "Comments")
Bid Method:	Bid down the interest (penalty)
Redemption Period:	2 to 3 years (See "Comments")
Sale Date(s):	Varies by county
	Cook (Chicago)—April
	Champaign (Urbana)—October
	Adams (Quincy)—last Mon. in October
	DuPage (Wheaton)—1st week in December
	Peoria (Peoria)—October
Statute Section(s):	35 Illinois Compiled Statutes 205/238, 200/21-350, 355, 385
Over-the-Counter?	No

Comments:

1. *Redemption period:* Illinois law provides that property sold at a tax sale may be redeemed within two years of the date of the sale. However, if the property sold was improved (i.e., had a house or other structure on it) with one to six units, it may be redeemed within two and one-half years from the date of sale. However, the *purchaser* of property sold at a tax sale may extend the redemption date to three years by filing with the county clerk of court (where the property is located) a written notice describing the property, stating the date of the sale, and specifying the extended redemption time.

2. Notice how the Illinois statute sets forth the payment due, depending upon the redemption time. Statute 35 ILCS 200/21-355 provides in pertinent part:

   > Any person desiring to redeem shall deposit with the county clerk . . . an amount equal to the following:
   >
   > (a) the certificate amount . . .
   > (b) the accrued penalty, computed through the date of redemption as a percentage of the certificate amount, as follows:
   > (1) if the redemption occurs on or before the expiration of 6 months from the date of sale, the certificate amount times the penalty bid at sale;

(2) if the redemption occurs after 6 months from the date of sale, and on or before the expiration of 12 months from the date of sale, the certificate amount times 2 times the penalty bid at sale;

(3) if the redemption occurs after 12 months from the date of sale, and on or before the expiration of 18 months from the date of sale, the certificate amount times 3 times the penalty bid at sale;

(4) if the redemption occurs after 18 months from the date of sale, and on or before the expiration of 24 months from the date of sale, the certificate amount times 4 times the penalty bid at sale;

(5) if the redemption occurs after 24 months from the date of sale, and on or before the expiration of 30 months from the date of sale, the certificate amount times 5 times the penalty bid at sale;

(6) if the redemption occurs after 30 months from the date of sale, and on or before the expiration of 36 months from the date of sale, the certificate amount times 6 times the penalty bid at sale.

Now let's examine the potential rates of return, given different redemption times. Assuming that the penalty rate was not bid down (i.e., that you received it at the maximum 18%), here's what you would have (rounded to the nearest whole number):

Year 1		Year 2	
Redemption after Month:	**Rate of Return**	**Redemption after Month:**	**Rate of Return**
1	216%	13	50%
2	108%	14	46%
3	72%	15	43%
4	54%	16	40%
5	43%	17	38%
6	36%	18	36%
7	62%	19	45%
8	54%	20	43%
9	48%	21	41%
10	43%	22	39%
11	39%	23	38%
12	36%	24	36%

Year 3

Redemption after Month:	Rate of Return
25	43%
26	42%
27	40%
28	39%
29	37%
30	36%
31	42%
32	40%
33	39%
34	38%
35	37%
36	36%

3. The above numbers are startling. You will not be the first investor to see those returns and say, "Wow, I'm going there!" In addition, since "deep-pocket" investors will want to sink as much money as they can into those kind of returns, expect most areas to bid down that penalty number lower than 18%. The deep-pocket investors *need* to get a lot of liens, because they have a lot of money to place. As such, they're willing to bid the interest rate down to 10%, 9%, 8%, 7%, or even much lower (also knowing that some will redeem in a month or so and they'll get a much better rate of return). What I've found at numerous auctions is that if you are patient (i.e., you may have to sit there for the better part of a day), alert, and willing to get a lien on a vacant lot, you can generally spend what you want and get a decent rate (say, 15% to 17%).

INDIANA

Sale Type:	Lien
Interest Rate:	10% to 15% penalty (See "Comments")
Bid Method:	Premium bid
Redemption Period:	1 year (See "Comments")
Sale Date(s):	Varies by county (must be Aug., Sept., or Oct.)
	Marion (Indianapolis)—August
	Allen (Ft. Wayne)—September
Statute Section(s):	I.C. 6-1.1-24
Over-the-Counter?	No

Comments:

1. *Interest Rate/Penalty:* Indiana charges a penalty rather than an interest rate, and the amount depends on the redemption time. Indiana law provides that the redemption fee will be calculated as follows:

    1. On the minimum bid
        - 10% of the minimum bid if redeemed not more than 6 months after the date of the sale.
        - 15% of the minimum bid if redeemed more than 6 months but not more than one year after the date of sale.
    2. On the *difference* between the successful bid price and the minimum bid (referred to as Tax Sale Overbid)
        - 10% per annum interest from the date of payment to the date of redemption.

    Let's start with the minimum bid, or the amount owed to the county and where bidding will begin. If you get any liens at the opening bid (as I did at the 2001 sale in Marion County), your rate of return will be excellent. Since it is a penalty format and is graduated depending on your redemption time, your return is better if the lien is paid off faster. The chart on the next page will set forth your return (rounded to the nearest whole number):

Redemption after Month:	Rate of Return
1	120%
2	60%
3	40%
4	30%
5	24%
6	20%
7	26%
8	22%
9	20%
10	18%
11	16%
12	15%

Like other states with outstanding rates of return, expect competitive bidding on most (not all) liens. As a general rule of thumb in any state, the vacant lots and lower-class houses will get the least amount of competitive bidding (most of the time no bidding at all). If you bid over the lien amount (which is a premium amount but which is called an "*overbid*"), you will only receive 10% per annum on that overbid amount. For example, if you buy a $1,000 lien for $1,500, you will receive the penalty and rate of return (as set forth on the table above) on $1,000, and 10% simple interest on the premium of $500. As you can see, this overbid will reduce your overall rate of return. However, since your penalty rate is outstanding and 10% on an overbid is not too bad either, you'll probably be happy in any case.

2. *NEW LAW:* Property owners *cannot* redeem after one year (the old system allowed them to redeem after one year and pay a higher penalty). In addition, if the lien is not redeemed after one year, the lien buyer must apply for a tax deed within six months from that expiration date or forfeit his or her purchase money.

3. *Unique bidding system:* The premium system used is not unique. However, how premiums are sold is (at least for the larger counties like Marion). The county official will list a group of 25 liens on an overhead screen. If you desire to bid on any of the liens shown in that group, you must yell out the number of the

lien you wish to pursue. The county official will then reannounce that lien number, the address, and the lien amount, and then open the bidding. If no one bids against you, you get it at the minimum bid (i.e., the lien amount). While this sounds like a chaotic system (since several people could be yelling at the same time), it actually ran very efficiently (probably because of the politeness of the midwestern folks in attendance).

4. *General comments:* I attended the 2001 sale in Marion County (Indianapolis) and found it one of the best run, most professional systems in the country. It ran like clockwork. In addition, the people were very friendly and very helpful. I suppose it's the midwestern ethic, since the people in Iowa are the same (as opposed to the government employees in Philadelphia and D.C., where officials treat you like you're a nuisance!).

   One disadvantage, however, to Indiana is that each county has townships, and each township has its own tax assessor. This makes your research more difficult since the township assessors are not accessible online, and you must go to each township to gather information about any particular property.

5. *New Web site:* Marion County now is making the list of auction properties available online at http://www.indygov.org/treas/taxsale/index.htm.

IOWA

Sale Type:	Lien
Interest Rate:	24% per annum
Bid Method:	Random selection, rotational (See "Comments")
Redemption Period:	2 years (See "Comments")
Sale Date(s):	3rd Monday in June
Statute Section(s):	Code of Iowa, Chapters 446, 447.13
Over-the-Counter?	No

Comments:

1. *Bid method:* Technically, the state is a "bid down the ownership" state. What this means is that if two or more persons want a particular lien, they can bid down how much of the property will be security for the lien. For example, they can bid down the ownership to 80%. This means that if the property owner does not redeem, the lien holder could foreclose on only 80% of the property! To effectively prosecute the foreclosure, a lien holder would have to file a court

action to sell the property and divide the proceeds 80/20! What a mess, right? Fortunately, county treasurers don't like this system either. I have attended sales in three Iowa counties and spoken with county treasurers in four other counties; *none* of these seven counties used the "bid down the ownership" system. All of these counties used either a random selection or a rotational bidding system. Thank heavens!

2. *Redemption period:* The Iowa foreclosure system is not "self-executing." What this means is that the redemption period does not automatically terminate. The lien holder has a right to file (with the county treasurer) a "90-day Notice of Right of Redemption Affidavit" 1 year and 9 months from the date of the sale. If done at that time, this would give the owner exactly 2 years to redeem and not lose the property.

3. *Cancellation of certificate:* The county treasurer may cancel any lien certificate if the holder has not taken any action (i.e., issued his or her 90-day notice) on the certificate after 3 years from the date of issuance of the certificate. If so, you will have made a nice donation to the county—your lien amount! As you may recall, Florida is the same, although it has a 7-year time frame. Any lawyer will tell you that the law punishes those who "sleep on their rights." That is, if you have legal rights on a particular matter, you either pursue those rights or you will eventually lose them.

4. *General comments:* I found the county officials in all seven Iowa counties that I dealt with to be extremely nice, friendly, and helpful.

KANSAS

Sale Type:	Deed
Interest Rate:	N/A
Bid Method:	Premium bid
Redemption Period:	N/A
Sale Date(s):	Varies by county
	Cowley (Winfield)—December
	Douglas (Lawrence)—May
	Johnson (Olathe)—late fall
	Leavenworth (Leavenworth)—October

Sedgwick (Wichita)—July
Shawnee (Topeka)—August
Sumner (Wellington)—May
Wyandotte (Kansas City)—August

Statute Section(s):   K.S.A. Section 79-2801
Over-the-Counter?   No
Comments:

Kansas is one of the best deed states in the country. Counties typically start the bidding for the properties at the lien amounts, although some counties allow you to bid *below* the lien amount! For example, Leavenworth County only requires a $50 minimum bid, and Sedgwick County does not have a minimum bid. Keep in mind, as always, the quality of what you are buying. I went to the 2001 Kansas City sale and picked up a few vacant lots for $75 each, and one small house for $4,100 (which needed a lot of work).

KENTUCKY

Sale Type: Lien
Interest Rate: 12% per annum
Bid Method: Premium bid
Redemption Period: 1 year
Sale Date(s):   April to May
Statute Section(s):   K.R.S. Section 134.460
Over-the-Counter?   No
Comments:

LOUISIANA

Sale Type: Deed (a hybrid state)
Interest Rate: 12% per annum plus 5% penalty
Bid Method: Bid down the interest
Redemption Period: 3 years
Sale Date(s):   January to April
Statute Section(s):   L.R.S. Section 47:2181, 2183

Over-the-Counter?   No
Comments:

If redemption occurred in year one, the rate of return for the investor would be 17% (redemption after 1 year) to 72% (redemption after 1 month). The worst-case scenario would be if redemption occurs just before the end of the redemption period. For example, if redemption occurred after 35 months, the rate of return would be 13.7%.

MAINE

Sale Type:	Deed
Interest Rate:	N/A
Bid Method:	Sealed bid (See "Comments")
Redemption Period:	N/A (for the deed sale)
Sale Date(s):	Varies by county
Statute Section(s):	Maine Revised Statutes, Title 36
Over-the-Counter?	No

Comments:

1. Property taxes are collected at the city level, rather than at the county level. Accordingly, city ordinances control the sale procedures. If taxes are unpaid, the city will lien that property. Under state law, the owner has 18 months to redeem. If not redeemed, the redemption period automatically terminates, and the city will now own the property.
2. Once the city owns the property, *the city may retain ownership* or sell the property by way of sealed bid. Additionally, even if the city bids the property, the city can reject all bids as inadequate. Maine, then, is one of the worst deed states (from the investor's perspective).

MARYLAND

Sale Type:	Lien
Interest Rate:	6% to 24% (varies by county)
Bid Method:	Premium bid
Redemption Period:	After 6 months (See "Comments")

Sale Date(s):	Varies by county
	Baltimore City—May
Statute Section(s):	Annotated Code of the Public Laws of Maryland Section 14-817, 818, 820, 831, 833, 844 (See also county code sections for statutes relating to interest rates)
Over-the-Counter?	Yes

Comments:

1. As you can see from the above notes, the state gives the counties (and City of Baltimore) great leeway in administrating their own lien sales. The best areas for rates of return are Baltimore City (24%), Prince George's County (20%), Garrett County (20%), and Montgomery County (20%).

2. *Bid method:* Like many other states, Maryland uses a premium bidding method. However, unlike most jurisdictions, Maryland counties do not require the investor to pay the full amount of the bid at the time of the sale. Rather, the investor need only pay for the opening bid (like other states, comprised of back taxes, penalty, and interest) after the sale, not the *full* amount of his or her bid (which would include the opening bid plus the overbid or premium). So when is that overbid (which they call "surplus" or "residue") to be paid by the investor? If the lien is redeemed, the investor *never* pays the surplus! If the lien is *not* redeemed, the investor must pay the surplus before he or she can foreclose on the lien and get a Treasurer's deed.

3. *Redemption period:* The redemption period in Maryland is not self-executing; the investor must actively pursue redemption by filing a complaint at the county level to foreclose the right of redemption. The investor can do this after six months of the date of the sale.

MASSACHUSETTS

Sale Type:	Deed (hybrid state)
Interest Rate:	16% per annum
Bid Method:	Premium bid
Redemption Period:	6 months (but not self-executing)
Sale Date(s):	(See "Comments")
Statute Section(s):	Annotated Law of Massachusetts Sections 45, 62
Over-the-Counter?	No

Comments:

My staff has contacted several Massachusetts counties, including those for Boston and Cambridge, and was told that these areas *did not have* tax sales! Since we've heard that from more than one county, Massachusetts is probably not a great place to look for investing.

MICHIGAN

Sale Type:	Deed
Interest Rate:	N/A
Bid Method:	Premium bid
Redemption Period:	N/A
Sale Date(s):	Varies by county (See "Comments")
	Saginaw (Saginaw)—August
	Genesee (Flint)—March
	Ingham (Lansing)—infrequent, check
	Kent (Grand Rapids)—infrequent, check
	Wayne (Detroit)—end of May
Statute Section(s):	Public Act 123 of 1999; Act 206 of Public Acts 1893 (Sections 140-143)
Over-the-Counter?	No

Comments:

On July 22, 1999, Michigan enacted a new law (Public Act 123), changing the state from a lien state to a deed state. Each county has the option of administering its own sale, or allowing the state to conduct the sale.

MINNESOTA

Sale Type:	Deed
Interest Rate:	N/A
Bid Method:	Premium bid
Redemption Period:	N/A
Sale Date(s):	Varies by county
	St. Louis (Duluth)—February, June, October
Statute Section(s):	Minnesota Statutes Sections 281, 282

Over-the-Counter?   Yes (including by mail)
Comments:
1. In St. Louis County, most of the tax-forfeited land is forested.
2. *Financing:* Some counties, like St. Louis, will finance your purchase of these properties. St. Louis finances some purchases on a contract for deed basis for up to ten years at 10% interest.

MISSISSIPPI

Sale Type:	Lien
Interest Rate:	18% per annum (on the lien only, *not* on the premium)
Bid Method:	Premium bid (See "Comments")
Redemption Period:	2 years
Sale Date(s):	Last Monday in August (lien sale)
	First Monday in April (deed sale)
Statute Section(s):	Mississippi Code of 1972, as amended
	Sections 27-41-55, 59; 27-45-3
Over-the-Counter?	No

Comments:
1. I bought liens in Jackson at the 2001 sale. While there were about 6,900 liens offered, only about 60 bidders were at the sale.
2. *Interest rate:* Notice that *not only is no interest paid on the premium (overbid), but the premium is not repaid either!* As such, any premium bid over the lien amount would reduce your yield. At the 2001 sale in Jackson, most of the liens were sold at premium bids.

MISSOURI

Sale Type:	Lien
Interest Rate:	10% per annum (plus 8% for any subsequent taxes paid)
Bid Method:	Premium bid
Redemption Period:	2 years
Sale Date(s):	4th Monday in August (most counties)
	Jackson county has two sales:
	Independence—September

Kansas City—October

Statute Section(s): Missouri Revised Statutes § 140
Over-the-Counter? No
Comments:

Bidder restriction: A bidder *must be a resident of the county* in which the sale is held. In order for a nonresident (i.e., someone from out of state or even out of county) to bid, that person must designate a resident agent for service of process (like corporations must do in each state) and have that county resident bid for him or her at the auction. Needless to say, this requirement, coupled with the low interest rate, makes Missouri one of the least attractive lien states.

MONTANA

Sale Type: Lien
Interest Rate: 10% per annum plus a 2% penalty
Bid Method: Random selection or rotational
Redemption Period: 3 years
Sale Date(s): July
Statute Section(s): Montana Code Annotated Sections 15-16-102; 15-18-211 through 216
Over-the-Counter? Yes
Comments:

Since part of the interest rate is a penalty, a lien redeemed in the first year would yield 12% (redemption after one year) to 34% (redemption after one month). After one year, the yield would be between 10% and 12%, depending on the month of redemption.

NEBRASKA

Sale Type: Lien
Interest Rate: 14% per annum
Bid Method: Bid down the ownership, rotational
Redemption Period: 3 years
Sale Date(s): 1st Monday in March
Statute Section(s): Revised Statutes of Nebraska Sections 77-1807, 1824

Over-the-Counter?   Yes
Comments:

1. *Bid method:* Technically, the state uses a "bid down the ownership" system. However, like Iowa, many counties will use a rotational system, since it is far better for all parties concerned.
2. *Over-the-counter:* I purchased a nice lien over-the-counter in Omaha in the summer of 2001 (at the maximum 14%, of course!).

NEVADA

Sale Type:	Deed
Interest Rate:	N/A
Bid Method:	Premium bid
Redemption Period:	N/A
Sale Date(s):	Varies by county
	Washoe (Reno)—April
Statute Section(s):	Nevada Revised Statutes Sections 361.590-595
Over-the-Counter?	No

Comments:

Nevada is one of the best deed states, since bidding typically starts at the lien amount (i.e., the back taxes, costs, penalties, and interest), and the tax deed sale will extinguish any other liens such as mortgages and judgment liens (special assessments such as a county's mowing lien survive, as in virtually every other state).

NEW HAMPSHIRE

Sale Type:	Deed
Interest Rate:	N/A
Bid Method:	Premium bid
Redemption Period:	N/A
Sale Date(s):	Varies by county
Statute Section(s):	New Hampshire Revised Statutes Annotated Section 80:24
Over-the-Counter?	No

Comments:

NEW JERSEY

Sale Type:	Lien
Interest Rate:	18% per annum
Bid Method:	Bid down the interest or premium (See "Comments")
Redemption Period:	2 years
Sale Date(s):	Varies by county
	Atlantic City—December
	Camden—January and June
	Burlington—September
	Trenton—March
Statute Section(s):	New Jersey Code Annotated Sections 54:5-32, 54
Over-the-Counter?	No

Comments:

New Jersey is a bit unusual in its approach to bidding. Generally, the bid method will be "bid down the interest." However, if a bidder bids the interest down to less than 1%, he or she may, in lieu of any rate of interest, offer a premium over the amount of taxes, assessments, or other charges. See New Jersey Code Annotated Section 54:5-32.

NEW MEXICO

Sale Type:	Deed
Interest Rate:	N/A
Bid Method:	Premium bid
Redemption Period:	N/A
Sale Date(s):	Varies by county
Statute Section(s):	New Mexico Statutes Annotated, Chapter 7 (Articles 35-38)
Over-the-Counter?	No

Comments:

New Mexico is *not a priority lien state!* Unlike most deed states, an investor who acquires the property at a tax sale takes the property *subject to any encumbrances* (i.e., a mortgage) on the land. Accordingly, an investor at a New Mexico sale must carefully review the title prior to purchasing the property.

NEW YORK

Sale Type:	Deed
Interest Rate:	N/A
Bid Method:	Premium bid
Redemption Period:	N/A
Sale Date(s):	Varies by county
	Albany—July
	Fulton—August
	St. Lawrence—October
Statute Section(s):	Uniform Delinquent Tax Enforcement Act
Over-the-Counter?	No

Comments:

1. New York may, but is not required to, start the bidding at the back taxes, penalty, and costs (i.e., a starting point of a certain percentage of the tax-assessed value). I was at the sale in St. Lawrence County a few years ago and found a number of decent properties (many were huge blocks of acreage). This particular auction was also a popular one; in my estimation, there were about 150 bidders.
2. The City of New York is also allowed to sell liens.

NORTH CAROLINA

Sale Type:	Deed
Interest Rate:	N/A
Bid Method:	Premium bid
Redemption Period:	N/A
Sale Date(s):	Varies by county
Statute Section(s):	North Carolina General Statutes Chapter 44A
Over-the-Counter?	No

Comments:

North Carolina is one of the better deed states, since bidding begins at the lien amount (back taxes, penalties, and costs). However, the state does have two minor disadvantages:

1. *Court confirmation:* Within three days from the date of the sale, the tax commissioner must provide the local county court with the report of all sales. Within 10 days following this filing by the commissioner, anyone claiming an exception or irregularity to the sale may challenge the sale.

2. *Upset bids:* In addition, anyone desiring to increase the bid amount may do so (called an "upset bid") by filing with the court. For you to do so, you must increase the winning bid by 10% of the first $1,000, plus 5% of any excess above $1,000. If an upset bid is filed, the court will negate the first sale and order a second sale, called a "resale."

NORTH DAKOTA

Sale Type:	Lien
Interest Rate:	12% per annum
Bid Method:	Premium bid
Redemption Period:	3 years
Sale Date(s):	2nd Tuesday in December
Statute Section(s):	North Dakota Century Code, Chapters 57-24, 38
Over-the-Counter?	No
Comments:	

OHIO

Sale Type:	Deed and Lien (See "Comments")
Interest Rate:	18% per annum (for lien sales)
Bid Method:	Premium bid (See "Comments")
Redemption Period:	15 days for deed sale (See "Comments")
Sale Date(s):	Varies by county
	Cuyahoga (Cleveland)—May
	Franklin (Columbus)—Every Friday
	Summit (Akron)—October

Statute Section(s):   Ohio Revised Code Sections 2329.17, 20; 5721.23; 315.251

Over-the-Counter?   No

Comments:

1. *Deed and lien sales:* Ohio is historically a deed state, but actually has both types of sales. Counties with populations of over 200,000 are also allowed to sell lien certificates. Check with each county to see which type of sale it uses.

2. *Minimum bid for deed sales:* Pursuant to Ohio Revised Code Section 2329.17, *no tract of land may be sold for less than two-thirds of the appraised value.* As such, no great deals will be found in Ohio. Based on the foregoing, Ohio would be one of the worst of the deed states for bargain-hunting investors.

3. *Redemption period for deed sales:* An owner may redeem his or her property by payment in full of all taxes and costs until the sale is confirmed by court—approximately 15 days. See O.R.C. Section 5721.23.

OKLAHOMA

Sale Type: Lien

Interest Rate: 8%

Bid Method: Random selection or rotational

Redemption Period: 2 years

Sale Date(s):   1st Monday in October (normal sale)

                         2nd Monday in June (resale)

Statute Section(s): 68 Oklahoma State Statutes Sections 3107; 3135

Over-the-Counter?   Yes

Comments:

1. The fact that Oklahoma has a very low interest rate is actually a benefit for those looking to acquire properties for pennies on the dollar. The reason for this is because far fewer liens will be sold to investors (who will not accept an 8% return). When that occurs, many properties end up in the county's inventory. I was in Oklahoma City a few years ago, and that area had several thousand properties held in inventory (some with redemption periods remaining, others that can be picked up free and clear from the county).

2. In Oklahoma City's "List of Lands Available," there are some 1,100 properties (as I recall) that one can make a bid to purchase. You can order this list from the county for $23.

3. The downside of this surplus in Oklahoma City is that the county does not have the assessed values listed (or other helpful information, for that matter). What you must do is make an offer to the county for each parcel. The county will then accept or reject that offer, perhaps with a counteroffer. However, since the information on these properties have been deleted from the county assessor's office Web site (http://www.oklahomacounty.org), you must now engage a broker to determine the values. In any event, it's still not a bad opportunity.

OREGON

Sale Type:	Deed
Interest Rate:	N/A
Bid Method:	Premium bid
Redemption Period:	N/A
Sale Date(s):	Varies by county
	Multnomah (Portland)—October or November
Statute Section(s):	Oregon Revised Statutes Section 311
Over-the-Counter?	Some counties in the past have allowed
Comments:	

As in Ohio, some counties may set the minimum bid as a percentage of the fair market or assessed value, obviously a disadvantage for an investor looking to buy real estate for a fraction on the dollar. In the past, however, many Oregon counties have *financed* purchases by investors! Check with each county for its rules regarding minimum bids and financing.

PENNSYLVANIA

Sale Type:	Deed (a hybrid state)
Interest Rate:	10% per annum where applicable (See "Comments")
Bid Method:	Premium bid (See "Comments")
Redemption Period:	Possibly 1 year (See "Comments")
Sale Date(s):	Monthly
	Allegheny (Pittsburgh)—1st Monday
	Philadelphia (Philadelphia)—3rd Wednesday

Statute Section(s):   Act of Assembly May 16, 1923, P.L. 207; Act of March 15,
                                 1956, No. 388

Over-the-Counter?   Some small counties have allowed

Comments:

I attended the July 18, 2001, sale in Philadelphia. The following summarizes my
notes for that city's sale:

1. *Bidding:* The minimum bid was $800.
2. *Right of redemption:* If the property is legally occupied 90 days prior to the sale,
   the owner has one year within which to redeem the property by paying the back
   taxes, and pay the investor the purchase price plus 10% interest. If the property
   is unoccupied or abandoned, there is no right of redemption.
3. *City administration:* All of the properties I intended to bid on were redeemed
   just before the sale (and there were some *very* nice properties). Philadelphia
   seems to be somewhat negligent in getting information back to investors in a
   timely manner. For example, the county employee informed my office over the
   phone that there would be 75 properties sold at the sale. However, when I received the list of the 75 properties a few days before the sale, some 11 properties had been listed as "STAYED" (*stayed* is the term used to indicate that the
   owner was given additional time to pay the lien and the property would not be
   offered at the sale). So, in actuality, only 64 properties would be sold.

I then went to the city's office to do my research. Unfortunately, the city only had
three computers for the public to access the information regarding the properties,
which were all taken. After waiting about an hour, I was able to jump on one computer and get the information I needed (i.e., assessed value, type of property, size,
etc.). I then drove to inspect about 8 properties.

At the sale, the auctioneer read the "updated" list of stayed properties and those
being pulled from the sale. Of the 64 remaining properties, another 34 properties
were removed from the sale, including all of the 8 on which I had intended to bid.
Out of our initial list of 75 properties, now only 30 properties would actually be sold!
The 34 properties were not redeemed by the owners, but were simply pulled from
the sale by the city. It was very disappointing, since I had just wasted two days. In addition, with the exception of the District of Columbia tax sale employees (who were
extremely difficult to deal with), the Philadelphia city employees were the worst I've
seen in the country.

PUERTO RICO (Commonwealth of)

Sale Type: Lien
Interest Rate: 20% penalty
Redemption Period: 1 year
Comments:

1. There's good news and bad news with Puerto Rico. The good news is that the high penalty makes Puerto Rico one of the best lien jurisdictions in the country. Since it is a 20% penalty, your rate of return would range from 20% (redemption after 12 months) to 120% (redemption after 1 month) or more (redemption earlier than 1 month)! The bad news is you need to speak Spanish. My Spanish is poor, and I didn't get very far trying to talk to someone about his or her sale. So, officially, it's a good lien jurisdiction. Actually getting information on sales, if available, is another story.

RHODE ISLAND

Sale Type: Deed (a hybrid state)
Interest Rate: 10% penalty plus 1% penalty for each month after month 6
Bid Method: Premium bid
Redemption Period: 1 year
Sale Date(s): August
Statute Section(s): Rhode Island General Laws Sections 44-9-12, 19, 21
Over-the-Counter? No
Comments:

Since Rhode Island operates with a penalty, if you were to acquire a lien without a premium, your rate of return would be between 16% (redemption after 12 months) and 120% (redemption after one month)! I have not been to a sale in this state, but my guess is that bidders are bidding premiums.

SOUTH CAROLINA

Sale Type:	Lien
Interest Rate:	8% or 12% per annum (See "Comments")
Bid Method:	Premium bid
Redemption Period:	1 year
Sale Date(s):	1st Monday in October, November, or December
Statute Section(s):	South Carolina Statutes Section 12-51-90
Over-the-Counter?	Yes
Comments:	

Interest rate: If redemption occurs in the first 6 months, the interest rate is 8%; if redemption occurs in the second 6 months, the interest rate is 12%.

SOUTH DAKOTA

Sale Type:	Lien
Interest Rate:	12% per annum
Bid Method:	Premium bid
Redemption Period:	3 years (within municipality); 4 years (outside municipality)
Sale Date(s):	3rd Monday in December
Statute Section(s):	South Dakota Codified Laws Titles 10 and 44
Over-the-Counter?	Yes
Comments:	

TENNESSEE

Sale Type:	Deed (a hybrid state)
Interest Rate:	10% per annum
Bid Method:	Premium bid
Redemption Period:	1 year
Sale Date(s):	Varies by county and year
	Knoxville—varies (February, fall)
	Nashville—June
Statute Section(s):	Tennessee Code Title 67
Over-the-Counter?	No
Comments:	

TEXAS

Sale Type:	Deed (a hybrid state)
Interest Rate:	25% penalty (See "Comments")
Bid Method:	Premium bid
Redemption Period:	6 months (nonhomestead, nonagricultural)
	2 years for homestead, agricultural
Sale Date(s):	1st Tuesday of each month
Statute Section(s):	Texas Tax Code Section 34.21
Over-the-Counter?	Yes (many counties)

Comments:

1. Texas is a hybrid deed state, which means that it is a deed state but operates like a lien state. In Texas, a winning bidder will receive a deed to the property; however, that deed is encumbered (i.e., subject to a right of redemption by the owner). For agricultural and homestead properties, the redemption period is 2 years. For nonagricultural and nonhomestead properties, the period is only 6 months!

2. Texas is different from most states in that
   - it has sales every month (as does Georgia) and
   - the sales are administered by law firms (don't worry, you don't pay the lawyers, the county does). As such, you will need to contact the county for the contact information of the law firm assisting the county.

3. *Effect of a penalty:* In Texas, the 25% is a penalty rather than an interest rate. Second, the penalty is not only on the lien amount but also on your premium and any costs associated with the administration of the lien/deed by the law firm and county. As such, you receive 25% on your aggregate total! This makes Texas one of the best states in the country for investors. Now let's look at the impact of a penalty return. The following chart will illustrate your rate of return on a nonagricultural, nonhomestead property, depending on the date of redemption.

Redemption after Month:	Rate of Return
6	50%
5	60%
4	75%
3	100%
2	150%
1	300%

UTAH

Sale Type:	Deed
Interest Rate:	N/A
Bid Method:	Premium bid
Redemption Period:	N/A
Sale Date(s):	May
	Salt Lake City—4th Thursday
	Some counties on 3rd Thursday
Statute Section(s):	Utah Code, Title 59
Over-the-Counter?	No

Comments:

Utah is a good deed state, since bidding typically begins at the lien amount (i.e., back taxes, penalties, interest, and costs).

VERMONT

Sale Type:	Lien
Interest Rate:	12% per annum
Redemption Period:	1 year
Sale Date(s):	Varies by county
Statute Section(s):	Vermont Statutes, Title 32, Section 5260
Over-the-Counter?	No

Comments:

VIRGINIA

Sale Type:	Deed
Interest Rate:	N/A
Bid Method:	Premium bid
Redemption Period:	N/A
Sale Date(s):	Varies by county
	Arlington does not have a sale every year.
Statute Section(s):	Code of Virginia, Title 58, Chapter 32

Over-the-Counter?   No

Comments:

Overall, Virginia is a good deed state, since bidding begins at the lien amount (i.e., back taxes, penalties, interest, and costs) and the tax lien is a priority lien (i.e., so long as notice was given to other lien holders, any other liens are wiped out by the sale). The sale must be approved by court confirmation, which is routinely given.

WASHINGTON

Sale Type: Deed
Interest Rate: N/A
Bid Method: Premium bid
Redemption Period: N/A
Sale Date(s):   Varies by county
                            King (Seattle)—December
                            Spokane—August
Statute Section(s):   Revised Code of Washington, Chapters 35, 60
Over-the-Counter?   No

Comments:

WEST VIRGINIA

Sale Type: Lien
Interest Rate: 12% per annum
Bid Method: Premium bid (but not on overbid)
Redemption Period: 17 months
Sale Date(s):   Varies by county between October and November
                            Kanawha (Charleston)—November
Statute Section(s):   West Virginia Code Section 11A-3-23
Over-the-Counter?   Liens—no; deeds—yes (See "Comments")

Comments:

1. *Bidding:* Notice that you do not receive any premium on any overbid (i.e., premium or surplus) amount.

2. *Over-the-counter.* If you wish to acquire properties, contact the deputy land commissioner at 304-343-4441. The land commissioner may have his or her own sales for properties owned by the county and may allow purchasing over-the-counter.

WISCONSIN

Sale Type:	Deed
Interest Rate:	N/A
Bid Method:	Premium bid (See "Comments")
Redemption Period:	N/A
Sale Date(s):	Varies by county
	Eau Claire—twice per year (spring and summer)
	Dane (Madison)—not held every year
Statute Section(s):	Wisconsin Statutes, Chapter 75
Over-the-Counter?	No
Comments:	

Wisconsin appears to be the least desirable of all the deed states, since the county may not accept bids less than the appraised value. Keep in mind, of course, that sometimes the county's appraised value may be significantly less than the true fair market value.

WYOMING

Sale Type:	Lien
Interest Rate:	15% per annum plus 3% penalty
Bid Method:	Random selection
Redemption Period:	4 years
Sale Date(s):	July, August, September (most in September)
	Laramie (Cheyenne)—1st week in August
	Teton (Jackson)—1st week in August
Statute Section(s):	Wyoming Statutes Sections 39-3-108, 39-4-102
Over-the-Counter?	Yes
Comments:	

SAMPLE STATE BIDDING, REGISTRATION, AND SALES RULES

PREAMBLE OF PUBLICATION FOR 2001B TAX SALE

**County of Los Angeles
Department of the Treasurer and Tax
Collector**

Notice of Divided Publication

Pursuant to Sections 3702, 3381, and 3382, Revenue and Taxation Code, the Notice of Sale of Tax-Defaulted Property Subject to the Power of Sale in and for the County of Los Angeles, State of California, has been divided and distributed to various newspapers of general circulation published in said County for publication of a portion thereof in each of said newspapers.

Public Auction Notice
Of Sale Of Tax-Defaulted Property Subject To
The Power Of Sale (Sale No. 2001B)

Whereas, on May 29, 2001, I, MARK J. SALADINO, Treasurer and Tax Collector, was directed by the Board of Supervisors of Los Angeles County, State of California, to sell at public auction certain Tax-Defaulted properties which are Subject to the Power of Sale. Public notice is hereby given that unless said properties are redeemed prior thereto, I will, on August 6 and 7, 2001, at the hour of 9:00 a.m. at the Los Angeles County Arboretum, Ayers Hall, 301 N. Baldwin Ave. Arcadia, California, offer for sale and sell at public auction to the highest bidder for cash or cashier's check in lawful money of the United States for not less than the minimum bid.

The minimum bid for each parcel is the total amount necessary to redeem, plus costs, as required by Section 3698.5 of the Revenue and Taxation Code.

Prospective bidders should obtain detailed information of this sale from the County Tax Collector. Pre-registration and a $1,000 deposit is required during the registration period. Registration will start on July 10, 2001, in the Treasurer and Tax Collector's Office, 225 North Hill Street, Room 130, Los Angeles, California and will end on July 26, 2001.

If the property is sold, parties of interest, as defined by Section 4675 of the Revenue and Taxation Code, have a right to file a claim with the County for any proceeds from the sale which are in excess of the liens and costs required to be paid from the proceeds. If excess proceeds result from the sale, notice will be given to parties of interest, pursuant to law.

All information concerning redemption, provided the right to redeem has not previously been terminated, will upon request be furnished by MARK J. SALADINO, Treasurer and Tax Collector.

If redemption of the property is not made according to law before 5:00 p.m. on the last business day prior to the first day of auction, the right of redemption will cease.

The Assessor's Identification Number (AIN) in this publication refers to the Assessor's map book, the map page, and the individual parcel number on the map page. If a change in the Assessor's Identification Number occurred, both prior and current Assessor's Identification Numbers are shown. An explanation of the parcel numbering system and the maps referred to are available from the Office of the Assessor, 500 West Temple Street, Los Angeles, California 90012.

A list explaining the abbreviations used in this publication is on file in the Office of the Treasurer and Tax Collector, 225 North Hill Street, Los Angeles, California 90012, or telephone (213) 974-2474.

I certify under penalty of perjury that the foregoing is true and correct. Executed at Los Angeles, California, May 18, 2001.

MARK J. SALADINO
Los Angeles County
Treasurer and Tax Collector
State of California

LOS ANGELES COUNTY TREASURER AND TAX COLLECTOR

GENERAL INFORMATION

2001B TAX SALE - AUGUST 6 AND 7, 2001

- You must pay for your purchase **IMMEDIATELY** upon being awarded the successful bid. No opportunity will be given for any successful bidder to go to the bank prior to completing the sale transaction.

- We will stop for lunch and periodic breaks. The breaks will allow you the time to complete your purchase at the cashiers' table. Parcels will be reoffered if the sale transactions are not completed by the end of the break. The auctioneer will announce when breaks and lunch hour will be taken.

- All sales will be for cash, cashier's check or bank issued money orders made payable to the Los Angeles County Treasurer-Tax Collector. No traveler's checks, non-bank issued money orders, personal checks and checks payable to another party or two party checks will be accepted.

- Should a successful bidder refuse to pay for the property they have bid on, their bidder card will be confiscated and/or voided and they will forfeit their right to further participate in the sale.

- **ALL SALES ARE FINAL.** Even if the successful bidder makes a mistake and bids on the wrong property, the sale will remain final.

- **CAUTION-INVESTIGATE BEFORE YOU BID.** The sale of these properties should not, in any way, be equated to real estate sales by licensed sales people, brokers or realtors. The County Tax Collector cannot guarantee the condition of the property nor assume any responsibility for conformance to codes, permits or zoning ordinances. An investigation may reveal that the property is in a street or alley, in a flood control channel or landlocked. Improvements that may be shown on the tax sale list may no longer exist at the time of the auction and a lien may have been or will be placed on the property for their removal. Streets shown as such on the maps offered by the Los Angeles County Assessor's office may or may not exist, but in some cases may be future streets. You should physically inspect the property before investing.

- The burden is on the purchaser to thoroughly research before the tax sale, any matters relevant to his or her decision to purchase, rather than on the county, whose sole interest is the recovery of back taxes. Tax defaulted property will be sold on an as is basis.

- No warranty is made by the county, either expressed or implied, relative to usability, the ground location, or property lines of the properties. The prospective purchaser must determine the exact location, desirability, and usefulness of the properties. Refund of any purchase or any payment on a purchase agreement will not be made.

- Tax defaulted parcels subject to the Tax Collector's Power to Sell can only be redeemed on or before the close of business on the last business day prior to the date of the sale. There is no extended right of redemption in the State of California.

- **MINIMUM BID:** The minimum bid is indicated on the auction list next to the legal description.

    (A)   The properties in this sale are in item number order. They will be auctioned in that order.

    (B)   Bidding will be in increments of $100 on bids between $100 and $5,000. Bids exceeding $5,000 will be offered in increments of $1,000 until the parcel is sold to the highest bidder. If the bid on any one item is more than $5,000, the successful bidder may pay for the property by depositing $5,000 or 10% of the purchase price, whichever is the greater, with the balance to be paid within 30 calendar days from the date of the auction.

    (C)   Title will not be transferred until the total bid price is received. If the buyer fails to pay the balance within the 30 calendar day period allowed, the deposit is forfeited as well as all rights to the property.

- Time permitting, unsold parcels may be reoffered at a reduced minimum bid.

- **LIENS:** A tax deed will cancel all private liens, i.e., Deeds of Trust, Mechanic's Liens, Judgements, etc., as well as all prior delinquent taxes. However, public liens such as Improvement Bonds, Demolition Liens, Weed Abatement tax liens, etc. **MAY NOT** be discharged with a tax deed. The county assumes no liability for any other possible liens, encumbrances or easements, recorded or not recorded. **ALL PROPERTIES SHOULD BE INVESTIGATED THOROUGHLY PRIOR TO PURCHASE.**

Pursuant to Section 3712 of the Revenue and Taxation code, the deed conveys title to the purchaser free of all encumbrances of any kind existing before the sale, **except**:

(A)   Any lien for installments of taxes and special assessments, which installments will become payable upon the secured roll after the time of sale.

(B)   The lien for taxes or assessments or other rights of any taxing agency which does not consent to the sale of the parcel at auction.

(C)   Liens for special assessments levied upon the property which at the time of the sale were not included in the amount necessary to redeem the property, and, where a taxing agency which collects its own taxes has consented to the sale were not included in the amount required to redeem from sale to the taxing agency.

(D)   Easements constituting servitude upon or burdens to the property; water rights, the record title to which is held separately from the title to the property, and restrictions of records.

(E)   Unaccepted, recorded, irrevocable offers of dedication of the property to the public or a public entity for a public purpose, and recorded options of any taxing agency to purchase the property or any interest therein for a public purpose.

(F)   Unpaid assessments under the Improvement Bond Act of 1915 (Division 10 commencing with Section 8500 of the Streets and Highways Code, which are not satisfied as a result of the sale proceeds being applied pursuant to Chapter 1.3 commencing with Section 4671 of Part 8 of the Revenue and Taxation Code.

(G)   Any Federal Internal Revenue Service liens, which pursuant to provisions of Federal law, are not discharged by the sale, even though the Tax Collector has provided proper notice to the Internal Revenue Service before that date.

(H)   Unpaid special taxes under the Mello-Roos Community Facilities Act of 1982 (Chapter 2.5 [commencing with Section 53311] of Part 1 Division 2 of Title 5 of Government Code) that are not satisfied as a result of the sale proceeds being applied pursuant to Chapter 1.3 (commencing with Section 4671) of Part 8.

NOTICE

THE TREASURER AND TAX COLLECTOR RESERVES THE RIGHT TO CONFISCATE ALL NUMBERED BIDDER CARDS REGISTERED TO ANY SUCCESSFUL BIDDER WHO FAILS TO TIMELY REMIT THE NECESSARY DEPOSIT OR PURCHASE PRICE, AS APPLICABLE, AT THE COMPLETION OF THE BIDDING ON EACH PARCEL SOLD.

UPON CONFISCATION OF BIDDER CARDS, NO SUBSEQUENT BIDS ON ANY REMAINING PARCELS MADE BY THAT BIDDER OR ANY CO-REGISTERED BIDDER WILL BE ACCEPTED OR RECOGNIZED BY THE AUCTIONEER.

ANY BID AT THE AUCTION IS MADE SUBJECT TO ALL OF THE FOREGOING TERMS AND CONDITIONS, AND BY BIDDING THE BIDDER ACKNOWLEDGES AND AGREES TO SUCH TERMS AND CONDITIONS AND EXPRESSLY WAIVES ANY OBJECTION, CLAIM OR RIGHT TO RESCIND A BID OR ANY PURCHASE ARISING THEREFROM.

ALL SALES ARE FINAL. INVESTIGATE BEFORE YOU PURCHASE

MARK J. SALADINO
TREASURER AND TAX COLLECTOR

::

LOS ANGELES COUNTY TAX SALE
REGISTRATION INFORMATION

**The sale will be held on August 6 and 7, 2001 at the
Arboretum of Los Angeles County, Ayers Hall
301 North Baldwin Ave., Arcadia, California**

All prospective buyers must be pre-registered in order to bid. Pre-registration will be held at the Tax Collector's Office at 225 North Hill Street, Room 130, Los Angeles, 90012 between 8:00 a.m. and 5:00 p.m., July 10, 2001 through July 26, 2001. **You must pre-register to participate in the sale.** There will be no registration at the auction. We will require valid picture identification at the time of registration i.e., valid driver's license, valid California ID card, valid military ID card. An official numbered, bidder card will be issued at the time of registration and is required to participate at the tax sale auction.

If you intend to register/vest for someone not present at the tax sale or time of registration, you must show power of attorney for each person you are representing. If you intend to vest as a company, corporation or partnership, you will need to provide certified copies of the document that gives you the authority to register/vest on their behalf. This documentation might be in the form of corporate minutes or resolution bearing the corporate seal, power of attorney, or partnership agreement.

The tax deed conveying title will be vested in the manner in which you register. We will not accept changes in vesting after you have completed your registration.

Samples of vesting for registration:

- A SINGLE MAN
- A SINGLE WOMAN
- A MARRIED MAN
- A MARRIED WOMAN
- AN UNMARRIED MAN
- AN UNMARRIED WOMAN
- A WIDOWER
- A WIDOW
- A MARRIED MAN AS HIS SOLE AND SEPARATE PROPERTY
- A MARRIED WOMAN AS HER SOLE AND SEPARATE PROPERTY
- HUSBAND AND WIFE AS JOINT TENANTS
- TENANTS IN COMMON
- A CORPORATION
- A PUBLIC AGENCY
- OTHER

ALL SALES ARE FINAL. Even if the successful bidder makes a mistake and bids on the wrong property, the sale will remain final. All sales of property must be paid for immediately. No opportunity will be given for any successful bidder to go to the bank prior to completing payment. All bidders interested in a particular parcel are encouraged to stay until they are certain that the property has been paid for and will not be re-offered. Should a successful bidder refuse to pay for the property they have bid on, their bidder card will be voided and they will forfeit their right to further participate in the sale.

Los Angeles County
TREASURER AND TAX COLLECTOR

BIDDER REGISTRATION FORM

Attention Bidders: Persons wishing to bid at the tax sale must pre-register **in-person**. A deposit of $1,000 in the form of a Cashier's Check or bank issued Money Order payable to the Los Angeles County Tax Collector is required at the time of registration. A Bidder Registration Form must be completed and submitted in-person with your deposit. Valid picture identification (driver's license, military identification or state identification card) is required for all registering parties. If you register or request vesting for someone else, you must provide a notarized copy of the power of attorney for each person you represent, along with your valid picture identification. If you register or request vesting for a public agency, company, corporation, or partnership, you will need to provide **notarized copies** of the document that gives you the authority to register and bid on their behalf, along with your valid picture identification.

BIDDER'S NAME: _____
signature(s) required below   REQUIRED FIELD (PLEASE PRINT CLEARLY)

8:00 AM TO 5:00 PM PHONE NUMBER (___)_____
                                        REQUIRED FIELD

VESTING NAME: _____
signature(s) required below

ADDRESS: _____

_____
              CITY   STATE   ZIP

PLEASE SHOW HOW TITLE IS TO BE VESTED

____ **HUSBAND AND WIFE AS JOINT TENANTS**   ____ **A SINGLE MAN**
      (REQUIRES BOTH SIGNATURES)

____ **AS TENANTS IN COMMON**   ____ **A SINGLE WOMAN**
      (REQUIRES SIGNATURES OF ALL PARTIES)

____ **A MARRIED MAN AS HIS SOLE & SEPARATE PROPERTY**   ____ **AN UNMARRIED MAN**

____ **A MARRIED WOMAN AS HER SOLE & SEPARATE PROPERTY** ____ **AN UNMARRIED WOMAN**

____ **A MARRIED MAN**   ____ **A CORPORATION**
                                                     (REQUIRES ARTICLES OF INCORPORATION
____ **A MARRIED WOMAN**   AND ORDER BY AUTHORIZED MEMBER OF THE
                                                     BOARD OF DIRECTORS GIVING YOU AUTHORITY
                                                     TO BID & VEST PROPERTY.)

____ **A WIDOWER (MAN)**   ____ **A PUBLIC AGENCY**
                                                     (REQUIRES CERTIFIED ORDER FROM THE
____ **A WIDOW (WOMAN)**   GOVERNING BOARD GIVING YOU
                                                     AUTHORITY TO BID & VEST PROPERTY)

____ **OTHER**

BIDDER'S SIGNATURE _____

OTHER SIGNATURES _____

DATE _____

PLEASE NOTE THAT THE PURCHASE OF TAX-DEFAULTED PROPERTY MADE IS AT YOUR OWN RISK. VESTING INFORMATION CANNOT BE CHANGED AFTER THE REGISTRATION PERIOD HAS CLOSED.

Tax Sale Details-Jefferson County, Co   Page 1 of 2

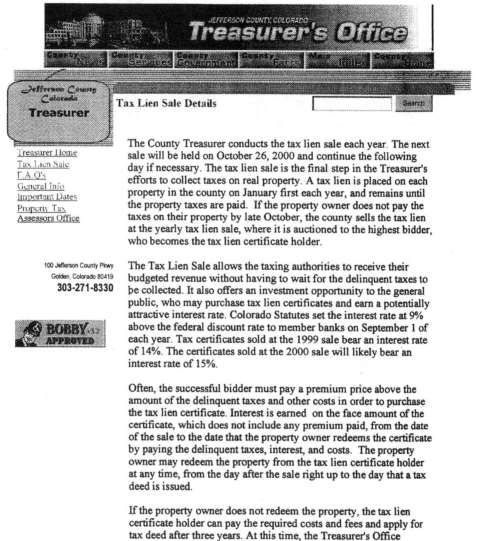

Tax Lien Sale Details

Treasurer Home
Tax Lien Sale
F.A.Q's
General Info
Important Dates
Property Tax
Assessors Office

100 Jefferson County Pkwy
Golden, Colorado 80419
303-271-8330

The County Treasurer conducts the tax lien sale each year. The next sale will be held on October 26, 2000 and continue the following day if necessary. The tax lien sale is the final step in the Treasurer's efforts to collect taxes on real property. A tax lien is placed on each property in the county on January first each year, and remains until the property taxes are paid. If the property owner does not pay the taxes on their property by late October, the county sells the tax lien at the yearly tax lien sale, where it is auctioned to the highest bidder, who becomes the tax lien certificate holder.

The Tax Lien Sale allows the taxing authorities to receive their budgeted revenue without having to wait for the delinquent taxes to be collected. It also offers an investment opportunity to the general public, who may purchase tax lien certificates and earn a potentially attractive interest rate. Colorado Statutes set the interest rate at 9% above the federal discount rate to member banks on September 1 of each year. Tax certificates sold at the 1999 sale bear an interest rate of 14%. The certificates sold at the 2000 sale will likely bear an interest rate of 15%.

Often, the successful bidder must pay a premium price above the amount of the delinquent taxes and other costs in order to purchase the tax lien certificate. Interest is earned on the face amount of the certificate, which does not include any premium paid, from the date of the sale to the date that the property owner redeems the certificate by paying the delinquent taxes, interest, and costs. The property owner may redeem the property from the tax lien certificate holder at any time, from the day after the sale right up to the day that a tax deed is issued.

If the property owner does not redeem the property, the tax lien certificate holder can pay the required costs and fees and apply for tax deed after three years. At this time, the Treasurer's Office notifies all who have an interest in the property that he has received an application for tax deed on the property. If no one redeems the property, the Treasurer's Office will issue a tax deed. In this instance, the tax lien certificate holder will not receive any interest or reimbursement of costs in addition to the deed to the property. It is important to note that Jefferson County very rarely issues a tax deed for improved property. Because the county does not own the

property but simply has a lien on the property, the county does not
guarantee or warrant any part of the tax lien process. The tax deed is
created by state statute and is not the equivalent of a general
warranty deed. It is each tax lien purchaser's responsibility to
understand the process and the risks connected with the process; to
understand the nature of the tax deed; to become familiar with the
value, circumstances, and condition of the property; and to
determine whether there is anyone with a hidden interest in the
property. Additional Tax Lien Sale information is presented at the
Pre-Sale Seminar held each fall.

Send mail to ckirby@co.jefferson.co.us with questions or comments about this Web Site.
Copyright © 2000, Jefferson County, Colorado. All rights reserved.
Last modified: January 09, 2001

Pitkin County Treasurer
506 East Main Street, Suite 201
Aspen, Colorado 81611
(970) 920-5170
Carol L. Foote, Deputy
Judy James, Deputy
Kristine Dillingham, Deputy

THE INTEREST RATE FOR TAX LIEN SALE CERTIFICATES SOLD IN 2001 PERCENT

The annual Tax Lien Sale for delinquent real estate taxes will be held on November 8, 2001, in the Commissioner's Meeting Room. The Meeting room is located in the Pitkin County Courthouse, 506 East Main Street in Aspen, Colorado. The sale begins promptly at 9:00 A.M.

A list of delinquent real estate parcels will be advertised in the Aspen Times Weekly for a three-week period. The publication dates for the list are October .

An updated list of delinquent properties will be available the morning of the Tax Lien Sale with all paid parcels deleted.

All parties interested in bidding at the Tax Lien Sale should check in at the Treasurer's Office prior to the sale to receive a bidder's number. Each bidder must provide the Pitkin County Treasurer's office with an affidavit stating that he or she is not an employee of Pitkin County, nor are they a family member or the agent of a Pitkin County employee. By Colorado Statutes, county employees are not allowed to bid on or own Tax Lien Certificates.

Pitkin County conducts their Tax Lien Sale by a rotation method. We follow the order of parcels as they appear in the Aspen Times. Parcel number 1 will be offered first to bidder number 1, parcel number 2 will be offered first to bidder number 2, etc. Tax Lien Certificates of Purchase sold in 2000 earn 15% per annum when redeemed. Overbids or premium bid are accepted but are not refundable and do not earn interest. When calculating your bid totals, you must add a $4.00 Treasurer's fee to each successful bid.

All successful bids must be paid for by cash, cashier's check or certified check by 2:00 P.M. on the day of the sale. Personal checks will not be accepted without a letter of credit on file.

The Pitkin County Treasurer's Office will be closed for approximately 1 to 2 hours after the sale, so we can tally up each bidder's totals and balance. We ask that you do not interrupt our office at this time.

Pitkin County mails 1099 Interest Earned forms to all tax sale buyers. In order to complete our records, each tax sale buyer will be required to furnish the Treasurer's office with their Tax Identification number or Social Security number and their permanent mailing address and telephone number.

Pitkin County gives the investor the option of allowing their Tax Lien Certificates of Purchase to be held for safekeeping in the Pitkin County Treasurer's vault. The investor will receive a safekeeping receipt from the Treasurer's office, and upon redemption of the certificates, the investor will realize a much faster return of their investment and earned interest. The redemption check is mailed to the investor along with a copy of the redemption certificate showing the amount invested and the interest earned.

If the owner of the property involved in a tax lien sale does not pay the current taxes on the property by June 15, the investor will be notified by the Treasurer's office of the amount due and will be given the opportunity to pay them and endorse them on the tax lien certificate of purchase. Payments of subsequent taxes earn the same rate of interest as the certificate.

A Tax Lien Certificate of Purchase does not give the investor any ownership rights to the property. It is only a tax lien on the property that earns interest for the investor until redeemed.

A Treasurer's Deed may be applied for three years after the date of the tax lien sale if the property has not been redeemed. A deposit will be required to cover the cost of the title search, advertising and postage for notice to all parties having an interest in the subject property. The majority of properties are redeemed. Pitkin county has issued only a few tax deeds on real estate to an investor since the 1950's.

IMPORTANT NOTICE

Pursuant to Federal Law, the Federal Deposit Insurance Corporation (FDIC) and the Resolution Trust Corporation (RTC), when acting in the capacity of receiver or successor to a failed financial institution, may not be liable for payment of any penalties or fees associated with the failure of any person to pay property taxes when due. Because the FDIC and RTC are unable to guarantee identity of all real property of the FDIC or RTC subject to exemption from penalty interest, the Treasurer of Pitkin County is unable to definitively advise those interested in bidding at the 1996 tax lien sale of which properties may be so effected. The Treasurer has attempted to withhold from sale those tax liens of which we are informed by the FDIC or RTC to which their own investigation of the status of liens offered for sale and obtain their own analysis of the applicability of Federal Law.

It is the buyer's responsibility to know the quality of the property on which they are paying the taxes and receiving a lien. Particular attention should be given to the impact of a bankruptcy filing or the involvement of the Resolution Trust Corporation, either of which could place a cloud upon the tax lien sale certificate. The recommendation of the Treasurer is that you consult with private legal counsel prior to the tax lien sale.

SUMMIT COUNTY TREASURER
INFORMATION ABOUT THE 2001 ANNUAL TAX LIEN SALE

NOVEMBER 2, 2001 – 9:00 A.M.

HOLIDAY INN – SUMMIT COUNTY
1129 North Summit Boulevard
Frisco, Summit County, Colorado

SALE
Doors will be open at 8:00 a.m. for registration. Sale will commence at 9:00 a.m. with instructions. Settlement will take place at the County Treasurer's Office, 208 Lincoln Avenue, starting at 1:30 p.m. Each bidder must complete a registration form prior to the start of the sale. Registration information will be used for Certificate issuance. Bidding will be by number. If you plan on coming to the tax lien sale, please pre-register. This will assist in starting the sale promptly. No one will be admitted to the "round-robin" sale after the commencement of the sale.

YOU ARE NOT BUYING PROPERTY!
Successful purchasers will receive a tax lien Certificate of Purchase on tax liens they have purchased. The certificate represents a lien on the property. The owner of the property has the right to redeem the lien at any time prior to the issuance of a Treasurer's Deed on the property. (Normally a minimum of 3 years after the sale.)

SETTLEMENT
Initial deposits will not be required for this sale. Sale settlement will occur at the Office of the County Treasurer, 208 Lincoln Avenue, Breckenridge, Colorado 80424, starting at 1:30 p.m. Settlement must be completed by 3:30 p.m. on the day of the sale. All settlement monies must be good funds. No credit card payments will be accepted. IF a purchaser fails to pay the amount due on sale day, the purchases will be canceled and re-sold. Non-sufficient funds in payment of purchases will cause all purchases to be canceled and re-sold. Payments must be made in the name of the buyer.

PROHIBITED BIDDERS
No County official, employee, immediate family member, or person acting as agent of same may participate in the tax lien sale. Bidders will sign "Non-Employee Certification." No person under the age of 18 may bid or purchase at this sale.

METHOD OF SALE
The 2001 Sale will be conducted in two parts. All liens under a certain amount (initially set at $1,000) will be sold "round-robin". Any vested interest liens will be pulled from the first part of the sale and put into the "Silent" Auction. There will be a break. Then, all liens over the "certain" amount, plus any vested interests, mining claims and other small dollar liens will by sold by "Silent" Auction. Each tax lien will be recorded on a separate sheet of paper and set on a table in the "Silent" Auction sale room. Auction sheets will be grouped by area of the county for ease of determining location. Each purchaser will be able to purchase the liens that he or she would like. Only the number of the buyer and the amount of premium, if any, will be needed for each bid. There will be no specific order nor any vested purchase requests. Special assessment liens will be combined with property tax liens and sold as a single certificate. You may participate in one or both parts of the sale. Mobile Homes will be sold at the "Silent" Auction Sale.

MINIMUM BIDS
Sale of the tax liens will be for the amount advertised, including the $4.00 certificate fee. Premium bids are those in excess of this dollar amount. After the initial bid is recorded, any additional bid will require a premium bid.

PREMIUM BIDS
There will be no specified premium bid amount. REMEMBER that you will NOT receive your premium bid back at time of redemption. NO redemption interest will be paid on your premium bid.

CERTIFICATE INTEREST RATE
The statutory certificate rate is twelve (12) percent. The annual rate of interest shall be 9 percentage points above the discount rate, which discount rate shall be the rate of interest a commercial bank pays to the Federal Reserve Bank of Kansas City using a government bond or other eligible paper as security, and shall be rounded to the nearest full percent. The commissioner of banking shall establish the annual rate of interest based upon the computation specified immediately above. Such annual rate of interest shall be so established as of September 1 of each year. Interest paid on redeemed certificates will be reported annually to the Internal Revenue Service.

CERTIFICATES OF PURCHASE

Certificates of Purchase will be issued to the purchaser as noted on the registration form. If desired, the Summit County Treasurer will hold certificates in the Treasurer's Vault and send a safekeeping receipt and a status report. Please note on the registration form if you are interested in this service.

SUBSEQUENT PROPERTY TAXES

Notices for subsequent year's property taxes will be sent to holders of unredeemed certificates. Tax sale lien sale certificate holders are **expected** to pay subsequent years property taxes. The amount due and paid will be endorsed on their certificate. Subsequent Tax Notices will be mailed in July or August of each year.

TREASURER'S DEED

Three years after the DATE OF SALE, the holder of an unredeemed Certificate of Purchase may apply for a Treasurer's Deed to the property. Additional information on the Treasurer's Deed process may be obtained from the Treasurer's Office.

SPECIAL NOTE

Because the Federal Deposit Insurance Corporation (FDIC) is unable to identify all real property of the FDIC subject to exemption from penalty interest, the Summit County Treasurer is unable to definitively advise those interested in bidding at the annual lien sale of which properties may be exempt from sale or as to which no lien for taxes may have attached. The Summit County Treasurer has attempted to withhold from sale those tax liens of which he is informed by the FDIC that the exemption does apply. The Summit County Treasurer has also attempted to withhold from sale those tax liens as to which the automatic stay provisions of the Bankruptcy Code apply. However, bidders should undertake their own investigation of the status of the liens offered for sale and obtain their own analysis of the applicability of Federal law. Upon determination that tax liens were sold for property subject to exemption or bankruptcy, the certificates will be redeemed as "SOLD IN ERROR" with penalty interest at the rate of 2 percentage points above the discount rate, which discount rate shall be the rate of interest at the Federal Reserve Bank of Kansas City, instead of the tax lien rate of 9 percentage points above the discount rate.

PRE-REGISTER

If you wish to attend the annual sale, you can save registration time by returning your registration form prior to sale day. A return envelope is enclosed for your convenience. Please pre-register if you believe that you will attend the sale. This will save everybody time in getting the sale started timely.

Thank you for your interest and participation in the 2001 Tax Lien Sale

**LARRY GILLILAND
SUMMIT COUNTY TREASURER
208 LINCOLN AVENUE
P. O. BOX 289
BRECKENRIDGE, CO 80424-0289
(970) 453-3440**

DIRECTIONS TO HOLIDAY INN SUMMIT COUNTY:

I-70 to Exit 203 (Frisco, Breckenridge). On Summit Boulevard, go to the 1st Stop Light and take a Left onto the Dillon Dam Road. Take the second Right into the Holiday Inn Parking Lot.

Remember to Register Prior to the Sale!

MARION COUNTY, INDIANA

2001 TAX SALE

INFORMATION AND PROCEDURES

PLEASE REVIEW THE ENTIRE CONTENTS OF THIS GUIDE!

NOTE: The Tax Sale item list will be available on the Treasurer's web page about July 5th. More information about this feature can be found on page 2 of this guide.

The following information and procedures **apply to Marion County only.** The statute governing tax sales in Indiana *(I.C. 6-1.1-24)* affords the County Auditor and County Treasurer options regarding the manner in which the Tax Sale may be conducted. Therefore, the exact procedures by which a county conducts a tax sale for properties with delinquent taxes and special assessments differ from county to county.

This public auction or "Tax Sale" of real property is required by Indiana law. While some unfortunate circumstances may exist which result in some properties being offered for sale,

> *it is nonetheless required that all properties with delinquent taxes, penalties, and special assessment liens for unpaid sewer user charges, delinquent weed cutting fees, delinquent solid waste service fees, or delinquent Barrett Law contracts, as specified by law, be auctioned at the Treasurer's Tax Sale.*

The Tax Sale enables the Treasurer to collect the revenue that has been levied for the operation of nearly 50 governmental units and school districts within Marion County. The staffs of the Marion County Treasurer and Marion County Auditor appreciate the attention of prospective bidders and buyers to the procedures governing this Tax Sale. Thank you for your participation. Your comments are welcome.

GREGORY N. JORDAN
MARION COUNTY TREASURER

★ ★ ★ ★ ★

GENERAL Points of Interest

The sale is to begin as a public auction at 9:00 a.m. Eastern Standard Time, Thursday, August 16, 2001. *(Tax Sale instructions will begin at 8:30 a.m. in the Public Assembly Room and will continue until the sale begins at 9:00 a.m.)* All times are Eastern Standard.

On Thursday, August 16, 2001, the sale will run from 9:00 a.m. to noon, followed by a one-hour lunch break, then the sale will continue from 1:00-4:00 p.m.

It is unlikely that we will be able to offer all available properties for sale on Thursday, August 16, 2001. If that is the situation, the sale will resume at 9:00 a.m. on Friday, August 17, 2001. The number of parcels left to offer for sale on Friday, August 17, 2001 will determine the need to take a lunch break.

On both Thursday, August 16, 2001, and Friday, August 17, 2001, the sale will be held in the Public Assembly Room (Room 230), 2nd floor of the City-County Building – 200 E. Washington Street, Indianapolis, IN 46204.

The "parcel number" identifies a property. There may be an owner and/or address advertised and/or read at the sale, but the parcel number identifies the exact property offered for sale.

Parcels will be offered for sale in Item Number sequence, as identified in newspaper ads. This means that "A" items (item numbers starting with A) will be offered first, followed by "B" items and then "C" items.

At the sale, parcels beginning with "A" will be offered in groups of 25 items at a time, such as items A00001 through A00025. Any bidder may call out an item number within that range. A call for a specific item number such as A00017 is considered a minimum bid for that item. Once the minimum bid is made, that item is auctioned to the highest bidder. If the item called for is no longer in the sale, that fact will be announced, and a call for another item within that group of 25 will be accepted. This procedure will continue until there are no more calls for item numbers within the group being considered. At that time the next group of 25 item numbers will be offered. After all "A" items have been offered once, parcels beginning with "B" will be offered, and then parcels beginning with "C" will be offered. Both "B" and "C" items will be offered on a first-asked, first-offered basis. Any bidder may call out one of those "B" or "C" items. A call for a specific "B" or "C" item number is considered a minimum bid for that item. Once the minimum bid is made, that item is auctioned to the highest bidder. If the item called for is no longer in the sale, that fact will be announced, and a call for another "B" or "C" item will be accepted.

After all "A", "B", and "C" items have been offered once, the Treasurer will open up the auction for all available items to be offered on a first-asked, first-offered basis. A call for a specific item is considered a minimum bid for that item. Once the minimum bid is made, that item is auctioned to the highest bidder.

Item numbers beginning with "A" were not in last year's sale. "B" items were in last year's sale but were not sold and still have delinquent taxes. "C" items have been identified by the Metropolitan Development Commission for redevelopment. "C" items that are sold have a maximum redemption period of 120 days rather than the one-year redemption that applies to "A" and "B" items.

A complete list of Tax Sale items available for sale will be available in three sources:

1. **Newspaper:** Properties available for sale will be advertised in *The Indianapolis Star* and the *Court & Commercial Record* on the following Fridays:

   > July 6, 2001
   > July 13, 2001
   > July 20, 2001

2. **Diskette:** The diskette will be available in Microsoft Excel and can be purchased from the Treasurer's office on or after July 3rd at the cost of $15.00 per diskette. The parcels that appear on the diskette will be the same as those parcels that appear in the first newspaper advertisement *(July 6, 2001)*. Updated tax sale lists will <u>not</u> be available on diskette.

3. **Web page:** Beginning on or shortly after Monday, July 2nd, the Marion County Treasurer's Web page will have the most current list of properties available for sale. The list will be updated daily and will be in the same format as the newspaper listing and the diskette. <u>A new feature has been added this year that will allow the list to be downloaded.</u> The Web address for viewing and/or downloading the list is www.indygov.org/treas/taxsale/index.htm.

An updated list of Tax Sale items still eligible for sale will be available from the Treasurer each day, beginning Thursday, July 5th, and each day thereafter until the Tax Sale ends on August 29, 2001. The list will include items available as of 8:00 a.m. on the morning it is printed. There will be a $3.00 charge per list to cover the cost of printing. Only the Tax Sale Item Number will appear on the list, so it will be necessary to have one of the original listings to be able to obtain other information about those unsold parcels.

The properties remaining unsold at the end of the sale on Friday, August 17, 2001 will again be offered on Wednesday, August 29, 2001 at 9:00 a.m. EST in Room 260 of the City County Building.

If a parcel is not sold on August 16, 17, or 29, 2001, it will not be offered for sale again this year.

On or before Tuesday, July 3rd, 2001, the Marion County Auditor will send a letter by Certified Mail to owners of all properties which at that time are eligible for the 2001 Marion County Tax Sale.

Any payment made to the Marion County Treasurer by an owner to withdraw a parcel from the sale or by a successful bidder at the sale must be paid by cash, by any **Certified Check,** by any **Cashier's Check** or by any **Official Check** that is issued by a financial institution. **NO MONEY ORDERS, PERSONAL CHECKS, OR BUSINESS CHECKS WILL BE ACCEPTED.** *(The Treasurer will not accept more than $7,500.00 in cash from any one bidder, for the period of July 2 through the duration of the sale.)*

The Tax Sale buyer's interest in the property is limited to a lien on the purchased property until: 1) the property is redeemed; 2) a Tax Deed is issued; or 3) six (6) months has elapsed after the expiration of the redemption period, whichever occurs first.

There is a one-year period following the sale of each "A" and "B" item (120 days for "C" items) during which the delinquent owner, occupant, or person with a substantial property interest of public record may "redeem the property", a term meaning to retain possession by paying all moneys owed to the county plus required fees.

Redemption of property purchased in a Tax Sale results in the parcel remaining in the current owner's name.

If a parcel sold in the "A" or "B" sale is not redeemed prior to one year from the date of sale (120 days for "C" items), the Tax Sale buyer may present the Tax Certificate to the County Auditor and receive a Tax Deed to the property granting title to the property to the buyer or assignee of the buyer.

A person who wants to redeem a property should contact the Marion County Auditor, Room 841 of the City-County Building, to have an exact calculation of the redemption cost made. That amount must be paid to the County Auditor within one year of the date of sale of an "A" or "B" item (120 days for "C" items). The redemption amount will be equal to the minimum bid required by the Treasurer, *plus* a redemption fee calculated on the minimum bid paid by the successful bidder (percentages listed below), *plus* 10% per annum interest calculated on the difference between the minimum bid and the amount paid by the successful bidder *(referred to as Tax Sale Overbid), plus* any taxes, penalties, and special assessments paid by the buyer subsequent to the date of sale, *plus* 10% per annum interest on those subsequent payments. (NOTE: The redeeming party does not have to repay the overbid amount, but they are required to pay the 10% per annum interest on the overbid amount.) The redemption fee will be calculated in two parts (three parts if taxes are paid subsequent to the Tax Sale):

1. On the Minimum bid –
   - 10% of the minimum bid if redeemed not more than 6 months after the date of sale;
   - 15% of the minimum bid if redeemed more than 6 months but not more than one year after the date of sale.

2. On the <u>difference</u> between the successful bid price and the minimum bid *(referred to as Tax Sale Overbid)* –
    - 10% per annum interest from the date of payment to the date of redemption

3. On any payments made by the Tax Sale buyer subsequent to the sale –
    - 10% per annum interest from the date of payment to the date of redemption

If, before redemption or the execution of a Tax Deed, it is found that the *sale* is invalid, the Tax Sale buyer is not entitled to a Tax Deed, but shall be entitled to a refund of the purchase price plus 6% per annum interest.

If, after the execution of a Tax Deed, it is found that the *deed* is invalid pursuant to *I.C. 6-1.1-25-12,* the Tax Sale buyer is entitled to a lien on the property in the amount of the purchase price, any taxes or special assessments paid subsequent to sale, and any amount due the Tax Sale buyer as an occupying claimant plus interest at 10% per annum.

Points of Interest *(primarily)* for Current OWNERS of Property Being Offered in This Year's Sale

The following schedule applies to payments made to the Treasurer by property owners wanting to prevent their parcels from being sold in this year's Tax Sale. The owner must make payment by **cash,** by any **Certified Check,** by any **Cashier's Check,** or by any **Official Check** that is issued by a financial institution. **NO MONEY ORDERS, PERSONAL CHECKS, OR BUSINESS CHECKS WILL BE ACCEPTED.**

July 2, 2001 Through August 14, 2001 – Owners must pay all delinquent taxes, penalties, and delinquent special assessments due on their parcel(s) *plus* $25.00 of the Tax Sale Administrative Cost;

August 15, 2001 – **No payments will be accepted on Tax Sale items** so that the Treasurer can make necessary preparation for the conduct of the sale to begin on August 16, 2001;

August 16, 2001, and after – Owners must pay all delinquent taxes, penalties, delinquent special assessments, *plus* the November 2001 tax installment, plus the November 2001 solid waste service fee (if applicable), *plus* other current special assessments (if applicable), *plus* the Tax Sale Administrative Cost of $25.00. If the parcel is sold before the owner makes the full payment, the owner will have to wait to redeem the parcel through the Marion County Auditor's office until approximately one week after the parcel has been sold.

Payments made by owners on the dates of public auction (August 16, 17, and 29) must be in full – no part payments – and will be collected by the Treasurer after 8:00 a.m. in the room in which the auction is being conducted.

Prior to August 15, 2001, owners may make part payments toward the minimum sale price. There is no minimum amount of part payment required. After payment of the $25.00 Tax Sale Avertising Fee (which is included in the Administrative Cost), any part payments made will reduce the minimum bid amount and will save total redemption costs to the owner if the property is sold.

If a "B" item is not sold at the Tax Sale and the owner does not pay all charges due on the parcel, the County Auditor may issue a Tax Deed to the County 120 days after the sale ends.

If a "C" item is not sold at the Tax Sale and the owner does not pay all charges due on the parcel, the Metropolitan Development Commission may request a Tax Deed from the County Auditor 120 days after the sale ends.

Points of Interest *(primarily)* for BUYERS
of Property in This Year's Sale

Every Tax Sale buyer will be required to have a bidder number in order to bid on a parcel in the public auction. The two types of bidders will be: *Cash Bidders* and *Bid Account Bidders.*

Successful bidders are **not** allowed time to "go to the bank" to secure funds to pay for their purchase(s).

Cash bidders will be assigned a yellow bidder paddle with a bidder number in the range of 500-999. To obtain a bidder number the bidder must provide his/her name and address (as they are to appear on the Tax Sale Certificate), phone number, and Social Security Number (or Federal I.D. number). A cash bidder will be paying for each property as each is purchased. Payment must be made by **cash,** by any **Certified Check,** by any **Cashier's Check** or by any **Official Check** that is issued by a financial institution. Qualified checks must be for the exact amount of purchase. **NO MONEY ORDERS, PERSONAL CHECKS, OR BUSINESS CHECKS WILL BE ACCEPTED.** *(The Treasurer will not accept more than $7,500.00 in cash from any one bidder, for the period of July 2 through the duration of the sale.)*

Bid-account bidders will be assigned a white bidder paddle with a bidder number in the range of 100-499. To obtain a bidder number the bidder must provide his/her name and address (as they are to appear on the Tax Sale Certificate), phone number, and Social Security Number (or Federal I.D. number), *and* they must establish their account with qualified funds that may be deposited with the Treasurer in Room 1022 of the City-County Building through August 15th or in the Public Assembly Room on the day of the Tax Sale. Tax Sale purchases will be charged to the bidder's account by presenting the bidder number at the conclusion of each successful bid. If a deposit bidder's balance with the Treasurer becomes too low to make subsequent purchases, the bidder will be required to deposit additional acceptable funds before making additional purchases.

Beginning on or shortly after Monday, July 2nd, the Marion County Treasurer's Web page will have the most current list of properties available for sale. The list will be updated daily and will be in the same format as the newspaper listing and the diskette. A new feature has been added this year that will allow the list to be downloaded. The Web address for viewing and/or downloading the list is www.indygov.org/treas/taxsale/index.htm.

The minimum bid that will be accepted on any property must be equal to all taxes, penalties, and special assessments presently due on the parcel – including the November 13, 2001, property tax installment and solid waste service fee (if any) – plus a $175.00 Administrative Cost.

The $175.00 Administrative Cost includes an Advertising Fee of $25.00 and a Title Search Fee of $150.00 that is charged with each sale and is to enable the Marion County Auditor to secure such a service so that all interested parties of public record may be informed by the Auditor of the impending issuance of a Tax Deed to a different owner. The search remains the property of the County Auditor.

After a minimum bid has been received for a particular item number, we will allow the next bidder, if any, to bid an amount which is equal to the next even $25, $50, $75 or $100 figure. After that point in any bid, the minimum increase in bid price will be at least $25.00.

No one should bid in this Tax Sale who does not have the correct type of payment at the time of becoming a successful bidder. A high bidder who fails to immediately pay the bid price in acceptable funds must pay a penalty of 25% of the amount of the bid (subject to prosecution - *IC. 6-1.1-24-8*).

All sales are final! There will be no refunds or exchanges. Prospective buyers are urged to research available properties thoroughly to aid in identifying the exact piece of property identified by the parcel number. Research may include, but not necessarily be limited to, a review of:

- liens recorded with the Marion County Recorder;
- plat maps in the appropriate Township Assessor's office;
- orders of the Department of Metropolitan Development concerning demolition orders and unsafe buildings;
- sewer user charges, solid waste service fees, and/or weed cutting charges that have not been certified to the Treasurer by the Department of Public Works; and
- Barrett Law assessments that are delinquent but not yet certified to the Treasurer.

The IRS may claim redemption rights in properties sold which are subject to Federal tax liens pursuant to a right of redemption established under *26 U.S.C. §7425* which is different than that provided under Indiana Statute.

If a successful bidder buys a "pig in a poke", the buyer will get just that.

Concerning deposit bidders – the Treasurer will refund any excess of deposits over purchases when the bidder advises the Treasurer that no more purchases are planned. Such refund will be made by County check within several days of the request to close the account.

Tax Sale buyers run a risk of trespassing if they make a purchase and attempt to enter the premises or exercise any ownership rights during the redemption period which is prior to the time a Tax Deed is issued in the buyer's name.

At the conclusion of each parcel sale, the Treasurer will issue a receipt for the amount paid. (Receipts for deposit bidders will be held by the Treasurer until the bidder closes out his/her account with the Treasurer.)

After 4-6 weeks from the date of sale, the buyer may present the Tax Sale receipt to the Marion County Auditor, Room 841 of the City-County Building, in order to receive a Tax Certificate evidencing the buyer's lien against the property.

While the minimum time to exchange a Tax Certificate for a Tax Deed to an unredeemed property is one year for "A" and "B" items (120 days for "C" items), the maximum time for such action is six (6) months after the expiration of the redemption period.

The Tax Sale buyer's lien expires six (6) months after the expiration of the redemption period .

A Tax Sale buyer may pay any taxes, penalties, and/or special assessments which become due on the parcel subsequent to the Tax Sale but before the redemption period expires. Such payments can be made by requesting a bill in person from the Marion County Treasurer. It is the Tax Sale Buyer's responsibility to record any such payment in the Auditor's office if the buyer expects to be reimbursed when the property is redeemed.

If redemption is accomplished, the buyer will be reimbursed for recorded payments of subsequent taxes, penalties, and/or special assessments plus interest at the rate of 10% per annum.

If the parcel is *not* redeemed and the Tax Sale buyer surrenders the Tax Certificate to receive a Tax Deed, all delinquent taxes, penalties, and/or special assessments which became due subsequent to the Tax Sale must be paid before the Auditor will petition the court to issue a Tax Deed to the Tax Sale buyer.

All buyers who are to receive payments as a result of redemption of property they have purchased will be required to complete Form 3435 to give the County Auditor sufficient information to be able to issue and report on Form 1099-INT the amount of interest and redemption fee received.

NOTICE TO PURCHASERS OF TAX SALE PROPERTY
Marion County, Indiana, Sale of Delinquent Tax Properties
Commencing August 16, 2001

No. 1 Preparation and Delivery of Tax Sale Certificates. Tax certificates are prepared by the Marion County Auditor, and the purchaser must contact the Auditor's Office approximately four (4) weeks following the sale to see if tax certificates are available. The purchaser **must** bring the tax sale bill for identification, and the purchaser **must** accept the tax certificate and sign a receipt, at the Auditor's Office, **Real Estate Department**, City-County Building, **Suite 841**, Indianapolis, Indiana 46204. (Phone 327-4646) (NOTE: THE TAX CERTIFICATE DOES NOT CONFER OWNERSHIP OF THE PROPERTY, AND THE PURCHASER DOES NOT RECEIVE TITLE TO THE PROPERTY UNTIL A TAX DEED IS ISSUED; also, the purchaser will not be entitled to a tax deed if he/she does not present the tax certificate to the Auditor within six (6) months after the redemption period expires.)

No. 2 THE PURCHASER'S INTEREST IN THE PROPERTY. INTEREST IS LIMITED TO A LIEN ON THE PURCHASED PROPERTY UNTIL: 1) THE PROPERTY IS REDEEMED; 2) A TAX DEED IS ISSUED; OR 3) A MAXIMUM OF SIX MONTHS AFTER THE REDEMPTION PERIOD EXPIRES), WHICHEVER OCCURS FIRST. IF THE PURCHASER FAILS TO REQUEST A DEED WITHIN SIX MONTHS AFTER THE PERIOD OF REDEMPTION EXPIRES, THE PURCHASER'S LIEN EXPIRES.

No. 3 Purchaser's Interest if Property is Not Redeemed. After the expiration of the redemption period (which is one (1) year from the date of sale for "A" and "B" items, and one hundred, twenty (120) days for "C" items), upon receipt of the tax certificate, and at least three (3) months after the issuance of the post-sale notice by the Auditor, the Auditor will petition the court to direct the Auditor to issue a tax deed. The court will issue an order if the court finds that the following conditions exist:

(1)   The time of the redemption has expired.
(2)   The tract or real property has not been redeemed.
(3)   All taxes and special assessments, penalties, and costs have been paid.
(4)   The notices required by law have been given.
(5)   The petitioner has complied with all the provisions of law entitling the purchaser or the purchaser's assignee to deed.

To receive a tax deed, the purchaser should present the tax certificate to the Auditor's Office, being sure that the Auditor has the purchaser's and/or assignee's correct phone number, post office assigned address, and federal I.D. number or social security number. If tax statements are to be sent to a different place and/or person, that information should also be listed on the tax certificate.

A tax deed grants the purchaser fee-simple title, free and clear of all liens and encumbrances, except those liens granted priority under federal law and the lien of the State or a political subdivision for taxes and special assessments which accrue subsequent to the sale. However, the title is subject to all easements, covenants, declarations, and other deed restrictions and laws governing land use, including all zoning restrictions. In addition, the purchaser may initiate an action in Marion Circuit Court to quiet title to the property. Any appeal from the order to issue the tax deed must be filed in the Marion Circuit Court not later than sixty (60) days after the date of the court's order to issue the tax deed.

No. 4 Purchaser's Interests if Property is Redeemed. Any person may redeem the property at any time before the redemption period expires. When tax sale property is redeemed, the Auditor will notify the purchaser and ask that the tax certificate be delivered to the Auditor's Office as soon as possible so that the purchaser may receive a refund of the purchase price, including overbid, plus interest at the rate of ten percent (10%) on the minimum amount due if redeemed within six (6) months from date of sale; or at the rate of fifteen (15%) on the minimum amount due if redeemed from six (6) months to one (1) year of sale. In addition, the total amount required for redemption includes any other actual costs plus ten percent (10%) per annum on the amount by which the purchase price exceeds the minimum amount due.

The Auditor will also refund to the purchaser any subsequent taxes paid and **recorded in the tax sale register**, plus ten percent (10%) per annum. Upon receipt of the tax certificate, the Auditor will process a claim refund request within three (3) to four (4) weeks, and a refund check will be mailed to the purchaser. Also, the purchaser may be requested to fill out a Form W-9 so that the Auditor may issue tax form 1099-INT showing yearly interest for tax purposes.

NOTICE   The Auditor has obtained the consent of the Internal Revenue Service to conduct the tax sale, but the Internal Revenue Service (IRS) may claim a right of redemption different than that provided under Indiana law. For additional information, contact the IRS at (317) 226-6707.

No. 5 Payment of Subsequent Property Taxes. In order to receive a deed, a purchaser must pay all subsequent property taxes and special assessments on the tax sale property. When subsequent property taxes are paid by the purchaser, the purchaser **must deliver the paid tax receipt stamped, "Paid by Tax Sale Buyer",** to the Auditor's Office, **Real Estate Department,** City-County Building, Suite 841, for recording of the payment in the tax sale register.

No. 6 Purchaser's Interest if Sale is Invalid. If before redemption or the entry of an order for execution of a tax deed, it is found that the sale is invalid, the purchaser is not entitled to a tax deed, but shall be entitled to a refund of the purchase money and any taxes/special assessments paid subsequent to the sale, plus six percent (6%) interest.

If after the entry of an order for execution of a tax deed, it is found that the deed is invalid pursuant to IC 6-1.1-25-12, the purchaser is entitled to a lien on the property in the amount of the purchase price, any taxes or special assessments paid subsequent to sale and any amount due the purchaser as an occupying claimant, plus interest at ten percent (10%).

Martha A. Womacks
Martha A. Womacks
Marion County Auditor

TREASURER OF MARION COUNTY, INDIANA
RECEIPT TO BIDDER FOR FUNDS DEPOSITED WITH TREASURER FOR USE
AS AN OPEN ACCOUNT FOR PURCHASE OF TAX SALE PROPERTY

BIDDER NO.

_181_

BIDDER NAME: The Lobbs Companies

TAX ID #: _____ **PHONE:** _____ **CONTACT:** _____

ADDRESS: _____

CITY: _____ **STATE:** _____ **ZIP:** _____

_THE TREASURER ACKNOWLEDGES RECEIPT FOR DEPOSIT TO BIDDER
ACCOUNT FOR PURCHASES DURING TAX SALE FOR THIS AMOUNT ._ ➔

$ 2,000 ⁰⁰

[ ] CURRENCY
[ ] CERTIFIED CHECK
[✗] CASHIER'S CHECK
[ ] EFT

**RECEIVED BY MARION
COUNTY TREASURER** B. A_____ **DATE:** 9/6/01

PLEASE NOTE: _ALL REFUNDS FROM YOUR BIDDER DEPOSIT ACCOUNT FOR MONEY NOT
USED DURING AUCTION WILL BE MADE BY COUNTY TREASURER CHECK._

White - Bidder/Agent
Yellow- Accounting
Pink - Bidder Envelope

MCT-711 7/01

Audubon County Treasurer

Court House • 318 Leroy, #5 • Audubon, Iowa 50025
Office: (712) 563-2293 • Fax: (712) 563-2556 • Driver's License: (712) 563-3051

The annual Tax Sale of parcels with delinquent taxes is held the third Monday in June each year in the Audubon County Treasurer's office. The Treasurer's office will not act as agent for individuals purchasing at tax sale. It is necessary to attend in person or to send a representative. A list of available parcels is published in the Audubon County Advocate Journal, PO Box 247, Audubon, IA 50025-0247 (712/563-2661) the first full week of June each year.

Properties known to be involved in bankruptcy or published but paid prior to tax sale will not be offered for sale.

Parcels are listed as Regular Tax Sale, advertised one time, taxes being one year or less delinquent or as Public Bidder properties, advertised more that one time and being more than one year delinquent. A Tax Sale Certificate is issued for each parcel sold for the full amount of the taxes, interest, fees and costs due. If more that one party is interested in the same property, a bid down procedure begins. A parcel can not be sold for more than is due, therefore, the party willing to pay the full amount due for the least amount of ownership interest is the parcel, acquires the certificate. In the event a lottery system is used, each person may have only one chance for each drawing. No MINORS are allowed to bid.

There is a $100 per certificate fee due to this office to assign any privately held certificates. If the parties are located out of town or state, a signed, notarized affidavit of assignment must be submitted to this office with the fee.

The certificate holder is responsible for requesting the amount of subsequent taxes, without notice from this office. Subsequent taxes may be paid 14 days after the payment becomes delinquent. There is a $2.00 per parcel charge to provide written tax information.

All certificates purchased by individual-bidders at a Regular Tax Sale cancel in three years. The three- year period begins the day of the sale. Public Bidder purchases cancel in one year.

Public Bidder certificates must be held for nine months before the 90 Day Notice of Expiration of Right of Redemption and Application for Tax Deed can be served. Regular tax sale certificates must be held for one year & nine months prior to service. All parties with a recorded interest in the property, anyone in possession and the city in which the parcel is located, if applicable, must be served. Once Notice has been served and FILED IN THE TREASURER'S OFFICE, the parties served have 90 days to redeem the certificate. If not redeemed in the 90 day period, a tax deed can be issued. Your attorney can advise you as to the legal implications of a Tax Sale certificate. This office does not handle service of the 90 Day Notice for privately held certificates. Attorney fees cannot be recorded, however, the cost of the search and actual cost of service may be added to the certificate, if stated in the affidavit and filed before the certificate is redeemed.

Peggy J. Smalley
Treasurer

REGISTER OF BIDDERS
JUNE 18, 2001 ANNUAL TAX SALE
AND SUBSEQUENT ADJOURNMENTS THEREOF

CURRENT LEGISLATIVE CHANGES CONCERNING TAX SALES:

Treasurer <u>may</u> collect a registration fee at the tax sale to cover the cost of holding the tax sale. Treasurer <u>shall</u> collect an assignment fee of $100.00 for the assignment of tax sale certificates. Provides that if a tax sale certificate holder does not take action for issuance of a deed within 90 days of the expiration of right to redemption period, the tax sale certificate is cancelled.

Date _____

Name _____

_____

_____

Address _____

_____

_____

County of Residence _____

State of Residence _____

Telephone (_____) _____

Deed is to be issued to:

Name or Names: _____

Husband & Wife? _____ Yes _____ No _____ Not Applicable

Joint tenancy with right of survivorship? _____ Yes _____ No

Address: _____

_____

Tax Sale parcels are published on Thursday (the first full week in June) in the Audubon County Advocate Journal, P O Box 247, Audubon, IA 50025-0247 (712-563-2661).

Number: _____ (office use only)

Harrison County Treasurer's Office

Vicki Argotsinger, Treasurer

111 North 2nd Ave.
Courthouse
Logan, Iowa 51546

Tax Dept. 712-644-2750
Auto Dept. 712-644-2144
Driver Lic. 712-644-2750
Fax: 712-644-2643

NOTICE TO ALL TAX SALE PURCHASERS

The Code of Iowa, Chapter 446, requires that County Treasurers conduct Tax Sales of delinquent properties the third Monday of June each year. The sale is held in the Harrison County Courtroom at 10:00 a.m.. This year's Tax Sale date is June 18, 2001.

The Notice of Tax Sale will appear in the Missouri Valley Times-News. The list is published the first Wednesday of June. You may obtain the publication by calling (712) 642-2791.

You must complete a bidder registration form. If you have a representative bidding for you or your company, the appropriate forms must be filled out.

You must complete a W-9 form. We will file a 1099-INT with the Internal Revenue Service and with you if your interest earnings on Tax Sale certificates exceed $600.00.

Payment must be by personal check, money order, or cash. The amount must be the same as presented at the Tax Sale, plus $10.00 for each certificate issued.

You may register by mail, but you or a representative for you must be present to bid at the Tax Sale. A bidder may represent only one person/company and a person/company may be represented by only one bidder.

Any parcel with one year or more taxes owing is included in the Public Bidder Sale. Any parcel with one year or less taxes owing is included in the Regular Tax Sale.

When more than one person offers to pay the total amount due and all parties concerned do not wish to bid less than 100% interest in the parcel, a random drawing will be done. The bidder number drawn will have the choice to purchase the taxes. If the bidder declines, another number will be drawn.

When more than one person offers to pay the total amount due and one party requests a per cent of interest bid down, the County Treasurer will enter into the bid down process.

All properties purchased at the Tax Sale will have a Tax Sale Certificate issued and subsequent taxes should be paid by the certificate holders each year until the property is redeemed or until a Tax Sale Deed is issued.

After the Tax Sale has been completed, all Tax Sale purchasers must go to the Treasurer's Office. Payment for tax purchases will be made, and all registration forms and W-9's will be left in the Treasurer's office. A $10.00 fee will be assessed for each parcel purchased.

The Tax Sale Certificates will be issued within 10 to 15 days. The original certificate will be mailed to you. Please keep the certificate in a safe place. A $10.00 fee will be assessed to issue a duplicate certificate. The original certificate must be returned to the Treasurer after notification of redemption. A copy of the Tax Sale Certificate will be retained in the Treasurer's Office.

Subsequent taxes may be paid after October 15th and after April 15th. You will not be notified of these amounts. It is your responsibility to obtain the amounts from the Treasurer's Office. All subsequent taxes will be added to your Tax Sale Certificate and earn 2% interest per month.

The County Treasurer is required to notify the title holder of record for each parcel sold at Tax Sale.

The Tax Sale purchaser will be notified when the property is redeemed. Return the original Tax Sale Certificate to the Treasurer's Office and we will issue you a check and a redemption certificate.

A Tax Sale Certificate does not entitle the holder to any right, title, or interest in the property purchased.

A Tax Sale Certificate does not clear the property of tax liens.

The Tax Sale Deed conveys right, title, and interest in the property. A Tax Sale Deed will be issued following the redemption period after due process of law has been completed. The County does not assist in the Tax Sale Deed process.

The title holder of record retains the right to redeem within a specified period of time. If the sale remains unredeemed after this period has expired, the purchaser may begin proceedings to obtain a Tax Sale Deed to the parcel. For parcels sold at Regular Tax Sale, the 90-day notice of right of redemption may be issued one year and nine months from the date of sale. For parcels sold at Public Bidder Sale, the 90-day notice of right of redemption may be issued nine months from the date of sale.

The Treasurer may cancel the Tax Sale Certificate three years after issuance if action has not been completed which qualifies the certificate holder to obtain a Tax Sale Deed.

This document has been prepared to provide general information and guidelines relative to Tax Sales and Tax Sale redemption's. It is not an all-inclusive listing of statutory requirements, procedures, or policy, or is it to be construed as a legal opinion of the laws governing Tax Sales.

To protect your interests as a Tax Sale buyer and to determine your rights and remedies, we recommend you consult legal counsel.

Please contact my office with questions or concerns. (712) 644-2750

Thank you for your interest in the Harrison County Tax Sale.

Vicki Argotsinger
Harrison County Treasurer

Harrison County Treasurer's Office
Vicki Argotsinger, Treasurer

111 North 2nd Ave.
Courthouse
Logan, Iowa 51546

Tax Dept. 712-644–2750
Auto Dept. 712-644-2144
Driver Lic. 712-644-2750
Fax: 712-644-2643

HARRISON COUNTY ANNUAL TAX SALE
REGISTER OF BIDDERS

The undersigned do hereby register as bidders at the annual Tax Sale and subsequent adjournments thereof, and do hereby acknowledge receipt of a copy of the NOTICE TO TAX SALE PURCHASERS OF THE TERMS AND CONDITIONS GOVERNING THE TAX SALE, and do further hereby acknowledge and agree that by placing a bid at the Tax Sale and subsequent adjournments that she/he will comply with and be bound by the aforementioned Tax Sale terms and conditions. Said Tax Sale to be held June 18, 2001.

Said NOTICE TO TAX SALE PURCHASERS OF THE TERMS AND CONDITIONS GOVERNING THE TAX SALE is based on the 1996 Code of Iowa and amendatory acts thereof.

DATE: _____

NAME: _____

ADDRESS: _____

_____

COUNTY OF RESIDENCE: _____

STATE OF RESIDENCE _____

TELEPHONE: _____

NOTE: All Tax Sale Certificates of Purchase and Tax Sale Deeds will be issued in the name or names as shown above.

To: Vicki Argotsinger
Harrison County Treasurer
111 North 2nd Avenue
Logan, Iowa 51546

AUTHORIZATION TO REPRESENT BIDDER

I / we, (please print) _____

(Bidder's name, as it appears on the registration form)

authorize (please print) _____

to act as my / our personal representative at the Harrison County Tax Sale held on

June 18, 2001.

_____

(Signature

_____

(Address)

_____

(City, State, Zip Code)

Date: _____

Subscribed and sworn before me this _____ day or _____, 2001.

_____

(Signature of Notary)

MONONA COUNTY TREASURER
PO BOX 415
ONAWA, IOWA 51040

PH 712-423-2347   *PH 712-423-2702*
TREASURER   *AUTO*

The annual tax sale is held at the Monona County Treasurer's Office at 9:00am on the third Monday in June, for as long as any bidders are present. The sale is adjourned on a daily basis.

Please be prepared for the sale, and know the parcels in which you are interested. Information can be obtained from the Treasurer's Office any time prior to the Sale.

The delinquent list is published in an official county newspaper, usually the first week in June. The official newspapers for Monona County are the Onawa Sentinel, Onawa Democrat and the Mapleton Press. The following rules apply;

> *1.Payment must be by personal check, money order or cash. The amount must be the same as that shown in the newspaper, plus $10.00 for each certificate issued.*

> *2.You may bid by mail. In case two mail bidders want the same parcel, the one with the earliest postmark will be awarded the parcel.*

> *3.Any parcel on which more than one year of taxes is owing, MUST be sold at the tax sale. There will be a one-year redemption period. Parcel which have one year or less of taxes owing may also be purchased. These will have a 2-year redemption period.*

> *4.The Tax Sale Certificate will be issued within 10 days, and will be mailed to you. They must be kept in a safe place, as they must be returned upon redemption. If you lose the original, a duplicate certificate may be issued for a $10.00 fee.*

> *5.Iowa law requires me to notify all owners that their property was sold at tax sale and that they have a certain time frame in which to redeem the property.*

> *6.During the time that you hold a Tax Sale Certificate, you will earn 2% interest per month or an equivalent of 24% on a yearly basis on the total monies invested.*

> *7.You must complete a W-9 form, so that we have the information needed to file*

1099 INT to you and to the Internal Revenue Service. Without a completed W-9 form, you will not be able to bid in any parcels at the tax sale. Only the actual amount paid to you will be filed and if it exceeds $600.00 in that tax year. Any lesser amounts, we are not required to file and report.

8. The Certificate does not give you a legal right to the property. There are legal steps to be taken either 9 months, or 1 year and 9 months after the tax sale purchase, depending on the years of taxes purchased at tax sale. I will include that information with your Tax Sale Certificate(s).

9. You may pay the subsequent taxes, and these will also earn 2% interest per month. These subsequent taxes can be paid anytime after October 15th and April 15th. I will send the amounts due for each certificate prior to those dates.

10. If and when the owner redeems the property, I will notify you to surrender the tax sale certificate(s) to me. I will then issue a check to you for the amount due, including interest earned. I will send a Redemption Certificate to you also so that you will see the breakdown of tax and interest.

I invite you to contact the Treasurer's Office with any additional questions you may have regarding Tax Sale.

Lawrence J. Framke
Monona County Treasurer

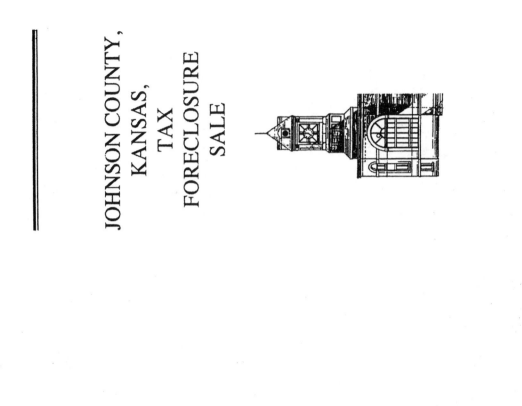

JOHNSON COUNTY, KANSAS, TAX FORECLOSURE SALE

ohnson County Legal Dept.
11 South Cherry St., Suite 3200
Olathe, Kansas 66061-3441

- The buyer is responsible for taking any necessary legal action to obtain possession of the property, such as by filing an eviction proceeding.

- For twelve months after the deed is recorded, a legal challenge may still be made questioning the procedures which the county followed. If such a challenge is successful, the property could revert to the original owner, in which case the court would order the purchase price refunded to the buyer.

This brochure is provided by the Johnson County Legal Department for general informational purposes. It is not intended as legal advice or as a complete statement of the law regarding tax foreclosures. The procedures described in this brochure are subject to change at any time, dependent upon changes in state law and county policies.

Johnson County does not discriminate on the basis of race, color, national origin, sex, religion, age, and/or disabled status in employment or the provision of services.

5/97

County tax sales are held to help collect unpaid taxes. This brochure will help you understand the process and the research you will need to do if you are interested in purchasing property at the tax sale.

Before the Auction

- Several properties will be offered for individual sale at the auction.

- *You are responsible for researching the properties which interest you to determine if they are suitable for your use.* Some examples of research you may want to do are determine the location and type of property; check with the city for zoning and building limitations; check with the county appraiser for assessed value and current tax rates; check with the register of deeds for easements and restrictive covenants; and *view the property.*

- A list of the properties, as well as the date, time and location of the auction and registration requirements will be published in the *Johnson County Sun* and the *Olathe Daily News* once a week for three weeks prior to the sale.

- For a minimal copy fee, you may obtain a list of the properties at the Johnson County Legal Department. Properties are listed by parcel identification number and by legal description; addresses are listed where available but are not warranted.

- Booklets containing maps of the properties are also available at the Johnson County Legal Department for a minimal charge.

- The amount of tax listed for each property in the sale ad is the amount of delinquent taxes owed, plus interest, *not* the assessed value.

- Ownership of the property remains with the current owner(s) until the sale. Therefore, you **may not** enter the property without the permission of the owner(s).

- The current owner(s) may redeem the property at any time prior to the time of sale.

The Auction

- Properties are sold at public auction to the highest qualified bidder. The county may bid on properties up to the amount of taxes and interest it is owed.

- Some properties may sell for less than the taxes owed; some may sell for more.

- Registration prior to the sale is required. Registration will be held the morning of the sale, as advertised.

- Generally, state law prohibits the following people from buying at the auction:
  a. those who owe delinquent taxes in Johnson County;
  b. those who have an interest in the property, such as the owners, mortgagees, relatives, or officers in a corporation which owns the property; and
  c. those who buy the property with the intent to transfer it to someone who is prohibited from bidding.

- All bidders must execute an affidavit, under oath, that they meet the statutory qualifications for bidding on tax sale property.

- Properties will be sold by legal description and by county parcel identification number.

- **PROPERTIES ARE SOLD "AS IS." THERE ARE NO WARRANTIES.**

- All the properties must be paid for by the stated time on the day of the sale. Only cash or a cashier's check will be accepted.

- The buyer must pay the fee for filing the deed with the register of deeds.

- The buyer will receive a receipt for payment on the day of the sale.

After the Auction

- The court will hold a hearing approximately three weeks after the auction to determine whether to confirm the sales.

- Some properties sold at the auction are subject to a federal lien. A deed will not be issued for those properties until the expiration of the federal redemption period of 120 days -- *if the federal agency chooses not to redeem the property.*

- For properties not subject to a federal lien, the Sheriff will issue a Sheriff's Deed after the court confirms the sale.

- All other liens which were of record will be extinguished upon confirmation of the sale; however, covenants, restrictions and easements of record are not extinguished, and the buyer takes the property subject to those encumbrances.

- The buyer is responsible for any taxes and assessments which are not included in the judgment, including the full amount of taxes assessed against the property for the calendar year in which the auction is held.

TAX FORECLOSURE AUCTIONS

Revised 05/08/00

GENERAL INFORMATION   <u>SEDGWICK COUNTY</u>, KANSAS

<u>LEGAL BASIS</u>: In the State of Kansas, Counties are allowed to sell real property having delinquent real estate taxes at the conclusion of the Judicial Tax Foreclosure Procedure via OPEN AUCTION (No sealed bids). Properties are sold to the highest QUALIFIED bidder.

<u>PUBLICATION NOTICES</u>: "Notice of Sale" is published in the officially designated County newspaper, the DERBY DAILY REPORTER, 788-2835. Copies are available in the County Treasurer's Office, 1ˢᵗ Floor, Courthouse.

<u>LOCATION, TIME, DATE</u>: Tax foreclosure auctions are held in the Jury Room adjacent to the 1ˢᵗ floor lobby of the County Courthouse, 525 North Main, Wichita, Kansas. The date is determined four to six weeks prior to the sale date and is announced through publication in the DERBY DAILY REPORTER or may be obtained by calling the Treasurer's Office, 383-7414.

Owners, heirs, and lien holders of record have the right to redeem properties through close of business the day prior to the sale date. Therefore, PROSPECTIVE BIDDERS ARE CAUTIONED THAT THEY CANNOT BE SURE THAT ANY GIVEN PROPERTY WILL ACTUALLY BE SOLD AT AUCTION UNTIL THE SPECIFIED SALE DATE.

ALL SALES ARE FINAL UNLESS SUCCESSFULLY CHALLENGED IN COURT. <u>Prospective bidders should adequately acquaint themselves with the properties in which they are interested prior to the auction</u>. Suggested inquiries might be considered in the areas of: special assessments - County Clerk's Office (383-7691) or respective City Clerks' offices; zoning and building restrictions - respective County or City building, planning and inspection offices; plat maps - County Clerk's Office; deed information - County Clerk's Office or Register of Deeds' Office (383-7511).

If a person desires to purchase a property prior to auction, that transaction is strictly between that person and the owner of record. To stop the tax foreclosure process, the full amount of taxes and interest plus court costs must be paid. The mere transfer of title, even having the deed recorded, will not stop the proceedings nor the sale. Only when all taxes and court costs are paid will the property be deleted from the sale.

BUYERS OF TAX FORECLOSURE PROPERTIES ARE RESPONSIBLE FOR THE FULL AMOUNT OF TAXES FOR THE YEAR OF THE SALE, REGARDLESS OF THE DATE OF SALE. <u>BUYERS ARE RESPONSIBLE FOR ALL CURRENT AND FUTURE SPECIAL ASSESSMENTS ON THE PROPERTY.</u> BUYERS ARE NOT RESPONSIBLE FOR ANY DELINQUENT TAXES.

Sale of properties sold at a tax foreclosure auction can be challenged after the sale through District Court by owners or lien holders of record at the time of sale. The County may defend the sale with appointed counsel. Buyers may, at their own expense, engage their own attorney if they wish to be represented during such action. If the court should decide in favor of the plaintiff and set aside the sale of the property, the court will direct the County regarding refunding the full purchase price plus any legally required interest.

TAX FORECLOSURE AUCTIONS

TERMS OF SALE   **SEDGWICK COUNTY, KANSAS**

Bidders MUST BE REGISTERED AND HAVE A BIDDING NUMBER to participate in the bidding. Registration will begin approximately one (1) hour prior to sale time. To register, a person must provide two pieces of positive identification showing name and address (with an attached photograph on one piece), provide their telephone number or other verifiable contact method, and provide their signature certifying they are not the record owner of any real estate upon which there are delinquent ad valorem or special assessment taxes. Only then will a bidding number be issued.

SUCCESSFUL BIDDERS WILL BE HELD RESPONSIBLE FOR THEIR BIDS AND MUST NOT DEPART THE AUCTION WITHOUT MAKING PAYMENT IN FULL FOR THEIR PURCHASES(S). IF NOT, LEGAL ACTION MAY BE TAKEN AGAINST YOU TO ENFORCE YOUR BID AND YOU MAY BE INELIGIBLE TO BID AT FUTURE SALES.

Any purchase or combination of purchases having a total sale (bid) price of $350 OR less must be paid in cash or cashiers check. You must have exact change. Any purchase(s) having a total sale (bid) price of more than $350 must be paid as follows: $350 cash or cashiers check, and either your personal check, cash or cashiers check for the balance.

There will be a $30 charge assessed for a returned check. Further, if a check is returned, the issuer will be granted no more than seven calendar days from the date of notice to redeem the check and pay the returned check assessment with cash or cashier's check only. Returned check notice will be via first class mail.

According to K.S.A. 79-2804, the Sheriff is required to register the deeds for properties purchased at Tax Foreclosure auctions prior to delivering them to the buyer. Therefore, the filing fee for registration of the deed(s) will be collected from the buyer of each parcel at the time of sale.

A receipt of purchase will be given at time of payment. A Sheriff's deed will be mailed to successful bidders as soon as "Confirmation of Sale" is filed with the Clerk of the District Court and the deeds are recorded with the Register of Deeds office. This usually requires a waiting period of approximately 90 days after the date of sale. This waiting period allows all checks to clear and the settlement of any disputed sales (challenges) in court. The County desires to conclude the case in the most expeditious, legal manner possible. It also may take additional time for prior years' delinquent taxes to be purged from the property record.

If a successful bidder purchases property with an occupied building, the purchaser is responsible for handling this instance in a considerate manner. The County is NOT RESPONSIBLE FOR EVICTION.

PURCHASERS ARE RESPONSIBLE FOR PAYMENT OF THE FULL YEAR OF TAXES (ad valorem and any "specials") for any tax foreclosure auction held during that year. The taxes are not pro-rated to sale dates. "Specials" can be added up to August 26th of each year. "Specials" which purchasers will pay as part of that year's taxes may be announced at the sale, however all specials may not be listed.

Wayne County Treasurer: Proceedure   **Page 1 of 2**

Wayne County Treasurer
Raymond J. Wojtowicz
Procedure When Purchasing a Tax Lien Certificate

FAQ -Tax Lien Sale

Procedure When Purchasing a Tax Lien Certificate:

- Purchase Tax Lien certificates at Wayne County Tax Lien Sale.
- The property owner has the right to redeem at any time prior to the date of the next annual tax lien sale by paying the amount of the sale, plus 1 ¼% interest per month. Once the property has been redeemed, the holder of the purchase certificate will be notified by the State Treasurer to surrender the original purchase certificate and will receive a refund for the amount paid by the owner to redeem.
- After the one-year redemption period, if owner of property has not redeemed, prior to the next annual tax lien sale, the purchaser must surrender his/her purchase certificate to the Office of the State Treasurer, and the tax deed will be issued.
- Once the tax deed has been issued by the State Treasurer, before the holder of the tax deed may acquire title to the premises, the following must be done:

    - Under the law, he/she must serve notice upon all parties of interest of record and persons in actual open possession of the premises or land through the sheriff.
    - File proof of such notice with the County Treasurer.
    - Persons with a redeemable interest have six (6) months after proof of services is filed to redeem by depositing in the County Treasurer's Office a sufficient amount for redemption.

    Service of notice must be made within five (5) years from the date that a deed could be issued. The tax deed holder cannot take absolute possession of the properties purchased until he/she has served the notice in accordance with the provisions of Section 140 to 143 inclusive of Act 206 of Public Acts 1893 as amended.

    Persons with a redeemable interest during the six-month period after proof of services has been filed, can do so by payment of the purchase price, plus 50% interest, plus the cost of service of the sheriff's notice, and /or cost of publication. Redemption may only be made by depositing guaranteed funds for the proper amount in the County Treasurer's Office.

- If the purchaser wishes to protect his/her original purchase, they should make purchases at subsequent tax lien sales until a Writ of Assistance (By the Courts) or other process for the possession of land; or quieting title (Through the Courts)

**Wayne County Treasurer
Raymond J. Wojtowicz
FAQ -Tax Lien Sale**

Procedure When Purchasing a Tax Lien Certificate

General Information:

What is the Annual Tax Lien Sale?

Each year on the first Tuesday in May, properties delinquent in the third year after assessment are subject to tax lien sale. At the 1999 tax lien sale the unpaid 1996 taxes will be sold. **The tax lien sale is not an outright sale of the properties. It is a sale of the lien for the unpaid taxes and charges.**

It is to be noted that an individual bid at the Tax Lien Sale has no bearing on taxes levied by the City of Detroit.

When will the next Tax Lien Sale be?

An informational meeting for the Annual Tax Lien Sale is held each year on the first Tuesday in May. The actual Tax Lien Sale is conducted at the end of May each year.

Where is the Tax Lien Sale held?

The delinquent taxes are offered for sale at the Office of the County Treasurer in each county. The Wayne County Treasurer's Office is located on the 5th floor in the International Building, 400 Monroe, Detroit, Michigan.

When and where do you advertise the Tax Lien Sale?

A listing of the description of properties going to sale are published in a local paper, that is contracted by the State for three consecutive weeks beginning the end of February of each year.

When can I register? Is there a fee?

Registration begins the first day of the Tax Lien Sale. There is no fee to register. You will receive a purchaser number on the day of registration.

Wayne County Treasurer -FAQ

What form of payment is accepted?

ONLY CERTIFIED CHECK, MONEY ORDER, OR U.S. CURRENCY WILL BE ACCEPTED FOR PAYMENT.

How do I purchase a tax lien?

The tax lien sale is a competitive sale. The tax lien covering the properties is sold to the person who will pay the accumulated taxes and charges and take the least undivided interest in the premises.

Each parcel will be offered separately in the same order as they appear in the tax list and tax records, unless they may be paid or lawfully withdrawn. Only after the sale number has been read will a bid be honored. Gestures will not be recognized.

The successful bidder at the tax lien sale receives from the County Treasurer a certificate indicating his/her purchase of the delinquent tax lien.

What if there is more than one bidder?

When there is more than one bidder, the sale will be made to the person offering to take the smallest undivided interest, and pay the taxes and charges as offered. Purchasers should state the interest they are bidding, such as 99/100, ¾, ½, etc.

What happens to the liens that are not sold at the Tax Lien Sale?

Any description that has not been sold at the County Treasurer's sale is bid off in the name of the State and may be purchased at the Office of the State Treasurer, Bureau Local Government Services. State bids may be purchased at the department any time prior to the 20th day of April of the year following the sale.

I Purchased a Tax Lien certificate at the Sale. What is my next step?

The property owner has the right to redeem at any time prior to the date of the next annual tax lien sale by paying the amount of the sale, plus 1 ¼% interest per month. Redemption may be made at the County Treasurer's Office in the county where the lands are located.

If the owner redeems the lands, the holder of the purchase certificate will be notified by the State Treasurer to surrender the original purchase certificate and will receive a refund for the amount paid by the owner to redeem. It usually requires about 6 weeks to process the redemption and refund.

If the owner prior to the next annual tax lien sale does not redeem the tax lien sale item, the purchaser must surrender his/her purchase certificate to the Office of the State

Treasurer and in return they will issue you a tax deed.

After I acquire the tax deed from the State Treasurer do I then gain ownership of the property?

A TAX DEED IN ITSELF DOES NOT CONVEY ABSOLUTE TITLE TO THE PREMISES.

Before the holder of the tax deed may acquire title to the premises, under the law he/she must serve notice upon all parties of interest of record and persons in actual open possession of the premises or land through the sheriff. If service cannot be made, notice must be published in a legal newspaper. After notice has been served, you must file proof of such notice with the County Treasurer, and then wait the statutory period of six months before beginning court action. Service of notice must be made within five (5) years from the date that a deed could be issued.

The tax deed holder cannot take absolute possession of the properties purchased until he/she has served the notice in accordance with the provisions of Section 140 to 143 inclusive of Act 206 of Public Acts 1893 as amended.

What further action do I take once I have served notice?

The purchaser should, if he/she wishes to protect his/her original purchase, make purchases at subsequent tax lien sales until a Writ of Assistance (By the Courts) or other process for the possession of land; or quieting title (Through the Courts) has taken place.

After absolute possession has been taken of the property, the purchaser should immediately pay all delinquent taxes.

Frequently Asked Tax Sale Questions

1. *What is a Tax Sale?*
2. *When and where is the tax sale held?*
3. *How often are public tax sales held?*
4. *Is there a deed sale in addition to a lien sale?*
5. *When and where is the tax sale advertised?*
6. *How and when to register for the tax sale?*
7. *What types of payments are accepted at the sale?*
8. *Is there a deposit required before the sale?*
9. *How does the bidding process work?*
10. *What type of document is issued at the sale?*
11. *Are there are any other expenses in addition to the cost of the lien?*
12. *Does the county handle the foreclosure procedure?*
13. *What happens to the liens that are not sold at the Tax Lien Certificate auction?*
14. *Can a person bid on Tax lien Certificates without attending the auction?*

Top of Page

What is a Tax Sale?

When a property owner fails to pay Real Property taxes as of April 1 (1st half) or August 1 (2nd half) and the taxes remain unpaid by the following February, the property is offered at a Tax Sale.

At the Tax Sale, an investor can pay the delinquent taxes to the County which places a tax lien on the property. When the property owner decides to pay the taxes, (called "Redeeming"), he/she pays the investor the amount of the taxes plus 14% interest. (14% is the interest rate Douglas County charges on ALL delinquent taxes).

If the homeowner does not redeem the property within three (3) years of the purchase of the lien the investor may foreclose on the property.

Top of Page

When and where is the tax sale held?

The **First Monday** of March, 7:00 AM, Civic Center 1819 Farm St. - 7th floor, Omaha, NE.

Top of Page

How often are public tax sales held?

Public tax sales are held once a year on the first Monday in March.

Top of Page

Is there a deed sale in addition to a lien sale?

Douglas County does **not** have a deed sale. Douglas County has a Foreclosure Sale through the County Attorney's Office after the public tax sale is completed. The Foreclosure Sale is held randomly throughout the year. If no redemption is made a deed will be issued two years after the sale. For further information contact the County Attorney for time and location of foreclosure sales (402-444-7866).

Top of Page

When and where is the tax sale advertised?

It is advertised in the "Daily Record" for three consecutive weeks in February prior to the March sale. You may purchase a delinquent property list from the "Daily Record" located at 3323 Leavenworth Street, Omaha, NE 68102, their phone number is (402) 345 -1303.

A diskette, listing all liens to be sold, may be purchased through the Douglas County Treasurer's Office for $25.00. The diskette contains additional information not included in the "Daily Record". Contact the Treasurer's Office at (402) 444-7272 to purchase a diskette.

Top of Page

How and when to register for the tax sale?

Bidders are required to furnish name, address, telephone number, fax number (if applicable), and social security number or Federal ID number to the Treasurer's Office.

The information may be furnished in person at the Douglas County Treasurer's Office, 1819 Farnam St.-Room H-03 Omaha, NE 68183-0003 or by fax (402) 444-7699. There is no charge to register but you must register before the sale.

Top of Page

What types of payments are accepted at the sale?

Personal checks, cashier checks or convenience checks (**NO** credit cards).

Top of Page

Is there a deposit required before the sale?

No deposit is required.

Top of Page

How does the bidding process work?

At the beginning of the sale a round robin is offered. If a majority of the bidders **agree,** a round robin process will be used. If not, a standard auction will be held.

In a round robin- the bidders agree to buy the liens for the delinquent tax amount including interest and advertising fees. The properties are offered one by one to the bidders in a specific order. If a bidder accepts an offer, the following property will be offered to the next bidder in line. If a bidder passes up a property he/she forfeits that bid and the parcel is

http://www.co.douglas.ne.us/dept/treasurer/PT_TaxSale.htm   02/12/2001 offered to the next bidder in line (the bidder that passed will not get another opportunity for a parcel until the bid works full circle back to them).

In a standard auction - the winning bid amount plus the amount of taxes, plus interest, plus $5.00 advertising. In the case of duplicate bids on any parcel, the parcel will first be offered to the bidder who bids the smallest portion (undivided interest), of the same. If no person bids for less quantity than the whole, the sale will be decided by an acceptable method of lottery.

Top of Page

What type of document is issued at the sale?

A Certificate of Tax Sale is issued.

Top of Page

Are there are any other expenses in addition to the cost of the lien?

Yes, a ten dollar ($10.00) fee for the Certificate (which will be included in the redemption amount), and an additional ten dollar ($10.00) fee per Certificate, if you choose to re-assign a Certificate (this re-assignment fee is non-refundable).

Top of Page

Does the county handle the foreclosure procedure?

Douglas County does **NOT** handle foreclosure procedures. It is up to the individual bidder to follow through with the foreclosure if necessary.

Top of Page

What happens to the liens that are not sold at the Tax Lien Certificate auction?

Liens not sold at the Tax Sale are offered at private tax sales over the counter at the Treasurer's Office throughout the year (after May 1). A foreclosure sale by the County Attorney may be offered. Contact the County Attorney's Office at (402) 444-7866 for dates and times of the foreclosure sales.

Top of Page

Can a person bid on Tax lien Certificates without attending the auction?

A bidder or a bidder's representative **MUST** attend the sale to obtain a lien. When a representative attends the tax sale on behalf of a bidder they will use the bidder's permanent number. Only one bidder is permitted to attend the sale per company or investor.

Oklahoma County's
Web Site

BRIEF TAX LIEN SALE INFORMATION

Under mandatory statutes the County Treasurer must advertise and offer for "Sale" all real estate tax liens, which are delinquent in a local newspaper. A mailing list is not available. The information is on request only. Although designated as a "Sale", it is merely a sale of the tax lien of the County, acquired by virture of the delinquent taxes. It is not an actual "Sale" of the property, at this time. The "Sale" is conducted the first Monday in October. The amount received for the tax lien can only be for the same amount of the delinquent taxes plus interest, advertising and costs. At this time the County Treasurer will issue to the purchaser of the tax lien a "Tax Certificate" which evidences the payment. The certificate will bear eight per cent interest per annum until redeemed by the record owner of the property, or someone with a legal or equitable interest in the property. At the end of two years, from the date of the lien sale certificate, the certificate holder may then apply for, a tax deed to the property. Sixty days after application for tax deed is applied for, if no redemption has been made, a tax deed will be issued to the certificate holder. We do not check for other liens and encumbrances. That is the responsibility of the certificate holder.

If a lien is not sold, it is retained by the County and subject to a later sale, designated as a "Resale". If no redemption has been made of property liens still held by the County, an actual sale of the property is held approximately two and one-half years from the date of the Original October Tax Lien Sale. According to State Statutes this sale is to be held the Second Monday in June, after the publication of properties involved for four consecutive weeks prior to the Resale in a newspaper in the County. This sale is an actual auction for cash. If no one buys the Property at the "Resale", actual deeds are issued to the County, and the property is removed for the list of taxable properties in the County.

According to State Statutes, the County Treasurer may sell any property acquired by the County at Resale. This is subject to approval of the Board of County Commissioners at its discretion. The Board of County Commissioners has the power to reject any and all bids. Bids must first be presented in writing to the County Treasurer's Office.

There is a list available of all of the County Owned properties, in the Treasurer's Office for a cost of $20.00, plus postage.

Oklahoma County's
Web Site

LIEN SALE INSTRUCTIONS

➤Sale opens at 9:00 A.M. and declaration of sale is read as required by statutes.

➤All properties could have delinquent taxes that have not been advertised. Therefore, BUYER BEWARE, all delinquent taxes must be endorsed (paid) on the certificate when issued. If any one property has delinquent taxes that the bidder does not want to pay, then none of the certificates awarded to that bidder will be issued.

➤The amount of interest paid to the County is an annual eighteen per cent (18%) per year. The amount of interest earned by the certificate holder is an annual eight per cent (8%) per year.

➤Cost for issuance of the certificate is $10.50.

➤This sale is only a lien sale and not a transfer of title or property rights.

➤All property, although listed by publication for sale, upon which the taxes have been paid, will not be available for the lien sale.

➤If all taxes are paid by the record owner, or any person having a legal or equitable interest in said property, prior to issuance of tax certificate, no certificate will be issued and the bid canceled.

➤The sale hereby advertised involves manufactured homes, which may be subject to the right of a secured party to repossess. A holder of a perfected security interest in such manufactured home may be able to pay ad valorem taxes based upon the value of the manufactured home apart from the value of real property. If a secured party exercises this right, the holder of the tax sale certificate will be refunded the amount of taxes paid upon the value of the manufactured home.

➤Certificates are issued, as soon as possible, after the sale. Certificate holders will be notified by telephone and will have one week to pick-up their certificates, after which the county will assume the lien.

➤Bidders will be required to pay for any bids made with certified funds or cash.

LIENSALEINSTRUCTIONS   Page 2 of 2

Certificates will be issued only in the name of the original bidder.

➤No bidder may claim only a portion of his/her certificates. All must be picked up or none will be issued.

➤All bidders shall print their name, address and telephone number on the back of their numbered card.

➤Your numbered card may be used throughout the lien sale; however, should you desire to initiate an additional request form a new number will be required. To obtain your new number return your original card to the registration desk and your new number will be issued.

➤All cards must be turned in at the reception desk by the end of the lien sale.

➤If more than one person is interested in the same property, those bidders numbers are put together and one drawn to determine who receives the tax certificate. Bidders that have not picked up their certificates in the past will have to leave certified funds or cash for their successful bids immediately after the sale or certificates will not be issued.

➤Property will be offered on a first come first serve basis.

➤Current taxes should be endorsed to your certificate, as soon as possible, after January 15, 1999 and must be endorsed prior to the next year's publication.

➤The County Treasurer's primary function is tax collection. We make every effort to see that tax deeds, both resale and sale are issued in accordance with the Statutes, but the buyer assumes all responsibility and liability on purchase, the date the deed is issued.

➤In the event a bankruptcy is filed on any property on which a certificate has been issued, the Certificate Holder will be given the following two choices

a. SURRENDER YOUR TAX SALE CERTIFICATE AND BE REFUNDED THE AMOUNT OF MONEY THAT YOU PAID FOR THE CERTIFICATE WITHOUT ANY INTEREST. THERE IS NO STATUTORY AUTHORITY TO PAY INTEREST IN THESE SITUATIONS.
b. KEEP THE TAX SALE CERTIFICATE AND PURSUE YOUR RIGHT TO FILE YOUR CLAIM FOR PAYMENT THROUGH THE BANKRUPTCY COURT. PLEASE BE ADVISED IF YOU CHOOSE THIS OPTION YOU DO SO AT YOUR OWN RISK AND IT IS POSSIBLE THAT ALL OR A PORTION OF YOUR BANKRUPTCY CLAIM COULD BE DENIED BY THE BANKRUPTCY COURT. IF THAT SHOULD HAPPEN TO OCCUR THE COUNTY WILL NOT BE RESPONSIBLE FOR YOUR LOSS.

NOTE: To go back to the previous page, use the back button on your browser.

Oklahoma County's
Web Site

RESALE INSTRUCTIONS

THIS IS FOR INFORMATION ONLY AND SUBJECT TO CHANGE WITHOUT NOTICE

INTERPRETATIONS OF THE STATUTES OR COURT CASES SHOULD BE OBTAINED FROM YOUR LEGAL COUNSEL

The Resale of Real Estate for delinquent taxes will officially open in the office of the County Treasurer at 9:00 A.M. on the 2nd Monday of every June. The Notice of Resale of Real Estate for Taxes will be read as approved by the State Statutes.

The meeting will be reconvened at 9:30 A.M. in The Oklahoma County Sheriff Parking Garage, designated as part of the Treasurer's Office for purposes of the Resale in keeping with posted notice previously made.

➤ The Resale will continue from day to day between the hours of 9:00 A.M. and 4:00 P.M. until completed, recessing each day for lunch at 11:00 A.M. to 1:00 P.M.

➤ All Successful Bids Include the amount bid and any other taxes, cost, abstract fee, and Resale advertising. Once property is auctioned off, sale will stop. The bidder then pays for property by cash or check. The sale of property will continue once all transactions are complete.

➤ If paying by check, a $500.00 cash deposit will be required per property. Your deposit will be refunded when your check clears. In the event of insufficient funds or payment being stopped, your deposit will not be refunded, and the items will be presented to our District Attorney's Office to begin collection proceedings.

➤ Deeds on property sold will be sent to the successful bidder after the same has been filed with the Registrar of Deeds in the County Clerk's Office. The Treasurer shall collect $10.00 for each deed issued and an additional filing fee of $10.00. The successful bidder will be provided a certified copy of the deed while waiting for the original to be sent from the Registrar of Deeds. The certified copy of the deed on property sold from 9:00 A.M. to 11:00 A.M. will be available to the successful bidder during the lunch recess. On Property sold from 1:00 P.M. to 4:00 P.M , the certified copy of the deed will be available by 4:30 P.M. the same day.

➤ If payment is made in any form except cash the deed will not be issued until proof of funds collected is presented. Be aware the property is subject to redemption until the deed is filed

RESALEINSTRUCTIONS

with the Registrar of Deeds.

➤ If any person is bidding for someone else or in the name of any firm or corporation, it should be so reported to the Clerk of the Resale as the deed form prescribed by state statutes require such information.

➤ All property must be sold for a sum not less than two-thirds of the assessed value of such real estate as fixed for the current fiscal year, or for the total amount of taxes, penalties, interest and cost due on such property, whichever is the lesser. However, all statutory fees, costs due to advertising, abstracting and treasurer's cost will be due in addition to the final bid. If there is no bid, a deed will be issued to the County, but the County cannot bid.

**In accordance with court decisions, and not Statutory Law. Tax Deeds only affect satisfaction of the taxes as listed in the official Resale Advertising publications. Other classes of Taxes are not affected and all Taxes of every nature are to be paid in addition to the amount bid for any properties in the Resale. We will attempt to advise you of all types of Taxes that the Treasurer's Office knows is delinquent and payable at this time, but we will not guarantee the amount. A Resale Deed will not affect future installments as they become due on special assessments; such as paving, sewer, water, or any other lawful tax.

➤ The County Treasurer's primary function is tax collection. We make every effort to see that Tax Deeds, are issued in accordance with the Statutes, but the buyer assumes all responsibility and liability on purchase.

➤ Each buyer is responsible for knowing what property is bid upon and each property should be inspected by the buyer prior to entering a bid upon it.

➤ Each bidder should research the records and inspect the property that they are considering prior to entering a bid. Some Federal, State and City liens may still exist and be valid against the property.

➤ All property, although listed by publication for sale, upon which the taxes have been paid will not be called. Bidding will open and properties as listed in the newspaper will be sold in order or listing number.

**Notice: While the Treasurer's Office makes every effort to ensure the correctness of the information, any error contained herein does not constitute a waiver of any tax amounts by or for the County Treasurer's Office or the Taxpayer.

NOTE: To go back to the previous page, use the back button on your browser.

Oklahoma County's
Web Site

INSTRUCTIONS FOR
BIDS ON COUNTY OWNED PROPERTY ACQUIRED AT RESALE

➤ According to Oklahoma State Statute 68 § 3135, the County Treasurer may sell any property acquired by the County at Resale. This is subject to approval of the Board of County Commissioners at its discretion. The Board of County Commissioners has the power to reject any and all bids.

➤ Bids must first be presented in writing to the County Treasurer's Office.

➤ Each bidder should research the records and inspect the property which he/she is considering prior to entering a bid. Some Federal, State and City liens may still exist and be valid against the property.

➤ Upon receipt of the bid, the Treasurer's Office researches the property, taking into consideration, the location of the property, current market value, and any delinquent taxes that were due at the time the County acquired the property. Upon completion of research tentative approval or disapproval will be given. This procedure is used to save the bidder the publication costs if commissioners do not wish to sell the property or do not feel the price is sufficient.

➤ If permission to proceed is given, the Treasurer's Office will then prepare the official bid request. The bidder has an option of paying the full amount of the bid in cash or completing an affidavit and paying 10% of the purchase price in cash with the remaining balance to be paid by personal check. The Treasurer will collect an additional $100.00 \$150.00 in cash for estimated publication cost and recording fees. If a portion of the payment is by check or cashier's check, the deed will not be issued to the successful bidder until proof the check has cleared is presented.

➤ The Treasurer then sets the date, time and place for auction, and notice for publication is prepared. Said notice will include the legal description of the property, the amount of bid and the name of such bidder, stating that on that date and time, sale of said property so listed shall be made at such price and to such bidder. Subject to the approval of the Board of County Commissioners, unless higher bids are received at such sale.

➤ On the date of the sale, said property will be sold by the County Treasurer to the highest competitive bidder or to the original bidder if there be no higher price offered. The successful bidder is required to tender at least 10% of the final sales price plus costs and fees in cash, with the option of paying the balance by personal check, cashiers check or cash. Again, if the balance is paid by any means other than cash under no circumstances will the deed be issued until proof the item has cleared is received. The sale in any event shall be subject to the approval of the Board of County Commissioners in its discretion.

➤ Successful bidder not having money, Procedures as to awarding to the next highest bidder if this happens.

➤ Treasurer's Office then prepares "County Treasurer's Transcript of Proceedings" and accompanying documentation for presentation to the Board of County Commissioners for official action.

➤ If approval is given, the Chairman of the Board of County Commissioners will execute a deed conveying title to the purchaser of such property.

➤ Upon receipt of the executed deed the County Treasurer's Office will file the deed. After the deed is recorded, the deed is returned to the County Treasurer. The Treasurer will then contact purchaser of the property to pick up the deed.

➤ If there is excess publication money, it is refunded to purchaser after deed is filed.

BLAIR, GOGGAN, SAMPSON & MEEKS
ATTORNEYS-AT-LAW
A PARTNERSHIP INCLUDING PROFESSIONAL CORPORATIONS
OIL & GAS BUILDING
SUITE 1414
309 WEST 7TH STREET
FORT WORTH, TEXAS 76102-5113
(817) 877-4589
FAX (817) 877-0601

JUN - 0 1996

May 31, 1996

SHERIFF SALE INFORMATION:

The Sheriff Sale is held the first Tuesday of each month at 2:00 P.M. on the Weatherford Street entrance to the Tarrant County Courthouse.

No registration.

The Sheriff Sale is published in the Commercial Recorder, notice is posted at the Courthouse.

Your bid must be paid in full - by cash or a personal/business check will be accepted on the day of the sale - the personal or business check must be picked up the next day by 11:00 A.M. with cash or cashiers check.

You will receive a Sheriffs Deed to the property.

The minimum bid represents the taxes and costs due on the years in the Judgment. Taxes which become due after the Judgment was taken will be assumed by the purchaser as well as any paving, weed, demolition or board-up liens.

If a property is not sold it will go the City or School District whichever has offered it for sale, they will hold until after the redemption period expires, then they may attempt to sell. The redemption period is six months, unless a homestead or agriculture property then it is two years. If the owner redeems the property from the purchaser they must pay the purchase price plus 25% interest on the six months. If a homestead or agriculture property is redeemed it is 25% the first year and 50% if redeemed the second year.

You or a representative must be present to bid on the properties.

This is not a Tax Lien Certificate sale - the real property is sold.

CONSTABLE'S SALE

INFORMATION ON DELINQUENT TAX SALES

For information on the next upcoming sale please click here

These sales are held every first Tuesday of each month at approximately 2:00 p.m. on the Tarran County Courthouse steps. The address is 100 West Weatherford, Fort Worth, Texas. Sale notices are published once a week for three consecutive weeks preceding such sale in the Fort Worth Commercial Recorder. These newspapers may be purchased at the Tarrant County Courthouse and all Tarrant County Subcourthouses. Notices are also posted on the bulletin board located in the basement at 100 Wes Weatherford in Fort Worth. These sales are an open bid, but will start out with a minimum bid. The minimum bid begins with an aggregate amount of all taxes and penalties for all tax entities, court costs, Constable's fees and publishing fees or the appraised value of the property, whichever is less. If the property does not sell, ownership reverts to the entity that is the primary plaintiff of the suit as trustee for all entities involved. These properties may be subject to liens. A title search should be done on the properties you are interested in purchasing and you may want to consult an attorney.

Directly after the sale, a receipt will be issued to the purchaser and at that time we will collect the bid in full by either a cashier's check for the full (not over) amount made payable to Constable Zane Hilger, cash, or we will accept a personal check made payable to the Constable in the full bid amount. If a personal check is written, the purchaser must come to Constable Hilger's office located at 645 Grapevine Highway, Hurst, Texas, 76054, by 11:00 a.m. the next day. At that time we will exchange your personal check for a cashier's check or cash. If there has been time to prepare a Constable's Deed for the sale, you may pick it up then. If not, it can be mailed to you or we can call you when it is ready. Once receiving your deed, it must be filed with the Tarrant County Clerk located at 100 West Weatherford, Fort Worth, Texas.

There is a redemption period that begins once the deed has been filed. If the property is not exempt by homestead or agriculture, there is a six month redemption period. The defendant may come back within that six month period and pay the taxes as well as pay the purchaser what they bid on the property plus a 25% interest on that bid in addition to any other taxes that they have paid. However, the purchaser will not be compensated for improvements made on the property. If the property is exempt by homestead or agriculture, the redemption period is two years. If the property is redeemed by the defendant within the first year, the interest due the purchaser is 25%. If the property is redeemed within the second year, the interest due the purchaser is 50%.

CONSTABLE'S SALE

JUNE 5, 2001

BY VIRTUE OF ORDERS OF SALE ISSUED OUT OF THE COURTS IN THE CAUSE NUMBERS INDICATED, THE FOLLOWING REAL PROPERTIES ARE TO BE SOLD AT

Linebarger Heard Goggan Blair Graham
Peña & Sampson, LLP

This material is strictly for informational purposes only and does not provide legal advice or services. Use of any of the following information does not create an attorney-client relationship. You should not act on the information provided without seeking legal counsel of your choice. The law firm of Linebarger Heard Goggan Blair Graham Peña & Sampson represents a number of taxing jurisdictions. We do not represent taxpayers, purchasers of judgment property, or any other outside interests. For further information, please contact your attorney.

COMMONLY ASKED QUESTIONS AND ANSWERS REGARDING TAX SALES

When and where are your tax sales advertised?

When and where are tax sales conducted?

What if I purchase a property that is encumbered by a mortgage or other liens?

Is payment in full required on the day of the sale?

What is the bidding process?

What is the minimum bid I should expect to pay?

Does your law firm offer a financing program or any discounts?

Do you allow investors to invest at your tax sales without attending the tax sale?

What type of ownership document is issued at the sale?

What happens to the properties that are not sold at the auction?

How do I get a list of properties struck-off at auction and now held for resale?

How do I find out the results of a tax sale auction, including which properties sold, to whom, and for what amount?

What if I purchase property at a tax sale, and the former owners of the property then want to "redeem" the property?

If I purchase property at a tax sale and later become dissatisfied with the property, may I cancel the sale and have a refund of the purchase price?

Will I be able to get title insurance on property I purchase at a tax sale?

WHEN AND WHERE ARE YOUR TAX SALES ADVERTISED?

They are advertised three times prior to the auction in a newspaper published in the county where the property is located. In Harris County, that publication is the Daily Court Review. It is available online at www.dailycourtreview.com. The number for the Daily Court Review is (713) 869-5434 if you would like to subscribe.

In Dallas County, sale notices are published in The Daily Commercial Records. To subscribe to that publication, you may call (214) 741-6366. To be added to a mailing list regarding future tax sales in Dallas County, you may contact the Dallas office of the Linebarger Heard Law Firm at (214) 880-0089.

In Bexar County (San Antonio), notices are published in The Daily Commercial Recorder, to which you may subscribe by calling (210)736-4450. Their website is at www.dcci.com/PTP/crecorder.html for additional information.

In addition, some sales are posted on the website of this law firm at www.publicans.com.

WHEN AND WHERE ARE TAX SALES CONDUCTED?

Public Tax Sales may only be conducted on the first Tuesday of any month at the courthouse of the county in which the property is located. As to the specific time and location at the courthouse, you must refer to the published notice of sale in the newspapers referenced above.

WHAT IF I PURCHASE A PROPERTY THAT IS ENCUMBERED BY A MORTGAGE OR OTHER LIENS?

Our firm's practice is generally to conduct a title search prior to filing tax suits on behalf of our taxing unit clients and, if we discover an outstanding lien, the holder of that lien is generally made a party and served with citation with a view toward having the tax judgment and tax sale extinguish and terminate that lien interest. However, **there is no guarantee that all ownership or lien interests have been accounted for and extinguished by the judgment, nor can we guarantee against any other possible defects** in the tax sale or in the underlying judgment on which the sale is based. **ALL SALES ARE CONSIDERED FINAL BY THE OFFICER CONDUCTING THE SALE, AND ALL SALES ARE WITHOUT WARRANTY, EXPRESS OR IMPLIED.** We urge you to independently verify the quality of the title you expect to receive by commissioning your own title search and by engaging your own attorney to examine all papers on file with the court in the underlying tax foreclosure suit.

IS PAYMENT IN FULL REQUIRED ON THE DAY OF THE SALE?

The judgment amount and all associated costs that constitute the "minimum bid" must be paid. However, the time allowed for the collection of adequate funds varies among officers who conduct tax sales. Some allow 1-2 hours, while others require the full amount paid at the time the successful bid is made. In Harris County, payment must be by cash or cashier's check. If the cashier's check is for more than the amount of the bid, the Constable will refund the excess money. Many people find it convenient to bring a cashier's check made out to themselves for the amount of the minimum bid,

COMMONLY ASKED QUESTIONS AND ANSWERS REGARDING TAX SALES   Page 3 of 5

and cash for any additional amounts they are willing to bid. If an investor is the successful bidder then he/she can endorse the cashier's check to the Constable. In some other counties, the officers will accept personal checks. Your best bet is to call the officer and ask in advance.

WHAT IS THE BIDDING PROCESS?

There is no formal bidding process. Oral bids are made consecutively by whomever can raise the last bid made, the same as in auctions generally. **All sales will be to the highest bidder.** The officer begins by announcing the sale and the official minimum opening bid, and then asks for bidders. If you open the bidding by offering the minimum opening bid, then others may raise the bid. Then, you can decide whether you want to continue bidding against them by offering a higher bid(s).

WHAT IS THE MINIMUM BID I SHOULD EXPECT TO PAY?

The "minimum bid" varies from property to property. The exact minimum bid is determined by the officer conducting the sale prior to the sale, and is announced at the sale. Unless there are "credits", you should expect to pay an amount that is the total of all amounts due in the judgment, penalty and interest, attorney fees, court costs, title costs, Constable/Sheriff fees, and posting fees.

DOES YOUR LAW FIRM OFFER A FINANCING PROGRAM OR ANY DISCOUNTS?

No. However, we may offer a payment arrangement plan for successful buyers of property at a Tax Sale for tax years not included in the judgment (i.e. taxes which accrue after the judgment).

DO YOU ALLOW INVESTORS TO INVEST AT YOUR TAX SALES WITHOUT ATTENDING THE TAX SALE?

Yes, so long as they appoint someone to represent them and they have the adequate funds to be the successful bidder. The appointed person present and bidding simply designates to the officer the name of the person or company in whose name the deed is to be made.

WHAT TYPE OF OWNERSHIP DOCUMENT IS ISSUED AT THE SALE?

The successful bidder on a property will be issued a Constable's Deed or Sheriff's Deed within 4-6 weeks after the auction date. It is provided by § 34.01(n) of the Texas Property Tax Code that:

> "The deed vests good and perfect title in the purchaser or the purchaser's assigns to the interest owned by the defendant in the property subject to the foreclosure, including the defendant's right to the use and possession of the property, subject only to the defendant's right of redemption, the terms of a recorded restrictive covenant running with the land that was recorded before January 1 of the year in which the tax lien on the property arose, a recorded lien that arose under that restrictive covenant that was not extinguished in the judgment foreclosing the tax lien, and each valid easement of record as of the date of the sale that was recorded before January 1 of the year the tax lien arose. The deed may be impeached only for fraud."

For further information regarding the meaning of this statutory provision, please consult

your own attorney.

If taxes have accrued against the property since the time of foreclosure judgment (i.e. "post judgment taxes"), the tax sale purchaser is considered by the taxing jurisdictions to have taken title subject to any such post-judgment taxes.

WHAT HAPPENS TO THE PROPERTIES THAT ARE NOT SOLD AT THE AUCTION?

In some cases, if no bidder bids upon a property, the property will be withdrawn from sale. In other instances, the property may be struck-off to the taxing jurisdiction that requested the Order of Sale. The struck-off property would then be owned jointly by all taxing jurisdictions which participated in the tax suit, and then later will be offered for resale as struck-off property.

HOW DO I GET A LIST OF PROPERTIES STRUCK-OFF AT AUCTION AND NOW HELD FOR RESALE?

With respect to property located in most counties, your two best sources of information are: (1) the tax assessor-collector's office and (2) the office of our firm handling the business of taxing jurisdictions located in that county. There are some counties in which the taxing jurisdictions entertain "private resales" in that they will consider written offers to purchase on a case by case basis as those offers are received. Other counties utilize a sealed bid procedure from time to time.

In Harris County, along with some other counties, resales of struck off properties are conducted by a second public auction. Notices of those resale auctions are advertised in The Daily Court Review as they become scheduled, and those auction notices will also ultimately become available online at www.publicans.com (our firm's website) as and when scheduled. A list of Harris County properties is not currently published.

HOW DO I FIND OUT THE RESULTS OF A TAX SALE AUCTION, INCLUDING WHICH PROPERTIES SOLD, TO WHOM, AND FOR WHAT AMOUNT?

We regret that we cannot furnish this information. However, the underlying papers for each separate tax suit on file with the court in the district clerk's office are public records. Those papers will include an officer's return on the order of sale which will give all information regarding the sale outcome. You will need the cause number for the tax suit in order to retrieve the information.

WHAT IF I PURCHASE PROPERTY AT A TAX SALE, AND THE FORMER OWNERS OF THE PROPERTY THEN WANT TO "REDEEM" THE PROPERTY?

We cannot give you any legal advice regarding that matter, except to advise you to seek your own legal counsel if you are unsure of the redemption period applicable to the property and/or the amounts to which you are entitled upon redemption by the former owner.

COMMONLY ASKED QUESTIONS AND ANSWERS REGARDING TAX SALES   Page 5 of 5

IF I PURCHASE PROPERTY AT A TAX SALE AND LATER BECOME DISSATISFIED WITH THE PROPERTY, MAY I CANCEL THE SALE AND HAVE A REFUND OF THE PURCHASE PRICE?

The officers who conduct tax sales regard those sales as final and not subject to rescission due to the purchaser's mistake or dissatisfaction with regards to the property.

WILL I BE ABLE TO GET TITLE INSURANCE ON PROPERTY I PURCHASE AT A TAX SALE?

We cannot guarantee that title insurance will be available. Underwriting practices vary from one company to the next with regards to tax sale property. If the availability of title insurance is of paramount importance to you, we urge that you explore that matter with a title company of your choice prior to any tax sale purchase.

The foregoing material is strictly for informational purposes only and does not provide legal advice or services. Use of any of the foregoing information does not create an attorney-client relationship. You should not act on the information provided without seeking legal counsel of your choice. The law firm of Linebarger Heard Goggan Blair Graham Peña & Sampson represents a number of taxing jurisdictions. We do not represent taxpayers, purchasers of judgment property, or any other outside interests. For further information, please contact your attorney.

ACTION PLANS
Now Get Out There!

ACTION PLAN FOR LIEN INVESTORS

Date Completed

1. Read and study this book.   _____

2. Pick one to three counties in one or two states to work on (this could be counties that are close to you or have upcoming sales or allow sales over-the-counter).   _____

3. Speak with county officials in each county selected. Get their materials for bidding, registration, a list of liens available, etc.   _____

4. Calendar the auctions.   _____

5. Attend an auction.   _____

6. Buy a lien at an auction.   _____

7. Have your lien redeemed (i.e., get a check from the county!)   _____

8. Buy multiple liens at another auction or over-the-counter.   _____

ACTION PLAN FOR DEED INVESTORS

Date Completed

1. Read and study this book. _____

2. Pick one to three counties in one or two states to work on (this could be counties that are close to you or have upcoming sales or allow sales over-the-counter). _____

3. Speak with county officials in each county selected. Get their materials for bidding, registration, a list of properties available, etc. _____

4. Calendar the auctions. _____

5. Do research on selected properties (see section on doing research). These properties may be over-the-counter or for upcoming auctions. _____

6. View each property and take a picture of it if you like it. _____

7. For the properties in which you are interested, contact a local broker about a possible resale value and his or her terms of sale (i.e., commission, length of listing, advertising). _____

8. Bid on chosen properties either over-the-counter or at an auction. _____

9. Acquire a property. _____

10. If necessary, contact a local title company or attorney to "quiet the title" (see section on foreclosure). _____

11. Sell the property (either with or without a broker). _____

12. Repeat the process. _____

Share the message!

Bulk discounts
Discounts start at only 10 copies and range from 30% to 55% off retail price based on quantity.

Custom publishing
Private label a cover with your organization's name and logo. Or, tailor information to your needs with a custom pamphlet that highlights specific chapters.

Ancillaries
Workshop outlines, videos, and other products are available on select titles.

Dynamic speakers
Engaging authors are available to share their expertise and insight at your event.

Call Dearborn Trade Special Sales at
1-800-621-9621, ext. 4444,
or e-mail trade@dearborn.com

Dearborn™
Trade Publishing
A **Kaplan Professional** Company